D1265915

Flashes in the Night

FLASHES IN THE NIGHT

The Sinking of the *Estonia*

Jack A. Nelson

Apprentice House
Baltimore, Maryland

Library of Congress Cataloging-in-Publication Data

Nelson, Jack A. (Jack Adolph), 1930-
   Flashes in the night : the sinking of the Estonia / Jack A. Nelson.
     p. cm.
   ISBN 978-1-934074-21-3
   1. Estonia (Ship) 2. Shipwrecks--Baltic Sea. I. Title.
   G530.E79N45 2010
   910.9163'34--dc22
                                        2009048375

ISBN: 978-1-934074-21-3

Jacket Design: Gregg Wilhelm
Thank you to John McIntyre for additional editorial assistance.
Printed in the United States of America
First Edition
Published by Apprentice House

Apprentice House
Communication Department
Loyola University Maryland
4501 N. Charles Street
Baltimore, MD 21210
410.617.5265
www.ApprenticeHouse.com
info@ApprenticeHouse.com

This work is dedicated to the courage, stamina, and optimism of those who survived the terrible conditions of that all-night ordeal in which towering, freezing waves at times washed away companions clinging to the same raft they were on. The actions of the six survivors focused on in this book offer great lessons in life and living.

Without the help and cooperation of survivors we interviewed in Stockholm and Estonia, this book could not have been written. We are especially grateful for our Estonian colleague Valeria Kaspar of Tallinn, who trudged through Estonian ships and the streets of Tallinn talking to survivors and families of the fallen.

—JAN

TABLE OF CONTENTS

PROLOGUE

On a breezy September evening in Tallinn, Estonia, in 1994, the young British adventurer Paul Barney boards the luxury ferry *M/S Estonia* bound on an overnight voyage for Stockholm. Most of the 989 aboard — fun-seekers from Sweden, a group of Swedish judges, police officials on an excursion, and wide-eyed Estonians — consider the overnight voyage a wonderful party, sometimes called a booze cruise.

At midnight, crashing waves send the huge ship reeling over, with dance-floor revelers hurled into the walls and sleepers tossed from their beds. A few minutes later the huge ship goes down, with some leaping into the sea and others hanging onto life rafts. Only 137 survive.

Among those are Barney; Kent Harstedt, a rising young Swedish entrepreneur; and a pretty Swedish student, Sara Hedrenius. Before the night is over, the three find themselves thrown together on an overturned raft amid thunderous waves in what is to be Europe's worst peacetime maritime disaster of the twentieth century.

This is their story, and the story of the scandal and controversy that after more than a decade still surround the *Estonia* disaster.

1 · SURVIVE!

The tall Englishman with dark, unruly hair came jauntily up the gangplank of the *M/S Estonia*, jostling with others as he balanced his backpack. At age thirty-five, Paul Barney of the village of Pangbourne in the Berkshire region of England was nearing the end of a long journey. For two months, he had been in Sweden on a grant from the Winston Churchill Memorial Fund to study energy and recycling matters. On this three-month sabbatical from his job as a landscape architect, he was researching reed beds and their ability to cleanse water pollution, which had taken him as far as the Arctic Circle.

Making his way to the afterdeck rail, he leaned back and watched as the Estonia prepared to leave under a gray and foreboding sky. In a melancholy mood, he drank the last bottle of Estonian beer he had bought ashore and pondered his life. In earlier travels, he had backpacked across almost all the continents of the world. Each time he had returned home unfulfilled, but he had hoped this venture in Sweden would leave him satisfied. Instead, now he contemplated returning to the same home, the same job, the same friends. He gloomily admitted to himself that the same restlessness was still smoldering within him. He was not sure what he was looking for, but as yet he had not found it.

Only a few days earlier, he had learned of an environmental conference in Estonia and had gone on this ship because it fit his schedule perfectly. He would arrive back in Stockholm just in time to drive his rented car to Goteborg in southern Sweden, catch a ferry there to return to London, and ultimately return to his home nestled in the Berkshire Hills. In his bag, he carried gifts of vodka and dried meat and clothing for his sister's family.

During the afternoon, the weather had been gorgeous in Tallinn, under a mild autumn sun. Now outside the terminal, a brisk wind was whipping up dust in the parking lot and the arrivals held tight to their hats and their skirts. Although there were families with small children, most of the crowd was made up of groups traveling at discounted rates. Paul watched as a union delegation of sixty-eight Stockholm police officials got aboard, followed by other groups, like the nineteen Pentecostal Bible students from a school near Stockholm, thirty-three kitchen workers from a small Swedish town, and twenty-four Swedish judges returning from a legal conference.

Inside the terminal as travelers gathered to board the ship, a palpable excitement buzzed in the air. With the break-up of the Soviet Union a year earlier, many of the Estonians were journeying to catch their first glimpse of a bustling Western nation they had only dreamed of before. In fact, for most passengers this was to be an evening of fun, banquets, dancing and inexpensive liquor. Many passengers considered the overnight voyage a wonderful party, sometimes called a booze cruise.

Near a candy booth in the terminal, a stocky, square-jawed twenty-nine-year-old Swede named Kent Harstedt stood eating sweets he had bought. He chatted with his friend Jan Eric Pettersson, who was munching on a salami sandwich as they watched the crowd. Kent was leader of a twenty-three-person cooperative group from six nations on a conference that would continue on the ship that evening and finish up in Stockholm the next day.

At a kiosk, Kent stopped to browse a minute. He had already bought all the souvenirs he intended, but the old woman in black who motioned him over pointed to the coins and rings she had spread out on a cloth. The coins were ancient, and one caught his eye. She smiled broadly when he paid her with the last of his Estonian kronor.

"Because you are my first customer this afternoon, the coin will bring you luck," she nodded sagely.

With a laugh, he thanked her. Then, he and Jan Eric and a young Danish friend from the conference, Morten Boje, went to board the ship. As they approached the gangplank, Morten teased him about the coin. Morten, very blond with a boyish face, was the same age as Kent, and they had become fast friends during the conference. At the gangplank, Morten recognized a fellow conference attendee, a tall Lithuanian who was standing uncertainly, gazing at the white-capped sea.

"What's wrong? Does the wind bother you?" Morten called with a laugh.

The Lithuanian gave a somber shake of his head. "Ships and storms don't mix well."

"No worry," Morten assured him. "My friend Kent here has a lucky coin for the journey."

The Lithuanian proceeded stiffly on up the gangplank.

As the ship pulled from the dock a little after 7 p.m., a few others of the nearly one thousand passengers and crew wandered out onto the seventh deck to watch in the breeze as the lights of the ancient city of Tallinn, Estonia, fell behind in the dusk. On that Tuesday evening of September 27, 1994, the sea was dark and rising. Visibility was good and a brisk wind was blowing. When the lights of Tallinn fell behind, an occasional rain squall smattered against the large windows of the ship's restaurant and the dance lounge. The 803 passengers aboard were bound for Stockholm, most of them returning from overnight pleasure jaunts or business conferences.

Watching the lights of the city fade away, a pretty nineteen-year-old Swedish girl named Sara Hedrenius was in a contemplative mood. She had been in the seacoast city of Parnu, Estonia, visiting her father, who was president of a Swedish company that specialized in cleaning up oil spills. It had been a special time, with the previous day spent riding horses along the beach at Parnu. "It was one of those father-daughter talks that a dad only gets a couple of times during a lifetime," her father recalled later. When she boarded the ship, she didn't feel like partying. Instead, she had taken a quick tour of the ship, then canceled her cabin and headed for the cafeteria to claim a spot for the night. She had decided the only cabins left, the ones deep in the ship, were too noisy. A bench would do just fine.

Likewise, as the ship pulled away from the lights of Tallinn, Paul Barney had canceled his cabin, which was located below the car deck. On the way over to Estonia, he too had found the lower decks noisy and unsettling. It would be quieter and easier to simply stretch out on a padded bench in the cafeteria.

After 10 p.m., Paul left the cafeteria and went to the Admiral Pub looking for some company. It was mostly empty with no friends in sight. He ordered a pint of Guinness and began to read a book. He was about to leave when the young man and young woman he had met from the Bible group came in, spotted him, and pulled up chairs at his table.

As fundamentalist Christians, Mikael and Maria soon steered the conversation to questions of life, including man's purpose on earth, his destiny, death and God. Barney had felt irritated that they claimed to have all the answers, and he had challenged them.

"It is arrogant of you who are so young to rule out what I think and believe," he told Mikael, who was twenty-three. "You should leave a little space in your mind for doubts. Jesus cannot save you from everything." Mikael only gave him an indulgent smile.

It was a conversation that Paul Barney was to think of often in the ensuing hours.

"I hope I haven't made you upset," Mikael finally said as they waved goodnight.

"No, it was a good discussion," Barney replied.

The two youths then excused themselves and went off to their cabins below the car deck.

Among those settling down for the overnight journey was the Alexander Voronin family, Russians who owned a business in northern Estonia. Alexander was a large, burly man with a gray beard and shock of grizzled hair, accompanied on this business trip by his father-in-law and his fifteen-year-old son, Vasya. Originally, they had planned to fly to Stockholm, but they were warned that the airline might cancel their flight because of the wind, so they found themselves boarding the *Estonia*, overnight bags in hand, and sharing a cabin.

By eleven-thirty p.m., when the ship had left the calmer waters of the Bay of Finland, the weather began to worsen. On the bridge of the *Estonia*, Captain Arvo Andresson peered into the ink-black night and saw slashing rain and gale winds, some thirty miles off the coast of Turku, Finland. The storm had swept across the Baltic Sea from Sweden — nothing unusual in September, where autumn gales are routine. But this night, rare southwesterly winds of 50 to 60 miles per hour were to whip the waves as the ship plowed ahead toward

Stockholm.

Yet Captain Andresson was unworried. After all, the *Estonia* was huge and beautiful and proud. With eight enclosed decks, it looked like a luxury liner, featuring a casino, restaurants and pubs, a dance floor, a swimming pool, saunas, playrooms, cabins and almost anything one journeying overnight could ask for.

True, Captain Andresson had received a faxed weather warning advising him of the gale-force winds forecast for that night. But the 186-man crew was accustomed to high seas, and the captain knew that the 515-foot, 15,500-ton *Estonia* was certainly capable of handling any weather. It was an easy trip, no more than fourteen hours to go the 230 miles from Tallinn to Stockholm. He and the ship's other captain aboard, Avo Piht, had made the same journey hundreds of times.

In the Baltic Bar where a karaoke contest was going on, Kent Harstedt leaned against the mahogany counter and watched with a melancholy interest. Sandy-haired and with a ready smile, Kent was not drinking like the others. He had been seasick earlier in the evening, and the roll and yaw of the huge ship fighting the heavy seas was beginning to set his stomach a-flutter again. Behind him, Jan Eric Pettersson, taller and blonder than his friend, stood watching. Like Kent, he was an outgoing person, strong-minded and optimistic. He had almost missed the ship as it left the terminal when he tarried too long in buying a doll at a boutique.

Kent was a sometimes-student at the University in Lund in southern Sweden studying Southeast Asia and the Chinese language. In addition, he worked part-time as a consultant for the Cooperative Development and Research Institute in Stockholm. Despite his youth, he had been a member of the city council, in his hometown of Helsengborg in southern Sweden for six years, a job with minimal pay but considerable prestige. He had been elected when he was only eighteen. Those who knew him were predicting a considerable future for the young man in the Swedish government. He and Morten were the youngest of all those at the conference.

Kent's assignment as project leader of this group was to explore how the cooperative unions of Denmark, Finland, Sweden, Latvia, Russia and Estonia could work for mutual betterment. The afternoon session in Estonia was a prelude to an evening banquet aboard the ship, and then the conference would end in Scandinavia.

Kent had known Morten Boje when they were both in the military. The slender, blond twenty-eight-year-old Dane from Copenhagen was only a year younger than the Swede, and their youth, shared enthusiasm and political ambitions naturally pulled them together. Both Social Democrats, they had gotten along famously during their days at the conference in Tallinn. Kent, however, had more international experience. During the previous year, his foreign consulting assignments had taken him to forty nations. These included audiences with the Dalai Lama and with Yassar Arafat in Libya.

On the previous day's program for the cooperative group, each country's representative had to make a presentation. Morten won the prize for his comedy sketch about Denmark, promising more wind in the right direction and less sexual talk in the classrooms.

In the spacious cafeteria, travelers without cabins had claimed places for the overnight journey. Travel without a cabin cost only about fifty dollars for the round trip, much less for group excursions, and a cabin cost nearly double that. Many figured that to save the extra money, it was worth simply stretching out on a convenient bench or in a corner on the carpet for a few hours. In fact, for most passengers there was not much time for sleeping. The social life in the lounges and bars always lasted well past midnight, and the ship was due to dock in Stockholm at 9:30 a.m.

Paul Barney was one of those who chose to sleep in the cafeteria, planning to use his pile jacket for a pillow. As he looked for an inviting bench, he noted the spray from the rising sea splattering the windows. In his travels backpacking around the globe, he had endured numerous adventures, so he was not concerned. In the hallway of the modest Georgian mansion where he lived, a plaque and a tattered naval flag, protected under glass, commemorated the survival of his stepfather, Brian Henry, during a near-disaster at sea right after World War II. In March of 1946 Henry was aboard a Royal Navy ship that was swamped with mountainous seas in a killer typhoon in the South China Sea bound for Hong Kong. A major tragedy had been averted only with a timely rescue by a British cruiser. The ship had earlier survived the D-Day invasion in Normandy, carrying a load of a thousand soldiers ashore. The plaque beneath the threadbare flag read: "Ensign flown by HM's LCI (L) in typhoon, South China Sea, March 1946." When he was home, Paul Barney passed that plaque every day. He had often wondered what such an experience would feel like.

On a bench at the far end of the cafeteria, nineteen-year-old Sara Hedrenius was settling in to try to sleep. About thirty others had stretched out there to find their own places for sleeping. After a sandwich and a coke, she noticed the Englishman Paul Barney enter and settle onto a bench across from her. Two of the young people from a Bible college in Sweden were chatting with him, trying to get him to join them at the smorgasbord. The Englishman told them he really wasn't hungry but said he might see them later.

At about that time, forty-one-year-old Holger Wachtmeister

slowly made his way down the narrow stairways into the bowels of the ship to the first deck, far below the waterline and even beneath the car deck where the dozens of cars and heavy trucks were carried. He was feeling pleased because earlier he had bumped into his sister, Wanda, at the information desk, neither knowing that the other was aboard. They had enjoyed a leisurely dinner together in the ship's Poseidon Restaurant. Holger had been in Estonia to explore the possibility of starting a business there.

Wanda Wachtmeister, at age thirty-five, was a worrier, who always read the safety instructions and ran through potential emergencies in her mind, locating exits and expecting the worst. On this night, with the crash of the waves pounding against the hull of the ship, she was particularly concerned. As she parted from her brother, she had commented on the trucks the ferry was carrying jammed into the car deck. "I hope they are fastened securely so it doesn't happen with us as it did with the *Jan Heweliusz*," she told her brother. Just a year earlier the Polish ferry ship *Jan Heweliusz* had gone down during a storm in the south Baltic Sea with a loss of 52 lives. After this unsettling remark, Wanda made her way to her cabin on the sixth deck. Far below, on the first deck in cabin 1048, Holger was thinking of his sister and her concerns and about his potential business as he drifted off to sleep.

As the ship had pulled away, the head bartender, Paul Andersson, stood looking out the window at the white-capped sea. From the scuttlebutt of the other crew members, he knew it would get worse from a predicted storm. Across the empty dance floor he spotted a friend, a young disc jockey who usually worked at radio station KUKU in Tallinn. Because the pay was good, the disc jockey sometimes worked the *Estonia*'s trips playing records and keeping things lively with his patter. The *Estonia* bartender walked over and greeted him.

"Tonight's going to be slow because of the storm," the disc jockey said. "Everybody goes to bed early when it's windy like this."

Paul Andersson agreed with a shrug. There would not be many tips tonight.

It was obvious that for most passengers that the storm had put a damper on the planned evening of revelry. With the heavy roll of the ship, some had fallen sick already.

Almost all the Swedish passengers spoke English, but most of the three hundred or so Estonians aboard knew only their own language and perhaps Russian. Only a few months earlier their nation had seen the last of the Russian occupation troops that for nearly fifty years had walked the streets of Tallinn, checking identities and enforcing their dour presence. Normally a stoical people, the Estonians on the ship that evening had shown their excitement in their eyes ever since the ship had pulled away from Tallinn.

For several years, the passenger ferries to the western Baltic States had offered a risky gateway to freedom for Estonians under the thumb of Russian troops. Desperate Estonians at times had sought to escape to the West by hiding themselves among the truck containers. Sometimes this meant being crushed to death as the cargoes shifted.

For the Estonians, there was a special relationship with the Finns, partly because of the closeness of their languages. Under five decades of Soviet rule, the Estonians looked to Finland as a window to Western society. They even watched Finnish television to learn what was happening in the rest of the world. After the Russians departed, Finns flocked in increasing numbers as day trippers to the Estonian capital in order to take advantage of the bargains there. Vodka at three dollars a bottle was about one-eighth what it cost in

Helsinki, and other prices were comparable.

By late 1994, the Russian soldiers had gone and Estonians for the first time began to be able to afford the journey. On board most were not able to celebrate much, but with their Estonian crowns they were able to buy small things in the duty-free shops. Wide-eyed, they were out to experience life in the West, and they peered curiously into the Poseidon Restaurant, with its white linen tablecloths and candles on the tables, where most of them could not afford to eat.

In the Admiral Pub on deck five, a small brass bell dangled above the bar on a foot-long chain that glittered in the low light. Each time the bartender received a sizable tip, he clanged the bell lustily amid laughter. When the bell was not ringing, it swung back and forth with each roll of the ship. On the pub walls, dozens of pictures of famous steamships that had plied the world's seas provided a nautical decor.

The ship itself served as an on-board center for numerous groups that held meetings each evening in conference rooms going and coming between Stockholm and Estonia. In addition, growing numbers of Finns, Swedes, Norwegians and other Europeans were taking these pleasure ships to what had become slightly-exotic Estonia for a cheap vacation. On this night, the Swedish groups included, along with the others, fifty-six retirees from the small city of Norrkoping south of Stockholm, part of a national pensioners' club. The Norrkoping retirees were so excited to be going to Estonia that they arrived at lunchtime, nearly six hours before sailing time. They had considered going to Poland, but had decided the Estonia trip was safer.

One member of such a group, Tom Johnsson, was a tall, heavy-shouldered man of thirty-three. Tom was one of sixty-eight representatives of the Swedish Police Union on an official visit. During their stay in Tallinn that day, the police union officials had visited their colleagues in the Estonian capital and had given them gifts. Then, they had returned to the ship, where the conference continued in the meeting rooms. Following dinner, some went to the pub, where the famous Swedish singer Pierre Isacsson was performing. Others headed for a shopping spree in the duty-free store to buy things before it closed at midnight. Prices in the shop were only about half what they were in Stockholm, sometimes far less

Just before midnight, Tom, who worked in the foreign affairs section of the Stockholm police union, left the others. Instead of going to the bar, he headed down to his cabin, number 4405 on deck four next to the lobby.

At 9:30 p.m. Kent Harstedt had decided he had time to take a sauna before the banquet. After an earlier meeting, he had bought Swedish cigarettes for his mother and a bottle of alcohol for his father in the duty-free shop. Now he ran down the narrow stairs to get to the sauna, which was next to the pool. At the sauna, he found Jan Eric, and they drank a beer as they sat in the steam. Unfortunately, his queasiness returned with the motion of the ship.

They did not talk about the storm. As they left the sauna, they realized they were late for the banquet upstairs. As they passed the pool next to the sauna, nobody was swimming there. But Kent noticed large waves sloshing over the sides and up to the wall. For a moment, he wondered if there was a wave machine in the pool. He was feeling worse and decided that the ship was swaying more than earlier. They rushed up the spiral stairs to change, with Kent urging the easy-going Jan Eric, whose room was around the corner, to hurry so as not to miss the dinner ceremonies.

At the banquet, the smorgasbord was loaded with shrimp, meats and cheeses of all kinds, and plentiful fruit and desserts. All the conference attendees had been looking forward to this sumptuous meal, because in Estonia the conference had taken place in an isolated spot in the woods south of Tallinn. Conditions had been poor, with cold showers and simple food. Breakfast each day had been porridge with melted butter. Now, everyone was ravenous.

There in the banquet room, the wind beat against the windows, and they could feel the rolling of the ship grow stronger. Kent noticed that when he went through the smorgasbord line it was difficult to walk straight. He filled his plate with shrimp, lox and eggs, grabbed a beer, and made his way to the table where Jan Eric and another friend sat. As he prepared to eat, however, he felt his stomach rising in his throat.

"I must be getting seasick," he said. This seemed odd, because he wasn't normally susceptible to seasickness. He turned to Jan Eric. "How do you feel?"

"I feel fine," Jan Eric replied. "But I took a seasickness pill."

"Have you any more pills?"

"No. Sorry."

For Kent Harstedt, there was no sign that the ship was in trouble, but the realization hit him that he truly was sick. He looked around and saw the Russians at another table laughing and drinking. Only one other conference attendee, Ruth, sitting across from him, also looked sick. His forehead felt sweaty, and his stomach warned him that he must leave quickly. He had been looking forward to a fantastic night on the ship, and now this. He rose, excused himself, told them he would be back soon, and stumbled to the doorway past all the beautiful food. There he paused and waved, and several of his friends returned the gesture.

In the corridors, he held on to the metal door handles of each room he passed to avoid the static electricity from the wine-red rug in the corridor. Other people he passed were holding on to the walls to keep their footing against the rolling of the ship. When he reached his room on the fourth deck, number 4316, he inserted his plastic room key and went in. He could not remember which bed his roommate, Alf Carlsson, had chosen. So he simply collapsed on the bottom bunk and lay back without removing his shoes. The whole room seemed to sway and spin, and he closed his eyes and slept.

At age sixty-two, Kent's roommate, Alf, was a senior statesman in another Swedish cooperative, with extensive international experience. He had spent many years in India and had a gentle, understanding way about him. As such, Kent was happy to tag along and learn from him. Their cabin was small, with a table and bathroom beside the beds. To avoid getting in each other's way, he and Alf tried to use the room one at a time for freshening up.

Meanwhile, after the business meeting, while most of the others went to the bar or the gambling lounge, Morten Boje had gone to his cabin to work on his laptop computer. He had never been to Stockholm and planned to see the city the following morning after they arrived. He wanted to awaken early and be alert when the ship entered the coastal waters of Sweden. For three hours just after daybreak, the ship would wind its way through the famous archipelago, one of the world's most picturesque voyages, where 25,000 pine-covered islands were almost touched by the ship as it skirted them through the maze. Passengers were nearly within shouting distance of brightly painted fishermen's homes. Most of those aboard planned to be awake to enjoy the sight.

At 10 p.m., however, Morten Boje had put on a jacket and tie and joined the others at the banquet. There was not a place left at Kent Harstedt's table, so he joined another group.

Morten had returned Kent's wave when his friend left, guessing from his appearance that he was sick. The main topic of conversation around the tables seemed to be the storm and the swaying of the ship. During the banquet, Morten visited with his Danish friend, Knud Olgaard, a sixty-seven-year-old politician with whom he shared his cabin. They agreed to turn in early so as not to miss the archipelago the next morning, and so went off to their cabin. When traveling by air, Morten was a nervous flyer, and that night he felt the same uneasiness as he tried to sleep. He lay awake listening to every sound of the ship straining against the huge waves. His Danish friend had joined him and had quickly fallen asleep. Morten finally convinced himself that in spite of the lunging of the ship and the sounds of crashing, that all was well.

Outside, the wind grew in intensity. The ship, its four engines straining to push into the face of the waves, lumbered like a wallowing beast against the short-chopped swells, heaving, dipping and yawing in an effort to make headway against the relentless pounding and slamming of the quartering waves on its bow. It was a sea that seemed determined to push the *Estonia* back. Occasionally in the rhythm of the storm's fury, a giant wave rose ahead as if some malevolent force had gathered its anger for a special assault on the ship. Such mountainous swells towered above the ship and sent spray flying across its decks as it slowly rose to the crest and in spite of its length heaved into the trough below.

2 · THERE'S WATER
ON THE FIRST DECK

11:40 p.m.

In the engine room of the *Estonia*, forty-three-year-old machinist Elmar Siegel had begun his shift as the ship pulled away from the harbor. The four large German diesel engines were purring and run by computers. Siegel's job was to monitor them from behind a thick window, and make adjustments when necessary on a large control panel. Occasionally he had to close a valve, add oil to a certain tap or give an infrequent check to the gauges. It was an easy job, one he enjoyed. Siegel was a short, sturdy, well-built man who had been at sea for nearly twenty-five years.

On this night, all was running smoothly. After an hour or so the heavy diesel smells of the engine room had begun to bother him, and he went to his cabin for a couple of hours of sleep. The smell of diesel still reeked from his clothes. He knew the sea was going to be heavy, but normally nothing would keep him from sleep.

Even though the seas had risen as high as a three-story building, with all engines throbbing at 24,000 horsepower the ship was bulling through the waves at 15 or 16 knots. Even so, the power of the waves had slowed her from its normal 20-knot speed. And Siegel knew that the captain had been hurrying to catch up with the *Mariella* and the *Silja Europa*, two other passenger ferries out of Helsinki bound for Stockholm.

At 10 p.m., both Captain Andresson and Captain Avo Piht had come to the bridge and consulted. Piht was not on duty at this time but was scheduled to take his winter competency exam at 5:00 the next morning. This meant he would be guiding the ship through the tricky maze of islands that made up the Swedish archipelago to show his mastery of the route. They spoke of the weather and of the first real storm of autumn that was building in front of them.

The captains talked with the helmsmen on duty, Peeter Kannussaar and Andres Tammes, who were scheduled to go off duty at midnight. The two captains shared a real concern that the *Estonia* was running almost an hour late. In addition to fighting the storm, they had left Tallinn nearly twenty minutes past the scheduled 7 p.m. departure time. The captains were well aware that company officials frowned on their ship arriving late in Stockholm. If they docked after the 9:30 a.m. scheduled arrival, passengers sometimes missed business appointments in the Swedish capital or airline and train connections. It was bad for the shipping line, and the captains were held accountable.

So Captain Andresson had decided to push ahead under full power to try to make up lost time. Thus, all four giant engines of the *Estonia* were still running smoothly at the high speed, with force enough to take the ship through eighteen inches of ice during the winter. Even though they had made good speed at 17-18 knots through the calmer waters of the Gulf of Finland, they were now entering the more treacherous waters of the open Baltic about thirty miles off the Finnish island of Uto. The southwestward wind had reached 25 meters a second, more than fifty miles an hour. This meant that the waves were pounding the bow of the ship and slightly on the port side.

Seafarers around the world know the Baltic Sea as nasty, mean water that can at times swamp even tested, seaworthy ships. Unlike the deep, open sea, the Baltic is relatively shallow water, which can make it highly unstable. In addition, the depths change sharply from shallow to deep, causing clashing waves and currents. The wave action speeds up over the shallower water and slows down over the deep. The conditions make for a treacherous voyage.

After a few minutes both captains left, and then half an hour later Captain Andresson returned to the bridge for a few minutes. His cabin was directly under the bridge, making it easy for him to pop in and out when he chose. With the heavy seas this night, he was on the bridge several times. No one saw Piht on the bridge after the 10 o'clock appearance. It is likely he went to his cabin to sleep in order to be fresh for his early-morning exam.

By now, the *Estonia* was in a line with the two other passenger ships bound for Stockholm, the *Mariella* and the *Silja Europa*, which were coming from Helsinki. Both of these were using only three engines and had dropped from their normal 20-knot speed to around 11 knots in deference to the strong headwinds and giant waves. Indeed, because of the conditions Captain Esa Makela of the *Europa* was considering slowing down even further by going to two engines instead of the three they were now using. In the past hour the *Estonia*, pushing full ahead, had passed and left the *Mariella* behind in the darkness, with its lights visible occasionally as it rose to the top of a swell.

Einar Kukk, a thirty-two-year-old second officer on another ship who was along for a training session that night, later recalled that the conversation on the bridge dealt mainly with the wind and the storm. The wind was 25 meters a second, the southern wind was turning westward, and new waves were coming head-on, whereas the old waves had hit the ship at a 40-degree angle to the port side. Kukk remembers no talk of the seasickness and growing concern of the passengers about the increasing sway of the ship. Nor was there any talk of slowing down. Kukk was simply there to learn the bridge procedures on the *Estonia* before returning to his own ship as second mate.

Shortly after 11 p.m. Captain Andresson went to his cabin. Kukk decided that he too would go to his cabin, regarding with some pity Peeter Kannussar and Andres Tammes, who still had another hour of duty. Kukk took a stroll by the pub and then went to his bed.

Twenty-four year old Silver Linde, tall, lean-faced and wearing a crewcut, was the last sailor to complete hourly rounds that night. He had been working on the *Estonia* for six months. At 11 p.m. after making rounds, he reported that all was well with the ship but that some of the crew in their quarters were seasick and some had been drinking. At 11:30 p.m., he started his third rounds from the bridge, and then to the seventh deck. This time is accurate because Linde activated a time clock with a plastic card as he left the bridge.

His responsibility was to check that all was well on the decks outside the public areas. Decks four, five and six, with the bar for dancing, the restaurants, the cafe, the pub, were not under his watch. But decks seven and eight, with personnel rooms and holding rooms for passengers who got out of hand, were his. And the lower decks, with the cabins and the car areas and the sauna and engine room, these were to be checked for fire hazards and for anyone who had wandered into off-limits areas.

On his 10:30 p.m. rounds that evening, he had spoken to an engineer from Stockholm, Michael Oun, slightly built, with thick curly hair and glasses, who had Estonian roots. Oun was commissioned to bring a truck load of clothing to aid the impoverished of Estonia, just emerging from the blight of communism. Oun looked worried by the heaving of the ship and the sounds coming from the battering of the waves.

"It's a little bit stormy," Linde had said.

"A little bit," Oun had agreed, trying to smile as he carried out this mission of mercy as a truck driver.

At that hour, Silver Linde had wondered why they were pushing so fast into a resisting sea. "Why are we going so hard?" he thought to himself. "Why are all four engines going? We don't usually have all engines going at once except when there is ice." But, he was only a seaman. It was not his responsibility and not his place to question the captain's decisions about speed.

But one of Linde's special responsibilities was the car deck. If anything was amiss, he was to make sure any moving car or truck was secured. As an indication of the importance of that assignment, he had to use his plastic card to turn the three watch clocks on that deck, one at the front of the deck, one in the middle and one in the rear. Until his 11:30 rounds, he had reported there were no problems. The round took him about twenty-five minutes.

When Silver Linde began his 11:30 round, he found all normal on the upper decks and in the machine room. The sauna had been closed. All was well on deck one, with the hallways quiet and the drivers in their beds. But just before midnight on the car deck, Linde was walking by the bow ramp when he felt a heavy bump that almost knocked him from his feet. It sounded like metal grating against metal.

It is likely that Linde had heard the bow visor being wrenched from its hinges and locks by the tremendous force of the huge pounding waves. Later investigators would only speculate what other breakdowns had occurred in the locking mechanisms of those great doors. But, one thing is certain. In such a short amount of time, this breakdown would allow a fatal gap to let the sea flow into the ship.

Alarmed, Linde quickly got on the radio to the bridge.

"What the hell is going on?" Linde asked.

"Stay there and see if you can hear that sound again," replied Peeter Kannussaar. "Check the controls."

On the wall the control box showed the green lights that indicated that the bow visor and loading ramp were closed tight. And he could also see that there was no water leakage coming around the ramp.

"Everything looks okay," he reported.

"Check decks one and zero too," Kannussaar ordered.

On those decks, Linde saw nothing out of the ordinary. But as he returned to the bridge, he climbed the stairs rather than take the elevator as he usually did. Later, he would wonder if this was a premonition or simple caution because of the unusual sounds. On his way up, he heard no other strange noises. Just at midnight, he returned to the bridge.

In the dance lounge shortly after midnight, a karaoke contest was going on in spite of the storm. From the crew's lounge came the loud, raucous sounds of a birthday party for one of the bar waitresses. Everything seemed to be in control. Peter Kannusaar turned his duties over to his relief, Tormi Ainsalu. Andres Tammes stayed on the bridge even though he was off duty, presumably because of the storm.

A minute or two later Captain Andresson also came back to the bridge. The captain was a calm master of the ship, according to Linde, never nervous, very professional, and trusted by his men.

On the bridge, nothing seemed out of order. The array of modern instruments showed nothing wrong. Second Officer Tormi Ainsalu and Fourth Officer Kaimar Kikas stood with Silver Linde staring through the wind-driven spray into the towering waves and the black night. The captain did ask them for their position, their speed, and the wind, and when told, he swore, "Dammit! We are still almost an hour late."

The captain apparently left the bridge again. A few minutes after midnight, someone called from down below and reported that more "blows" had been heard in the area of the car deck.

"Go down again and see what's happening," Ainsalu told Linde.

Linde started down the stairs, but when he reached the fifth deck, the ship lurched suddenly and he was thrown from his feet. He got up and again lost his footing and fell as he felt the ship list farther to the right. He got to his feet and started down once more to check on the source of the trouble. At the stairway, however, he was pushed back by a mob of people rushing up the steps, mostly drivers from the car deck, some nearly naked_as they rushed toward the seventh deck, which led outside. Pushing through them to the fourth deck, a driver yelled that water was already high in the cabins. With the turmoil of frightened passengers streaming upstairs around him, Silver Linde used his radio to report the facts to the bridge.

On his portable radio he called up to Ainsalu, "People are screaming that deck one is already under water! The stairs are full of people."

"Check it out!" yelled Ainsalu.

Linde swore back at him. "I cant," he shouted. "I can't."

Ainsalu had sounded shocked at the news as he ordered Linde to go find out where the water had come in. It remains a mystery why those on the bridge were not aware what was happening down below.

The video cameras on the bridge covered the car deck and showed everything that was happening there. By this time, the ship was listing heavily to starboard.

As Linde started to work his way downward through the stream of ascending passengers, the ship rose and careened to the side, throwing him off his feet as it remained at a 30-degree list.

From below, passengers poured up the stairs from their cabins, some in bedclothes, some who had grabbed coats as they fled, all frightened and panicked. Unable to get downward past the mob of terrified passengers, Linde struggled back up to the fifth deck.

Pushed against a wall by the panicked passengers, Linde considered his orders. It was impossible to get past the mass of frightened bodies jammed against the crowded stairwell. He realized he had lost his walkie-talkie radio in the shoving. Turning, he pushed his way into the crowed and started back up the narrow stairs. He passed people who were standing motionless in fear. He pushed along those who seemed frozen in front of him toward the exit, intent on getting out of the stairwell to help with the rescue work.

By that time, Silver Linde had decided it was too late for any checking. The game was over.

A few minutes earlier Henrik Sillaste, age twenty-five, one of the ship's maintenance mechanics, had been awakened in his cabin on deck seven by a call that one of the ship's toilets wasn't working. On checking, he quickly saw that air had seeped into the vacuum system and that he would have to go down to deck zero where the regulator was located. Since it was a two-man job, he intended to stop in the engine room to ask someone for help. As he headed down toward the engine room, he noted that a strange shudder passed through the ship, and he thought this unusual. In the machine room, he greeted his boss, Margus Treu, the thirty-year-old third engineer, and an engine repairman, Hannes Kadak, a baby-faced blond machinist, who was only twenty-three.

Treu was one of the first to hear the blows against the ship shortly after midnight. "I have worked on cargo ships, and I never heard anything like that," the engineer reported later. His first thought was that a car or truck had come loose on the car deck.

No sooner had Sillaste said hello than one of the men shouted and pointed to the television monitor. In the control room, the three crewmen, Margus Treu, Henrik Sillaste and Hannes Kadak, froze in stunned silence as they stared at the monitor. The surveillance camera was focused on the car deck, and they gasped in surprise as the television monitor showed water rushing in at the side and over the top of the loading ramp. There was so much water that instantly the men wondered if the bow ramp had opened, as had happened with the British *Herald Free Enterprise*. That ship had sunk in the English Channel only seven years earlier with a loss of 193 lives. Later, Hannes Kadak would compare the sight to a scene from a Superman movie in which a wall of water from a broken dam rushes over anything in its path.

At the same time, the men in the engine room could hear Silver Linde and the bridge on the radio as he was ordered down to check reports of further sounds below. Then they heard him say that passengers were fleeing upwards with hysterical accounts of water on the car deck.

By 12:12 a.m., there was furious activity in the control room. Margus Treu had identified three major crashes that he knew were not made by waves crashing against the side of the ship. There were other problems. For one, the ship was listing badly. Quickly the men turned on the pumps to try to get rid of the water. Soon, however, they could see that the water on the lower deck was almost knee deep. Only fifteen minutes earlier, Silver Linde had reported no water on the car deck, and the instruments had showed the bow visor and ramp locked. But now water was pouring in and rushing down the stairwells to the decks below.

In such emergencies, it was assumed that the engine room supervisor would come down and take charge. This responsibility fell to 34-year-old Lembit Leiger, who was somewhere else in the ship at that hour. "We had practiced for an emergency situation like this, and the rule was that the engineer in charge would immediately go to the machine room to lead the work," Kadak reported later. "Either Leiger didn't know the routine or the tilt was already too bad."

In the control room they turned on the pumps and waited, watching on the monitor as the water rose in the car deck and the angle of the ship grew worse. Minutes passed, and finally Margus Treu took charge. At 12:20 a.m., the second officer, Ainsalu, radioed down from the bridge: "Can we get the ship in balance again with the ballast tanks?"

On each side of the ship were great ballast tanks that could be pumped full of water to bring the ship to an even keel when it was loaded unevenly. On this night before leaving port, however, the ship had been loaded with a list to the right. Even after filling the port ballast tanks to even out the weight, instruments had shown it still had a two-degree list as they left Tallinn and headed out to sea. This turned out to be a grave error because the ship would be sailing in a northwesterly direction, with the winds and waves pounding on it from the left side, adding to the imbalance and providing no way to add weight to the port side. With a grim nod Treu turned the knobs to see if any more water could be added for additional weight on the port to help right the ship. But he shook his head and told the steerman that it was impossible because the port tanks were already full.

"Is it possible to pump out the drinking water to receive ballast?" asked the steerman, his voice impassionate.

"No. That is impossible," Treu replied.

At the same time, Treu glanced apprehensively at the four diesel engines that were beginning to whine as they struggled to keep the ship heading into the waves.

In their control room, Treu knew that the waterproof doors had closed to protect them there in the heart of the ship. Their floor was still dry, but on the monitor they watched the water rushing down the stairs and shafts and cracks to the decks below.

On the fourth deck, Einar Kukk had lain awake, somewhat troubled by the unusual sounds. Then came a noise that never in all his years at sea had he ever heard — a sharp, penetrating sound of metal giving way that brought him to his feet. As he quickly dressed, making sure to grab a warm coat, he could feel the ship begin to list to starboard.

He ran from his cabin, joining two Estonian passengers, but besides them the corridors there were empty. At the stairs those going up were calm. On deck five at the information desk, a group of passengers were gathered who were upset but not yet panicked. But by the time Kukk reached deck six the angle of the ship was so severe that he had to crawl on all fours. On that deck he saw mostly older people, most of them half-dressed. Some were screaming in fear, but without moving, hands over their faces and making no effort to get out from below deck.

From deep below in the ship Kukk could hear the crashing of the vehicles on the car deck sliding downward into each other as each minute the *Estonia* leaned farther and farther on its side. His plan was to reach the command bridge and offer what help he could, but now that was impossible. All that was important was to get out on deck — and survive.

When he reached the seventh deck, which opened to the outside, the ship was leaning so heavily that it was no longer possible to walk upright.

Then a strange event occurred. A giant swell lifted the huge ship, which sloshed the water in the car deck against the side that was up, and for a few moments the ship straightened.

In the engine room Henrik Sillaste watched on the monitor as the water rose on the car deck, until it was level with the car roofs and splashing at the camera lens. The monitor fogged up, and the picture became blurry. They still had heard no alarm given.

As the motors began to miss, Margus Treu fought frantically to keep them from dying. He knew that in such seas, if the engines died, the ship would die. Listing badly and without power, it would be helpless against the gigantic seas. As of yet, there was no water in the engine room, but Treu knew they were in deep trouble. He also knew that the engines were designed to run on a relatively even keel, and that if the ship leaned beyond 30 degrees, the oil pressure would drop and the pumps would cease to send oil to the sensitive parts.

Already smoke tendrils were rising from each engine. That meant that they were on the verge of burning out. At 12:25 a.m. Treu ordered Henrik Sillaste and Kadak to abandon the engine room. As they hurried to ascend the emergency exit, they exchanged disbelieving glances. After all, this ship was modern, well-designed, well-cared-for, and with a trained and competent crew. It was unthinkable that it could sink. This sense of utter disbelief that a great modern ship could fail in a storm and go down would be shared by most of those aboard in the next few minutes.

Margus Treu, in the engine room, watched with held breath as the left engines stopped. They were programmed to automatically shut off when the tilt of the ship reached 30 degrees. He tried to restart them, but it was useless. The speed of the ship now had dropped to around 5 knots.

A few seconds later he could hear the bridge send the command, "Full astern!" One of the mates carried out the command.

In later months some have speculated that had the *Estonia* given that command early on to back away from the waves instead of plowing directly into them, it might have saved the ship or delayed its sinking. Such post-mortem speculation often has belated answers, but the man at the wheel has not the advantage of months of pondering.

In any event, this command came far too late. A few seconds after it was given, engine number four — which by now was receiving no oil — gave out with a great banging, hammering noise, then ... silence and smoke. The ominous sound was followed quickly by the same deadly pounding and coughing signals from engine number three until it fell silent. A small auxiliary engine, however, kicked in and gave emergency power for the radio and lights on the ship.

It was 12:30 a.m. when the angle of the ship passed 45 degrees and the auxiliary engine shut down. But the crew on deck eight started the other emergency diesel engines there. The emergency Mayday call had been sent out only six minutes earlier.

Still Margus Treu continued to work at getting his engines restarted.

The emergency electricity was still on, and Treu made one last heroic effort to get the reluctant engines turning again, but there was no response. Finally with a groan he shrugged in defeat and sent the dramatic message to the bridge that he knew would doom the *Estonia* in such seas: "The engines have stopped!" he announced into his walkie-talkie. "I can't get them started."

An ominous sound followed that drowned out all other noises of the night — the ear-shattering wail of the "tyfon," the siren that was the last distress signal for those aboard. It was the death knell. It meant that the ship was going down and that all aboard needed to save themselves in any way possible. In another fifteen minutes the majestic *Estonia* would be at the bottom of the Baltic Sea.

It was to be Europe's worst peacetime sea disaster of the century.

3 · WHAT HAPPENED? WHAT HAPPENED?

12:02 a.m.

After sleeping more than an hour, Kent Harstedt awoke before midnight to a crashing sound somewhere below in the ship. It was the sound of metal grating on metal, something swinging from side to side. Slightly concerned, he rose, washed his face in cold water, brushed his teeth and went up the stairs to get some air and to see what was going on. Alf, his roommate, had not returned to the cabin.

Despite the violent pitch of the ship, his stomach felt more settled. He decided that there was still time to salvage the evening in spite of the swaying ship. From somewhere deep below, he heard a loud thump, and he wondered what it might be. As he went up the stairs, gripping the banister to secure his footing, he hoped he would find Jan Eric or his other friends.

In the restaurant lounge where a dance band was playing, he found Alf sitting next to a window. Alf, a lover of music, was still in the lounge while most of the others had gone to their beds. He wanted to be awake for the archipelago passage in the morning. They chatted a few minutes, and then Kent moved on through the lounge and found Jan Eric on the far side, drinking schnapps.

"How are you doing?" Kent asked.

"Fantastic!" Jan Eric beamed. "Sit down."

Alf wandered by on his way to bed, but when he spotted them he pulled up a chair. Only a few people remained in the restaurant, but two or three couples were trying to dance. With the motion of the ship they stumbled and had to catch themselves, adding a comic note to the scene.

Behind the bar several bottles tipped, sending the bartenders scurrying to catch them. In spite of their efforts, two bottles fell to the floor and shattered. The bartenders seemed not overly concerned, as if such accidents were to be expected at sea. The five-man dance band took a break, leaning their guitars and instruments in their stands. As the music ended, Alf said he was going to bed and excused himself.

Near the band, the guitars and saxophones began to tip as the ship swayed heavily again. The players ran to scoop them up and returned to their table holding the expensive instruments for safe-keeping.

Earlier, spray from the waves had been dampening the restaurant window. Now, they could see cascades of water splattering against the glass.

Jan Eric looked worried. "This is almost like the *Titanic*," he said. "Pretty soon they are going to serve champagne in the bar and the band will probably play 'Nearer, my God to Thee.'"

Kent gave a nervous laugh at this sarcastic pessimism. "Let's go up to the discotheque," he suggested.

"No, let's go the karaoke bar." Jan said. "If nothing is happening there, we can try the discotheque."

As they went through the foyer, they could see the ocean spray slashing against the windows. Several middle-aged people stood looking out, half in fascination and half in awe. As they watched, swaying, they steadied themselves against the roll of the ship.

At the karaoke bar, Kent and Jan Eric found a lively crowd of a hundred or so people, singing lustily. They were of mixed ages, but with many young people the same age as the men.

"This looks great," Jan Eric said. "We'll go to the discotheque later."

In front of the microphone stood the slim, graying figure of Pierre Isacsson, acting as master of ceremonies. The noted Swedish singer had been a popular recording star in the 1970s. Now, he was in charge of the twenty-seven entertainers aboard the *Estonia*. This night he wore a white suit that almost shimmered in the flickering bar lights, as he joked with the audience and introduced the next singers. Kent noted that the man could still work a crowd.

Kent and Jan Eric went to a corner of the bar near Isacsson. In spite of the storm, it was a convivial atmosphere, with everyone laughing and singing. Kent would remember this moment best, a jovial scene of people singing along with the karaoke machine and toasting their voyage. Even though many revelers had retired early because of the storm, a lively crowd was still gathered there in celebration. Drinks were ridiculously cheap on the *Estonia*, an attraction of the voyage, and for many it was an easy way to get away for a high time at little expense.

As Kent stood close to Pierre Isacsson, his mind went back. When he was only seven years old, his parents had taken him to a folk song festival in their home town of Helsengborg where Isacsson was performing as a national star. Song festivals are popular in Sweden, and the boy had been smitten with the singer. Isacsson was particularly famous for his song, "Then I will go down in my cellar." With a start, Kent realized that here was his long-time hero and star, whom he remembered as tall and stately, now thin and small, finishing his career as a ship entertainer.

So this is how my idols end up, he thought.

The entertainer had the crowd in the palm of his hand and kept the laughter and the songs flowing. When he recognized a plump blonde woman from the previous night's trip, he teased her into coming up to perform, where she won loud applause. If any lull occurred, Isacsson launched into a familiar tune and the audience enthusiastically joined in.

Kent ordered a Coke and took a seat on a tall bar stool, while Jan Eric stood behind him and ordered another beer. The uneasiness they had felt earlier left them as they enjoyed the camaraderie. They even joined in the singing, following the words of the songs on a large TV monitor that stood on the floor.

Above the bar, the little brass bell that swung from the ceiling to encourage tips swung back and forth with the motion of the ship. At times, it seemed to hang suspended for a long moment near the ceiling before it dangled downward again as the ship rolled back to level.

Oblivious to the storm, the crowd in the karaoke bar remained loud and exuberant, drowning out the sounds of the wind and of the waves that beat against the ship. Indeed, the pounding of the storm and rolling of the ship seemed to excite them like the thrill of an amusement park ride. They whooped with merriment, fighting to steady themselves at their tables or standing around the dance floor. As in the restaurant, several couples even tried to dance amid the violent swaying, laughing as they stumbled, and holding on to each other to keep from falling. This only added to the party atmosphere.

It was then that a group of workers from a Swedish oil company took the microphone and launched into a well-known song they had been practicing, "Thirty-four." It was a song everyone knew and most joined in. The words dealt with an old house at number thirty-four that was being torn down and was thus going to heaven. In the midst of the song, a crashing sound reverberated throughout the ship, and the room rolled enough to send Kent's stool toppling, nearly spilling him. He caught himself by holding onto the bar railing.

"Oy, what a wave that was," Jan Eric said as he reached for the wall to steady himself.

At the loud crash that echoed like cannon-fire, the heavyset woman who was leading the Swedish karaoke singers paused momentarily with a frightened look. After a momentary puzzled silence, they resumed their song.

A few seconds later, a dull boom shuddered from deep within the *Estonia*. Most of those in the karaoke bar could not hear it because of the noise in the room, but the ship continued to lean. Isacsson caught the microphone as it teetered, but now the television monitor began to roll away. The singer had an annoyed look on his face as he reached to control it.

Almost immediately a third boom reverberated through the ship, and the sea seemed to fling the giant ship sideways. The starboard side dipped sickeningly toward the water. The karaoke lounge swam in chaos. Bottles, glasses, mirrors, and television sets behind the bar hurtled through the air as projectiles, smashing into the bar and into the bar crew standing there. From the corner of his eye, Kent saw a pretty dark-haired barmaid struck in the head and shoulders by flying bottles. She screamed, raising her arms to protect her head, as the shelves behind her toppled over. As if in slow motion, he saw the girl struck and sinking to the floor as the room turned nearly on its side, with people and objects sent flying pell-mell down the inclined dance floor.

Isacsson, looking confused, made a desperate grab for the monitor as it tilted away from him. Then he stumbled and was sent sliding downward. As the floor continued to tilt, dancers on the floor struggled to keep their balance as they caromed off each other to the downside wall in a tangle of tumbling tables and chairs. Those standing without support were hurled helplessly downward, tumbling and flying against the pile there. A glass-and-wood wall room divider collapsed, smashing nearby bystanders to the floor.

Hanging on to the bar and frozen by what he was seeing, Kent watched the tangled mass of people, arms and legs protruding, jammed against the wall. He could see people bleeding, and twisted limbs that told him there were broken bones. Some appeared to be unconscious.

For a long moment, people, stunned into silence, stared uncomprehendingly at each other. The pause grew as they waited for the ship to right itself.

Kent had been one of the few able to hang onto something stable and keep his feet. The whole world seemed upside down, and it took a few seconds before he could grasp what had happened.

The screams and groans of pain and unbelief rose in a chorus. Like a splash of cold water in the face, Kent realized the actual horror of the situation. Loud gasps and screams of terror added to a palpable feeling of growing panic. People lay everywhere, piled on top of each other on the downward slope.

"What happened? What happened? What happened?" shouted one man over and over again amid the horror.

Those who were able began to help one another up the steep incline of the floor, toward the doors that led to the foyer. These doors opened to stairs up to the outside decks.

As the incline grew steeper, it was evident that the ship was not going to come upright. Screams and shouts of despair drowned out all other sounds, which created a greater panic.

The little brass bell no longer swayed from above the bar, but nearly touched the ceiling on the starboard side.

After a short time fighting to hang on to the bar, Kent let go and went sliding downward toward the pile of humanity. "What the hell is going on here?" he thought as he struggled to his feet.

At first his eyes went to the windows above them, one after the other. He saw that they did not open. He knew he must struggle up the tilted floor to reach the door that opened to the stairwell that led up to the outer deck. Around him, the screams and pleas for help drowned out all sounds as the lights flickered and dimmed. Kent reminded himself that he must remain calm and not join the panic.

He did not see Jan Eric, but a chain of people had formed to help each other upward toward the doorway. With these people, he was able to get through the door and out into the hallway. With a glance back, he realized that most of the injured in the pile below would have no chance to get out. Also, it was obvious that those who had had too much to drink and whose judgment and coordination were impaired had little hope.

In a matter of a few seconds, it became apparent their plight had now become a matter of living or dying. Gone were thoughts of helping others. Gone was chivalry. Instead, men stepped on each other and pushed women aside in their desperate struggle up the slanting floor to reach the door.

Ahead of him in the dim light, Kent could see Isacsson's white suit. He followed this, still talking to himself to help analyze the situation. In the foyer, he spotted Jan Eric standing stupefied. Kent could tell that he was panicked, and he called to him amid the turmoil.

"Jan, we have to help each other!" he pleaded. Jan Eric only stared at him without responding. Again, Kent shouted at him that they must work together, with no response. Finally, Jan Eric looked at him as if seeing him for the first time, then nodded, "Okay."

"Take it easy," Kent said. "Everything is going to be okay."

Across the foyer, they could see the stairs that led upward toward the seventh deck, which opened to the outside. The steep slope across the slippery rug that led to the stairs was almost impossible to negotiate alone. Those who attempted to run up in panic fell back atop others, who were also struggling upward. Using the wall for support, Kent was able to work his way to the stairs, grab hold and then reach back to help Jan Eric up. At the top, they paused to reach back and help others up the near-vertical incline. Many passengers refused help, as if in their fright they thought they would be hurt instead. These kicked and screamed and tried to get loose when the two friends tried to help them up. Many just sat on the floor and cried.

Once more, they felt the ship jerk farther to starboard. This sent some near the top of the stairs sprawling back down the incline, and increased the terrified wails of despair. The lights flickered again and came back on dimly.

Kent joined the others clambering up the last stairway to the outer deck. When a young woman in a red skirt paused in front of him, he bumped into her, stepping on her skirt and tearing it. In the process he stepped on her shoe, which went bouncing back down the stairs through the crowd.

"My shoe!" she cried. "I lost my shoe!"

She turned and began to retreat back down the stairs. Kent reached to stop her, but she eluded his grasp. "What's a shoe at a time like this?" he shouted at her, but she dodged into the crowd. He grunted in dismay that she would so foolishly throw away her chances of escape.

In the lower decks, the stairs were the only way out for those in cabins. It was the seventh deck that opened to the outside. The narrow stairs, now almost useless in such a steep incline, offered a deadly barrier for those caught below the outside deck.

Ahead of Kent and Jan Eric, the two flights of stairs to the seventh deck were a nightmare of people falling, begging, crying and screaming. Some worked together and helped people up the stairs, while others stood and cried. When Kent and Jan Eric finally broke out into the open air of the deck, the slashing rain and the wind seemed like a relief.

Kent studied the situation with a mixture of relief and dismay as he came out into the open air. After the terror of the enclosed quarters and people smashing against each other, the cold wind and the sea spray felt good. The decks were lighted, and for most the panic was eased as they emerged to the deck. Some stood waiting for instructions from the crew. Others were tearing at the life raft containers or trying to lower the lifeboats. A few, however, burst through the doorway and threw themselves over the railing into the dark sea. By now some crew members or cool-headed passengers were handing out life jackets or throwing them overboard for those already struggling in the cold water.

Jan Eric emerged through the door, and he and Kent spoke. Then Jan Eric hurried forward on deck, and Kent stayed where he was in order to analyze the situation to decide what he should do next. Without meaning to, they separated. As Kent studied the situation, the water seemed very far away, because the port deck had lifted as the starboard side had dipped to the water. He was not cold, still wearing the suit and tie that he had worn to the banquet.

There was no shortage of life vests. He could see them littering the deck in some places. He picked one up and carefully tied it, knotting it around his stomach.

The ship shifted downward once more, and the panic on deck was renewed. A few people at the railing began running to and fro, peering over as if to see where the boat was going next.

Near the door, lying with one leg twisted horribly at the knee, a nicely dressed woman about forty stared up at those passing, pleading. Her eyes fastened on Harstedt and she called in Swedish, "You, you have to help me. Give me a life jacket." He knew at least one leg was broken. She was a pretty woman, whom he had noticed earlier. Now as she cried, her mascara ran down her cheeks.

Kent Harstedt went over to her, and she grabbed his sleeve. "Are we going to die?" she demanded. "Are we going to die now?"

"No, there is more to come," he said solemnly, "and you and I are not going to die." He called out that an injured lady needed a life jacket, and someone threw one toward them. He helped her tie it on. He could see a crowd gathered around the steel boxes on deck that held the life jackets. Two crew members were throwing the life jackets right and left, and several lay unclaimed in the walkway.

With the ship holding its precarious list, Kent helped the woman to the rail of the *Estonia*. As she pleaded for more help, he turned away from her, feeling flushed with guilt, but determined to save himself. Around him, everything was chaotic. The rain and wind pounded at him, and now he shivered in the cold. People were streaming through the doors out onto the deck, crying for life jackets, screaming for help or just standing dazed and frightened. Faced with the angry sea beyond the rail, others simply sat down and cried hopelessly. Some poised on the rail, then leaped into the waves.

The very act of emerging on deck seemed to settle most people. Kent told himself that he must retain his self-control and find a lifeboat. He saw one man standing in the middle of the deck seeming to savor his last cigarette. Farther down the deck, Kent caught a glimpse of Jan Eric and he started to call to him, but there were so many people between them that he decided to climb up to one of the lifeboats instead. Kent started to work up the slippery deck toward the lifeboats on the high side of the ship. That was the last time he saw Jan Eric.

4 · IT'S A BLOODY EMERGENCY

A few minutes before midnight, the Englishman Paul Barney had returned to the cafeteria. It was dimly lit and quiet there, with most people sleeping. He noticed Sara Hedrenius across from him on a bench, a particularly pretty girl who was now sleeping. The benches were all taken, so Barney stretched out on the carpet in a corner, using his pile jacket as a pillow.

There in the corner, Barney, a light sleeper, was awakened with the first shudder of the ship. Still half asleep, he rose and wandered through the cafeteria. Because of the growing list of the ship, it was getting more and more difficult to walk, but in his half-awake state the danger failed to register with him. From below, the sound of the crash came to him, and then all the tables and furniture of the cafeteria smashed together on the low side of the room, jolting him wide awake.

At the same time, Barney noticed that Sara Hedrenius had snapped awake with the sounds. They did not speak, but each hurried toward the exit sign that marked the way into the foyer towards the stairs that led upward toward the deck. Barney shuddered at the sight of the frothy sea, the cold wind, and stinging rain that he could see through the window. He was reluctant to leave the warmth of the cafeteria. For a moment, he thought that they had run into a cliff of one of the islands near Sweden.

"I've got time," he assured himself, and he returned to where he had been sleeping and pulled on one of his boots. The other one had slid away into the jumble of furniture.

For a moment he gazed at the others in the cafeteria. Most of those sleeping had roused and sat half erect, frozen in fear and uncertainty. They were like soldiers who had come under fire for the first time and didn't know what to do.

By now, the ship was listing so badly it was difficult to stand. He realized the boot would do no good in the water. He jerked it off, and then stopped to pull on a heavy sweater and the pile jacket he had earlier used for a pillow.

Paul paused at the exit sign of the cafeteria while he tried to figure out what was happening. As he watched, a man came stumbling down the stairs into the foyer, terror in his eyes. Paul realized that the man was disoriented and going the wrong way. Right then, the Englishman resolved that the most important task for him in the next few minutes would be to keep his bearings and his wits.

Sara Hedrenius had been awakened earlier by the sharp swaying of the ship. But she wasn't feeling well and tried to go back to sleep. When the ship lurched, however, she was thrown violently from her couch. This time, fighting the fuzziness of sleep, she grabbed her glasses and her passport.

"If I drown, it will be easier to identify me if I have my passport," she grimly thought.

As she picked herself up, still uncertain what was going on, she noticed that the Englishman had gotten up from the carpet and was heading for an exit. As the ship lurched, she watched a heavy ashtray fly through the air and hit Paul on the hand. Suddenly with a start, Sara realized that something dreadful was happening and that time was short. She burst into a run toward the near exit that led to the stairway.

There, where walls were becoming floors, she found a scene of panic, with people screaming, pushing, sobbing uncontrollably or standing immobilized by fear. She squirmed through and tried to climb up the stairs, but the incline had turned to nearly straight up, and she fell back. Others grabbed her and they worked together to form a human chain. The chain broke, but Sara grasped the railing of the stairway and began to pull herself up, hand over hand. She did not turn to look down behind her. She fell backward and then struggled upward again and again, working up to the next deck, which led outside to the open air.

Inside the cafeteria, Paul had lost control of his emotions for one of the few times in his life. Waiting by the exit sign, an uncontrollable anger rushed over him when the ship seemed nearly on its side.

"What in the bloody hell is going on?" he shouted over and over, his British accent rising above the cries and screams of the night. He began to pound on the door in frustration and fear.

As if in answer, a message was blurted over the loudspeakers, but it was in Estonian, a language that fewer than half the passengers understood. Paul cocked his head, trying to understand what was being said.

Then, an Estonian passenger opened the door and said, "It's an emergency."

"I know it's a bloody emergency!" Paul shouted. Breathing deeply, he regained control and slowly asked the Estonian how long one could survive in such cold water.

"About four minutes," came the solemn answer.

Turning, Paul shouted to the walls: "How the hell can my life end like this? In a black ocean, in a damned cafeteria on the Baltic

Sea? What an incredibly stupid way for it all to end!"

The cafeteria lights flickered, went out and then slowly came back on, but dimly. In the light, Barney could see that water was pouring into the cafeteria.

"What the hell are people still doing in the cafeteria?" he shouted to the Estonian who had spoken to him. "Why are they only sitting there?"

"Don't even think about it," the Estonian said. "They are gone, done for."

Working together, the Englishman and the Estonian fought their way to the foyer and up the stairs to the open air. They were on the starboard side, which was dipping toward the water. As they emerged, they caught sight of a life vest hanging on the rail just above the surface of the water. But the deck was nearly vertical now, and covered with oil. The Estonian dashed through the doorway, slid down, jerked short against the railing, snatched the life vest, and put it on. The next second, the man was washed into the sea by a wave and bobbed away as a dark spot among the darker waves. Paul stood watching, wondering how long four minutes would be.

With a shrug, the Englishman stepped from the doorway and climbed upward toward the high part of the deck, through the rail, and onto the hull of the ship, which by now was almost horizontal. The side of the ship was white, and it was as if he was standing in a great field. Remarkably, the storm had paused briefly, although the waves did not diminish. A shaft of moonlight broke through the clouds, lighting his way. As he stood on the side of the ship, for some reason a great sense of relief swept over Paul Barney. He was resigned to his fate. Ahead through the falling rain, near the front of the ship, he could make out life rafts with people gathering around them. For the first time, a sense of hope came over him, a feeling that there might be a way to survive.

Walking gingerly in his stocking feet, he made his way along the hull. He avoided the cabin windows, telling himself that they might not have any glass in them and that he might plunge into depths of the ship if he stepped on them.

The ship was nearly two football fields long, and it took him minutes to work his way to the rafts. When he arrived at the nearest one, he found the two crewmen, Elmar Siegel and Paul Andersson, desperately trying to get a life raft they had inflated down the side of the ship and into the sea. When these rafts were inflated, an enclosed tent automatically popped up overhead for protection from the elements. In the panic, several people had already crawled inside the tent, making it almost impossible to move it along the sloping side of the ship. In spite of promises and threats, those inside the enclosure of the raft refused to get out.

The three men heaved and strained to move it inch by inch toward the edge. When they were almost there, a wave broke over them, plunging raft and all down into the water. As it descended, Paul Barney grabbed the edge of the doorway and pulled himself inside. Then, a second wave overturned the raft.

In the bitter-cold, dark water, Paul Barney felt everything go black. He was trapped inside. This must be the end now, entangled in a cold and watery grave. But instinct and anger took over. Furiously, he kicked and fought with his arms to rise to the surface, searching for the exit from the tent and upward to life.

5 · THIS SHIP CAN'T SINK, CAN IT?

Outside in the storm, Sara Hedrenius had found and hurriedly put on a life vest. Straining every muscle, she managed to pull herself up the slanting deck to the highest railing of the ship. Above the shrieking roar of the wind and the waves, she could hear the pandemonium below her. In the flickering light, she caught sight of a lone man on the deck below her trying to get one of the handles to lower a lifeboat that hung above them in steel davits. It was Kent Harstedt, struggling to get the handle to turn. But, the ship was already at such an angle that the release mechanism was jammed.

"Can somebody come and help?" he shouted, half in English and half in Swedish,

He looked at the pretty girl above him, holding on to the railing. Watching him, for some reason Sara Hedrenius became calm. Determined, she let go of the railing and slid down toward him on the deck. He was still wearing his suit and tie from the banquet.

From the other parts of the boat came cries of desperation and screams, but they were alone. Kent stood breathing deeply. Finally, he sized her up and gave a nod of approval. "You look calm," he shouted over the wind. "Maybe we can help each other. Shall we do this together?"

She nodded. "Sure, we can do that."

He held out his hand. "My name is Kent Harstedt."

"I'm Sara Hedrenius," she said, giving his hand a firm shake.

The pact was made. She had never seen him before, but it felt good to be throwing their fates together like this. They shook hands again to bind the agreement.

"Can you help me with this?" Kent askedl. Together they worked desperately to make the handle work. After another minute of furious work, the handle broke, jammed by the angle of the deck. With a shrug, they decided that it would be impossible to free the lifeboat.

They looked around.

The storm had intensified, and the rain beat against them. Angry, mountainous waves crashed constantly against the hull below them, covering them with freezing spray. On the deck below they could see men passing out life vests, throwing some into the sea, or helping others to put them on. They could see other people throwing themselves from the ship, or sliding down its side to be engulfed in the heaving sea.

"Do you think we're going to make it?" Sara asked.

"Absolutely. We are coming home, and we must believe this."

For a minute, they discussed what they should do. Kent stared at a man nearby who stood placidly smoking. It was Thomas Grunde, one of the Swedish oil company group, who had been performing in the karaoke bar when the ship lurched. Kent edged his way to him and asked him if he thought it was time to jump into the sea. "No, not yet," Thomas replied. "Wait till the boat gets lower in the water."

He nodded, and they looked upward to the railing. Steadying each other, Kent and Sara began to climb upward on the spray-slickened deck to find a better place to jump. They helped each other climb upward to the side railing, which had become a ceiling grill above them. Around them, others were clinging onto the railing, struggling to climb up, but it was nearly impossible to climb it alone. Kent pushed Sara up, and when she reached the hull where she could stand up, she reached a hand down to help him.

There on the side of the ship, Kent leaned over and shouted above the shriek of the wind, "If we make it through this, I promise to take you out to dinner in Stockholm next week!"

"It's a date!" she agreed through clenched teeth. In spite of — or perhaps because of — the chaos around them, they then paused to discuss which of the restaurants in Stockholm would be most suitable for their dinner date.

The side of the ship was now at a 45-degree angle into the frothing sea. Each moment, the ship sank deeper. They could see the two rows of windows beneath them that had been portholes on the side of the ship.

Hand in hand, they hurried on along the slanting hull, being careful not to step on the windows and looking for a better place to jump. They passed an inflated life raft that was being lowered down the side of the *Estonia*, but already more people were clutching to it than it could hold when launched.

The ship was still lit by deck lights. Then these flickered and went out.

With the ship's lights out, they could see better around them on the sea. On what seemed to be the horizon, they began to see lights appearing. Kent pointed to the lights and told Sara that they were probably fishing boats and that these boats would undoubtedly come to rescue them soon.

What they saw, however, were the small lights atop the life rafts that were already floating nearby. The containers that held the life rafts were rigged to open and send the rafts to the surface if the ship sank. Along with those that had been launched by survivors, these were now popping up from the starboard side, which had slowly dipped beneath the waves as the ship turned on its side. When the rafts surfaced, the tents also automatically opened to spread above the raft for shelter, and a small battery light came on atop the raft.

The rafts were six-sided, a bright orange color, with two doorways in the tent. About twelve feet across and with high sides, each raft was built to hold thirty-five persons. A small rope ladder was attached at each entrance of the raft, although in the darkness many of the survivors did not understand how the ladders worked. For instance, to close the openings in the rafts to keep the waves from washing in, the rope ladders had to be outside. It was not until morning that some survivors understood that the rafts even had ladders. Worse yet, in the mountainous seas, about half the rafts overturned, so that survivors had to climb on top and huddle in the indented area without protection from the sea.

When the ship's lights went out, the clouds that had covered the sky parted briefly and a near-full moon lit up the unfolding drama. For a moment, Kent and Sara stood looking up at the moon, with clouds skittering by. They could see others on the hull working grimly to get over the side and into the sea.

With the ship nearly on its side, it was difficult to reach the water without getting hurt on the way down the sloping hull. Kent reminded the girl that when they got in the water they needed to get away from the ship so as not to be sucked down when it went under. Waiting there with the spray soaking them and the wind pulling at their clothes, for the first time they began to realize how cold it was.

Oddly, they saw smoke coming from the front of the ship and Kent suggested that there was a fire inside. It is more likely, however, that the smokestacks had hit the water by that time and the diesel smoke was billowing from them. Margus Treu, the engineer, who escaped up the smokestacks, later told of the smoke that poured out when the stacks hit the water.

Perched there waiting for the proper moment to jump, Kent Harstedt and Sara Hedrenius listened to the alarm siren wailing in the night. The mournful sound pierced them to the core, and the thought came to Kent that the captain must be staying to the last to send the signal to abandon ship.

Finally, when it seemed they could wait no longer, each acknowledged with a nod that there was only one thing they could do — jump. The wet hull was as slick as glass. They held hands and carefully sidled downward along the hull to get nearer to the water. Below them, they could see a life raft tossing on the waves. Before jumping, Kent put his glasses into his pocket to avoid being cut if they broke. Sara had no pockets, so she kept her glasses on. At that moment, the bow began to rise as the *Estonia* entered its death throes.

Just before they jumped, Sara turned and called, "I'll see you next week for that dinner!" Then, together, as a wave splashed over them, they leaped toward the water.

It was not a freefall. Sara covered her head with her arms to make the bumps easier as they slid over the side of the ship. Each time she bounced over a porthole, she gasped in pain. Then everything went black, and she could feel herself being pulled down deeper into the the sea. Something had tangled around her leg, and she was being pulled down with the ship. This is how it ends, she thought. A picture came into her mind, crystal clear, of her mother.

"My mother," she recalled later. "I thought about how she has always been afraid of boats and the sea, and now she would be even more scared now that I was ... well, gone." It seemed as if she would never stop sinking. Sara even thought of opening her mouth to take in water as to ease the passage into death. Better to get it over quickly.

Kent Harstedt had fared no better. He was slammed against the hull, and he could feel the pain in his back. After bouncing down the side of the ship, he went into the water feet first. He entered a maelstrom that tugged one way and then the other by the force of the waves. Deep underwater, he became entangled in some ropes and was unable to rise back to the surface. He felt himself going down and down, dragged by the ropes. As he swirled round and round deep in the currents, helpless, Kent could not tell which way was up and which way was down. Although he struggled frantically, the rope on his foot held tight, and he gave up. He was angry that he was going to die so young. He felt dizzy, and it seemed as if he was being pulled deeper. Around him, the dark sea began to change color to a light blue like the Mediterranean, where he had once swum, and it became warm like that gentle sea. A soft and comfortable feeling came over him, and he bade goodbye to his parents. He felt the comforting blackness close around him.

Morten Boje, Kent's friend, had been trying to go to sleep in his cabin on the fourth deck deep in the ship. Half awake, he was vaguely aware of the groans of the ship's steel straining against the force of the storm. From the car deck below him, he could hear the sounds of a car alarm. He had a wistful thought that just like back home in Copenhagen, car alarms were likely to go off with no reason here as well. It is the violent sea, he reasoned, that had probably set off this alarm.

Immediately, there came the sound of metal smashing against

metal, a heavy dull thud from some distant part of the ship. Startled, he lay wide awake trying to figure out what was happening. In another minute, he gasped as he felt the foot of his bed rising and his head sinking. He could hardly believe the ship was in such a dreadful lean. Springing up, he snatched open his cabin door to the corridor. There, he saw a group of young women he had noticed singing and partying earlier. Now, they were screaming in terror, forced against the down side of the corridor by the list of the ship.

The hall floor was covered with broken glass. Morten quickly grabbed a pair of pants and boots and pulled them on as he shouted to his friend, Knud, to wake up.

When Knud tried to go back to sleep, Morten screamed at him, "Put on your shoes! There's glass in the hall, and we have to get out of here."

After Morten had his boots on and shook his friend, Knud still did not want to rouse himself. He mumbled sleepily and tried to turn back over. At length, Morten grabbed the man's shoes, pulled them on for him, and tugged him to the door.

In the corridor outside their cabin, Morten Boje faced an almost insurmountable problem. As they turned toward the stairwell nearest their cabin, a horrifying sight met them. The passageway was obstructed by heavy steel storage cabinets that clanged and crashed as they fell, blocking their way. Amid groans and screams, dozens of people were struggling to climb over and around the cabinets. Some people had been pushed flat against the floor, and Morten could see a woman caught beneath the cabinets. She had ceased to struggle.

Suddenly, water began to gush down the stairs. Morten leaped to catch a handhold and fought to climb over the cabinets. He reached behind him to give a hand to Knud. The ship was at such a slope that the stair railings could be used as a ladder. Around them, a chaos of screams and pleas for help filled the stairwell. Morten climbed hand over hand up the railing, aware that those who lost their grip would be gone. With the strength of youth, he pulled upward, ignoring those above him who could not hold on. Those people tumbled down past him, shrieking toward the scramble of humanity and rising water below.

The only thing he could hear was people screaming for help, but Morten blocked everything from his mind except the exit above that would lead to the open decks. It seemed that the stairs would never end, and he lost count of how many railings he had climbed or how much farther there was to go. At last, he could feel fresh air rush into his lungs, replacing the fetid smells rising from below — the smells of vomit and feces that accompany pure terror. He was near the doorway straight above him, but dozens of people were clinging there to try to squeeze out through the double doors, which had a vertical bar between. He noted sadly that those who tried to help others or clung to others were the ones who fell.

Pulling himself forward and up, Morten lay flat on the now-horizontal bar and reached back for Knud. A vivid picture etched itself forever into his mind of dozens of pairs of hands reaching toward him, begging for help. He put down his hand and helped one person up, then another. Still, he could not see Knud as he grasped yet a fourth person and lifted them up. The fifth person was Knud.

Forcing himself, he turned away then from all the hands reaching from below. He knew it was the only way he was going to live. By now, it was obvious that the *Estonia* was going under. At this angle, he knew it could not possibly last more than a few minutes. The sea was almost lapping at the doorway, and then he knew it would be too late for all those trapped below. With Knud, he struggled to the ship's railing.

There they could see the ship's great single funnel, which enclosed the four smokestacks near the rear of the ship, lying on the water. The ship was on its side. Dozens of people lay clinging on the flat surface of the hull, which was now in the horizontal position of the decks, frozen in fear. Some were huddled atop each other for warmth and comfort. Some of the passengers in the water were trying to climb onto the ship's funnel.

When Morten turned back, Knud was gone.

"We're sinking ... we're sinking," Morten told himself in despair. When he had reached the deck, he had expected to find a well-organized rescue effort under way, with crewmen handing out life jackets and launching boats. Instead, he could see panic and confusion everywhere, and the night was filled with and helpless shouts. Desperately, he searched over the hull and on the water for Knud, but he had disappeared. He knew then he would have to go on alone.

Not far from his feet, Morten saw a life vest lying on the hull near the edge of the water. Stretching carefully, he was able to grab the life vest and put it on. Morten began edging closer to the water, but before he could make any further decisions a huge wave towered above him and in a moment he realized that he was in the water, and without injury.

Elmar Siegel, the chief motor mechanic, who had come to his bunk to sleep and recuperate from the diesel fumes in the engine room, was stirred awake by the first blow that echoed through the ship. When the second blow came, he rolled from his bunk, realizing that the list was so bad that it was unlikely the ship would recover. He did not panic but stopped to dress himself warmly, pulling on a heavy crew coat. As he tried to open his cabin door, it was jammed by something that had fallen against it. Quickly, he turned and opened the window to his cabin and crawled out onto the deck. For him, it was fortunate that he was in crew's quarters, for the windows to passenger cabins remained tightly locked for safety reasons.

As a member of the crew, he had trained weekly on how to come out of the ship in darkness and through the corridors with the hydraulic walls closed. He wondered how the passengers unfamiliar with the ship would find their way out. In fact, some survivors claim that the lights went out and the corridors were completely dark. But most say that as the ship listed, the lights flickered, dimmed, then the emergency lights came on.

On the seventh deck, he saw a jumble of confused and dazed passengers milling about. Remembering his assignment for an emergency, Siegel headed for the lifeboats to try to unloose and lower them. With the ship in such a list, however, even with half a dozen of his mates tugging with him, it was impossible to get the lifeboats launched.

Siegel stood on the top deck above the spot from which Kent and Sara had jumped. Below him he could see crowds of people gathered at the railing, afraid to jump and not knowing what to do. He finally decided that it was useless to try to get the lifeboat loose. Even if it could be unfastened, it would smash into people below on the slanting deck, crushing some of them. He could hear people inside the lifeboat where they had crawled beneath the tarpaulin for safety. If the boat came loose, some of them would be killed in the fall.

The ship was continuing to list more and more each minute. The car deck was filled with water, and the pressure was bursting more and more of the porthole windows on the starboard side, which let the sea come flooding in. Almost on its side, the stern of the *Estonia* was going lower and lower in the water.

For Siegel, the issue was no longer in doubt. "Our ship has gone past the critical angle," he told himself. He knew he had to get off soon or it would be too late. He left his lifeboat station on deck eight and worked his way toward the stern. He passed groups of people standing crying; occasionally one broke away and leaped into the heaving waves in the darkness. Along the way, he stopped to open four or five raft containers, which popped open and inflated automatically. He spotted another crewman, Paul Andersson, and they began to work together to get rafts out of one of the steel bins. Elmar cursed himself for not bringing a knife to cut through the canvas straps that enclosed the bins. His fingers stung as he tore at the straps, and he used his teeth to help pull one loose.

At midnight, head bartender of the Baltic Bar, Paul Andersson, had finished his shift and made his way to the crew lounge. When the ship heeled strongly to starboard, he could hear things falling around the ship, so he knew there was trouble. At once, he thought that the trucks had shifted on the car deck, causing the heavy list, but he reassured himself that the crew below could handle the problem.

When the ship did not right, he ran the few steps to his cabin on deck eight. Now, sensing an emergency, he stopped to put on a thick sweater and crew coat. Like Elmar Siegel, he crawled through his porthole as the quickest way to the outside deck. He made it to his assigned emergency station that he had practiced so many times, but there he found he was useless — his station on the starboard side was under water.

At age thirty-two, Andersson was in good shape and often swam even on cold days at the beach near his home in Tallinn. He turned and worked upward on the slanting deck, then edged his way toward the stern, where he saw fellow crewman, Elmar Siegel, working to open a life raft bin. Working together, they managed to get four rafts inflated.

Andersson looked up as the deck lights flickered, went out, and then the emergency lights came on. He watched two men above him working to get the lifeboats loose, and knew at a glance that it was futile because of the slant of the ship. He did not take time to find a life jacket, but worked desperately to get the rafts loose. Then, as the ship sank lower, he and Siegel exchanged a nod. It was time to get off the ship in the last raft.

Studying the Situation, Andersson noticed several people slide down the side of the ship. The English passenger, Paul Barney, had spotted them working to loosen the raft. He trotted up and began to help shove the raft down the hull. It was difficult to move because of the weight of the people inside who refused to get out. Little by little, they moved it toward the edge. With the ship heeling farther over every minute, it was clearly time for them to get off.

They felt the ship lurch even farther to starboard. As the raft began to slide, a wave helped scoot it along and Paul Barney jumped inside. In a moment, a following wave smashed over the hull and swept the raft into the sea, along with those hanging onto it, including Siegel. When it landed, the raft was immediately turned upside down by a wave. Those inside it struggled to find a way out.

At the same time, some of those who had launched the raft were trapped beneath it. Siegel was running out of air, but finally was able to swim out and grab the rope on the side of the raft.

In the water, a few of those floundering nearby were able to crawl on top of the overturned raft. Those trying to stay afloat among the heaving waves screamed and added their shouts to the cries carried on the wind all around them.

6 · DEATH BY FREEZING IS GENTLER

When his raft hit the water and overturned, Paul Barney fought to get out from under it. He was trapped inside the upside-down tent, which was supposed to stretch over the raft for protection from the wind and the sea. In the icy blackness, he felt with his hands beneath him for the opening, bumping into others who were trying to get out. At last, he located the exit and managed to pull himself through and up to the surface.

"A life vest! A life vest!" he shouted, but his words were lost in the wind. In a moment, however, he spotted a life jacket floating only a few feet from his face. With a grunt of relief, keeping a firm grip with one hand on one of the raft ropes, he grabbed the vest, thrust his arms through, and made the ties fast. He pulled himself up on top of the overturned raft, where about a dozen others were huddling in water that reached their ankles as they sat.

Barney thought of the others trapped below in the tent-like upper part of the raft. Whether it was imagination or not he did not know, but it seemed that through the thick rubber bottom he could feel someone kicking. He turned away, banishing the thought.

Nearby he could see a young Estonian woman struggling in the water, and he reached over to help her into the raft. Wide-eyed, with black luxurious hair plastered against her neck, she was screaming hysterically.

"It's okay," Paul assured her. "You'll be fine. The worst part is over." As he spoke he wondered if she understood English. She was petite and pretty

Around the raft, a blizzard of Estonian paper money was swirling in the currents like a school of fish. Bemused, Paul muttered, "What a waste." In the next moment, he wondered how he could have such mundane thoughts at a time like this.

Nearby, beneath the surface where each had surrendered to their fates, Kent Harstedt and Sara Hedrenius each had a change of fortune. As the young man quit fighting and relaxed, he felt his left shoe come loose, and the rope that held him slipped away. The next thing he knew, he was sputtering and coughing, spitting water and gulping breaths of air.

In the water, something dark and soft bumped against him. It was a raft. He fumbled to grab at a rope that drooped from its side and hung tight.

At almost the same moment, Sara felt death loose its grip on her. She decided in her despair to breathe the water in deeply, but instead she found herself gulping air. Only a few feet from her, she saw a bobbing head and wondered who it was.

"Who is it?" she called.

As Kent clung to the raft, he heard the voice just behind him.

"Kent. Who are you?"

"Sara."

"Have you already forgotten me?"

"No, I haven't. Congratulations."

She was just behind him. She swam to his side, and hung on with him. The raft was upside down, with no light and, as they learned shortly, a puncture in it. It was already crowded with people. Nevertheless, Sara helped him up into the raft. He then reached down to pull her up, but his strength was gone. Another hand reached down and pulled Sara into the raft alongside him, and they embraced. Sara had lost her life vest in the fall, and they felt each other's warmth. Sitting there, each felt a new calmness, a sense of safety. Shivering in the cold, they continued their embrace for the warmth and the comfort it brought. Finding each other in the water like that, they both realized that their pact was more powerful than ever. That realization brought to each an overwhelming sense of peace. They knew they were not alone throughout this ordeal.

Seated on the raft, it seemed they had won their battle with the sea. There was a great but unspoken sense of elation. They had made it from the sinking ship and had managed to emerge from the near-fatal grasp of the currents below them. Surely they had won and had cheated an icy death. They could not have known that their ordeal was just beginning.

It was difficult to see the others in the darkness, but as the minutes dragged by the two newcomers estimated that probably twenty people were huddled atop the raft, sitting in knee-deep water. Most of the others were not calm. Several were screaming and in tears. Some were jumping up and down, waving, as if there were someone to see them. Worst of all, the night was filled with screams and calls for help from the dark waters around them. But, they could see no one.

Most of the others on the raft were so exhausted and despairing from their struggle that they did not speak to each other. Kent felt so tired that he could barely move, but he and Sara kept up nearly constant communication. Perhaps, this was to affirm that they were not alone, that they could buoy each other up, even kidding about the situation. But Sara warned Kent that she thought it would be many hours, perhaps even until daylight, before they were rescued. The shrieking wind and the cold water splashing over them served as a reminder that such a wait would not be easy. On a somewhat macabre note, she told him that a death by freezing was gentler than to die by drowning.

There, in the tossing raft, they realized for the first time just how furiously the sea churned. From the ship, the waves had seemed mountainous, at times towering above the bow before the vessel rose on the swells. Now on the tiny raft, they were hurled up and down like a roller coaster car, skittering down huge waves at times and at other times hovering in the troughs. Because the raft was heavily laden, its edge occasionally dipped under the waves, filling the whole raft with near-freezing water. When this happened, those swept by the water were rolled around the bottom, disoriented. It quickly became apparent that some were also being swept over the side. The raft was not as crowded as earlier. Cowering against the edge, Kent and Sara realized they must keep their grip on the rope that ran around the raft.

Paul Andersson, the crewman from the bar who had helped El-mar Siegel shove the raft into the water, seated himself beside Kent and Sara. Unlike most of the others, the two new arrivals seemed to be in control, and they exuded a sense of confidence. In the face of the cold wind and the water that splashed over them with each large wave, he put his arm around them both and pulled close.

"Are you from the crew?" Kent asked.

"Yes."

"What can we do? What should we do?"

"There is nothing to do," Andersson replied. "We can only wait and keep warm. We have to survive until help gets here."

At that moment, however, the question of a future was in grave doubt. With each passing moment, their ship was settling deeper into the Baltic, its nose rising higher in the growing moonlight. Through the darkness and the rain, they could see the tinkling red lights of the other rafts. Theirs had none, for it was overturned, and they clutched crab-like to its black bottom.

Worse, their raft seemed to be losing air.

"Dammit, it is punctured," someone cried.

"It is letting in water," someone else said quietly.

"We are going to sink," said a matter-of-fact voice.

7 · UP THE SMOKESTACK

In case of an on-board emergency, sea regulations say a ship's command bridge is supposed to warn passengers at least twice by loudspeaker and cabin phones in a common language. On this night, however, in the panic the messages were given in Estonian — while most passengers spoke Swedish or English. To be able to work on the ship, crew members were supposed to be able to speak at least Swedish or Russian in addition to their native tongue. In the excitement, however, those responsible gave the warnings and frantic instructions only in Estonian. Some passengers testified later that they heard no warnings at all, but perceptions in extreme emergencies are likely to be clouded. Numerous conflicting testimonies of events that night give ample evidence of that.

At about 12:20 a.m. the alarm siren began to sound. The alarm should have wakened everyone aboard, but for those still in their cabins it had to be a tragic awakening, for it was too late to reach the deck. By then the tilt of the ship was so great it was almost impossible to get up the vertical stairways. The horn continued its wail of distress until the bow of the *Estonia* lifted into the night sky and descended into the depths.

In analyzing the behavior of the survivors that night, a researcher from the Swedish Defense Research institute noted that there are definite ways people react to life-threatening emergencies. "We talk about the 30-50-20," he says. "Thirty percent react ideally, as we say. They not only save their own lives, but guide and help others as well. Fifty percent react by 'adapting,' which means they conform to the situation but usually manage to save only themselves. The remaining twenty percent are called 'non-adapters.' They panic and put themselves in greater danger than they actually were in to start with." Those who leaped into the heaving waves without life jackets fit the latter category.

It was a few minutes after midnight when Thomas Grunde and some of his group from their oil company where he was a supervisor had taken the floor to do the karaoke number of the old Swedish hit song of Per Myrberg's "Thirty Four," from the Sixties.

On Monday their company had sent fifteen members of their division to a conference in Tallinn. That afternoon Thomas had gone with a colleague to buy roses for Margareta, who was leaving another division in the company to start work as his assistant.

At dinner there was a small ceremony welcoming Margareta, after which she began to feel sick with the violent swaying of the ship. She went out on deck to get some air, had a drink of water, took some seasickness pills, and excused herself to go to her cabin.

In the bar without her, Thomas and the others launched into the song. When the group reached the chorus, they faltered as the sound of a great crash echoed from below them at the front of the ship. Some in the group gasped, while others laughed nervously. Thomas, however, thought it was only a giant wave against the hull. Then another blow, louder than the first, shook the ship, and it lurched violently to the side.

Thomas flew across the dance floor as if shot from a cannon and smashed head-first into a table. Stunned, he felt himself helped up by a co-worker. Around him there were terrified shouts and moans mixed with shocked silence. At that instant Thomas realized that he must get outside. Already the ship was tilting so badly that he had to crawl toward a door that led to the stairs and the seventh deck, which opened to the air.

The *Estonia* lay almost on its side at such an angle that it was difficult to stand. Once Thomas struggled to the deck, he could see people fighting their way upwards to grab onto the upper railing. He strained to leap upward but was thrown backward into a wall of the ship by the angle. He watched some men trying to get a life raft loose, but they were unsuccessful.

Someone threw out several life vests in their direction from a bin, and Thomas Grunde picked one up and put it on. Then the lights went out and he could hear the panic growing around him. He was concentrating hard on one thing: he knew he had to get away from the boat, farther out into the water so that he would not be sucked under when it sank.

Desperate, he forced himself to focus on his problem. Around him in the midst of the wind and rain there was pandemonium. Thoms then did an odd thing. He stopped to light a cigarette.

"If I'm going to have a last smoke, I'm going to have it now," he told himself. "There probably won't be another opportunity."

As he calmed himself, he focused on surviving. After a long drag on his cigarette, he threw it away with a flourish and pulled off his jacket. It was an expensive suit, he reminded himself wryly, and in its pocket there was a great deal of money. "If I'm going to swim, it will be easier without the jacket," he thought. "I'll be able to move around more."

Thomas looked back toward the stern and decided there would

be a better chance there. He had the notion that ships sink with the stern first. So in his dark pants, dancing shoes and white shirt, he began to work his way along the elevated port side toward the stern of the ship.

In the Admiral bar, the Estonian rock star/composer Urmas Alender had just taken a job singing on the *Estonia*. It was his first night of work. Popular on Estonian radio and television, he had been closely involved with the resurgence of Estonian folk singing in the 1970s. As a protest against the Soviet occupation, this "singing revolution" celebrated Estonian history and nationalism. His group Ruja had been recognized as one of the most important in the history of Estonian rock bands — with a strong expression of national ideals.

Going into the Soviet army had been unacceptable to him. To avoid it, he had stomach surgery that made him ineligible. At age forty, he was now resurrecting his career as singer and composer. He was collaborating with the noted Estonian poet Virve Osila — whom he had never met — on an album called *The Bird of the Soul*. Earlier that month he had written Osila in Stockholm, "The cassette is ready and in the nearest future I'll be bringing it."

On this trip Alender was bringing the tape with him.

When the *Estonia* swung on its side, Urmas Alender was standing by his heavy loudspeakers and sound equipment. In an instant it crashed down upon him, crushing him to the floor where he was standing. Injured and trapped, he was unable to move from the Admiral Bar, where he was to have begun his comeback as a composer and singer.

Like most passengers, crewman Timmo Vosa was asleep when he sensed something wrong after midnight. A twenty-five-year-old, he worked as a shop assistant in the duty-free store of the ship. It was one of the main attractions for travelers, especially for those from Sweden, where living costs were high. In the ship store, one could buy liquor, chocolate and endless luxuries for a fraction of what they cost in other places.

Trained as an orchestra conductor, Vosa had worked for a year as conductor for the Noarootsi Secondary School orchestra on a peninsula on the northwest coast of Estonia. He had found the isolation stifling, and when the chance came to work on the *Estonia*, he had jumped at it.

That night the sounds of the ship had troubled him in an uneasy sleep.

"When I awoke, it was obvious what was going on," he recalled later. The ship was listing heavily by then, nearly on its side. His books, clothes, cases, packages and everything in Vosa's cabin were in a pile against the wall. The door was over his head.

As an employee, he had been instructed earlier what to do in an emergency. He had been told to wear lighter clothes, as the heavier clothes weighed one down in the water. This turned out to be bad advice, for those with warmer clothes had a better chance of survival in the rafts. He grabbed a pair of sports trousers and pulled them on, surprising himself at how calm he was. Then he realized that his heart was beating so hard that it was pounding in his ears.

Peering through his cabin porthole, Vosa saw that water had risen almost to the opening. He locked it tight. He and his cabin mate managed to crawl to their cabin door and swing it open. In the corridor Vosa turned to the left and his roommate to the right — as they had been instructed to do in an emergency. On the way he stopped to close another porthole to keep out the water in a cabin where some Polish musicians had been staying.

When he reached the deck, it was a chaos of confusion, shouting and screaming. He tried to calm down some of those nearest him. Someone was handing out lifejackets, so he took one, put it on, and showed some of the frantic women how to fasten them securely. To help calm them, he pointed out the lights of ships on the horizon and told them that these ships must have heard the *Estonia*'s Mayday call. These ships would come quickly to their rescue, he assured them.

Standing at the railing, waiting with the storm beating at them, Timmo Vosa caught hold of the railing and clung to it. His legs dangled as he struggled to find something to stand on. He knew if he let go now, he would slip down the side of the ship to an open doorway below. Clinging next to him were a girl and a Russian man. He called out encouragement to them.

His hands grew painfully tired, and he felt his body growing numb with the cold. Even though he had never been religious, his thoughts now went to God. "I am not the kind of believer who goes to church and says prayers," he explained later. "Churchgoers are weak people who go to church to get support there. For me, God is just there. I am on good terms with him."

When the abandon-ship siren sounded only a scant four or five minutes before the *Estonia* slipped beneath the waves, most passengers were trapped hopelessly below deck. For the three crewmen in the engine room, however, there was another way out. A small door opened up into the funnel through which the smokestacks ran, and a vertical steel ladder ran up the side of the funnel to deck eight.

By the time that Margus Treu ordered his two subordinates, Hannes Kadak and Henrik Sillaste, out of the control room, the stairways were already impassable. In addition, the waterproof doors that kept the control room dry were closed, making the emergency exit the only way out.

Kadak, the young Estonian engineer, was the first of the three to attempt to go up the smokestack funnel. Because of the tilt of the ship, he was forced to grab on everything possible and wedge himself against the metal steps to maintain his hold. Grunting, struggling up, he could feel the heat from the pipes. Several times he burned his hands badly as he was forced to grasp them to keep from falling.

Just as he reached deck six, the lights went out. He caught his breath, not knowing what to do next. He fumbled with his hands against the funnel wall, looking for a door handle for an entryway into the ship. But then Sillaste caught up with him, told him they were only on deck six, and directed him upward toward deck eight. Then in a few seconds the emergency generators caught hold, giving light once more to continue on upwards.

By now the tilt was so great that the smokestacks were nearly parallel to the water. In the engine room, Treu was still trying to get the great diesels restarted. Finally he knew he must get out. The emergency siren was still wailing loudly.

"I have to get upstairs," he radioed the bridge. "I'll check the emergency diesel on deck eight."

As he started up the smokestack, Treu found the iron steps difficult to maneuver because the angle to the sea had become greater and the funnel swayed wildly up and down as the ship foundered. The lights were barely glowing, and the steps were not much help as he worked himself upward inch by inch. He dared not think would happen to him if the ship turned completely on its side, submerging the funnel.

By the time he reached deck eight and stumbled from the doorway, the ship was at nearly a ninety-degree angle, with the funnel caught by some waves. Strong black smoke erupted around the right smokestack as the seawater caught the hot pipes and the diesel fumes. The smoke rolled back up, stinging Treu's eyes as he emerged onto the heavily slanted deck. But he was able to make his way to the small emergency engine room on deck eight, where he learned that the emergency diesel generator was running but was leaking diesel because of the ship's tilt. After what seemed like only seconds, that engine also quit.

The tyfon siren, wailing like a foghorn, stabbed through the night even as the mouth of the funnel was covered by waves. Treu heard a voice in Swedish lament, "Why are they blowing that horn now? It's a little too late."

The sound was a dirge that floated out over the wind and the rain. For those already in the sea or still standing on the hull of the *Estonia*, it was a bitter reminder that a disaster was under way.

8 · MAYDAY! MAYDAY!

12:24 a.m.

It is impossible to know exactly what occurred on the bridge the last half-hour the *Estonia* lived. What is known is that Captain Andresson and perhaps the off-duty Captain Piht were extremely concerned about their schedule running late.

In the radio room, the first call for help received went out at 12:24 a.m. By that time, the engines had stopped and the ship was in a 30-degree list. It is still not known why the Mayday call went out so slowly. It is possible that attempts were made earlier, but perhaps equipment problems occurred with the radios. Perhaps Captain Andresson was reluctant to admit there was a problem he could not handle. Perhaps they were optimistic they could solve the problems themselves. Whatever happened, it was not done well, or in accordance with sea regulations.

The desperate conversation that went out over the air was on the international VHF emergency channel 16. The signal was weak and did not reach across the Baltic region as it should have. A small portable radio transmitter was on board the *Estonia*, and it is possible that the messages were sent on it instead of the regular radio. This would account for the weak signal. It might also help explain the delay in getting the message out. If the operators struggled for some minutes with the main radio before giving up and using the portable radio for the Mayday alarm, it would account for the time lost.

In addition, another unidentified ship in the area had inadvertently left its radio open on channel 16 that night. The weak coverage, however, could also have been because of another factor: The sinking took place in an area of relative radio silence where for some reason radio connection is difficult.

None of those on the bridge of the *Estonia* that night survived. But tapes played later for other crewmen identified the twenty-eight-year-old third officer, Andres Tammes, as the sender of the first message. The message was to the *Silja Europa*, first in Estonian, then in Finnish.

Tammes' watch had ended at midnight, but he apparently stayed on the bridge because of the storm. He was a young, good-looking Estonian who had gone to naval school in Tallinn. He had also attended the Kotka Naval School in Finland. In 1988, he had written a friend regarding his training: "Greetings from the Atlantic! I have now reached the point where I can no longer be called a sailor who hasn't been to sea. Before the journey everything went very fast. Only now I can really understand what had happened. The famous seaman and explorer Andres Tammes has started his first voyage!"

That first radio contact came at 12:24 a.m. Swedish time. It was weak and unclear. Tammes was a gentle, calm man, and the call that went out did not reflect the urgency of his message. The emergency call was in mixed Estonian, Finnish, Swedish and English in a low voice. The Estonian officers knew that the ships *Silja Europa* and *Mariella* were near, and the calls were to them.

"*Europa! Estonia! Silja Europa! Estonia!*" was the first message received by the ship *Europa*. It identified the target of the message first, and then who was sending it.

"*Estonia,* this is *Silja Europa,* replying on channel 16," answered the operator, Teijo Seppelin. For few seconds, he could hear no answer except radio static.

"*Silja Europa* ..." came Tammes' low, calm voice.

A long pause ensued.

"*Estonia?* This is *Silja Europa* on channel 16," replied the radioman. No answer. The operator could hear background sounds from the struggling ship. Then, as if he had not heard the reply, the *Estonia* operator tried to reach all the ships in that area, ignoring the emergency procedures.

"*Silja Europa,* Viking *Estonia.*" Tammes used the name of the Viking line to further identify his ship.

The obvious frustration of the *Europa* radio operator came through in his voice. "*Estonia? Estonia?*"

"Mayday! Mayday!" came the emergency call from Andres Tammes. It is the most frightening call a ship can send.

In the days of the telegraph, the standard international distress call became S-O-S, which was popularly understood to mean "Save our Ship!" Still universally recognized, it was chosen because of its ease on a telegraph key: three dots, three dashes, three dots. Generations of American servicemen learned that as "Dit-dit-dit Dah-dah-dah Dit-dit-dit." It replaced the earlier distress call used by the *Titanic* as it sank: "CQD," which meant, "Come Quickly, Distress."

In recent years, however, that telegraph-friendly distress call of "SOS" has been mostly replaced by the easier-to-say, "Mayday! Mayday! Mayday!" repeated three times. Tradition says it comes from the French word, "*M'aidez!*" which means "Help me." In maritime rules, there is a specific way to send an emergency call, and there are specific ways to respond. For one thing, all non-emergency radio traffic in the area is supposed to end. All pertinent messages should begin with the thrice-repeated "Mayday" phrase to alert any listener that a serious emergency is occurring. In the case of the *Estonia*, many people died that night because the general procedures were not followed.

After radio contact was made, more than a minute passed before the critical words were spoken that identified the crisis. In the confusion, the man with the microphone on the bridge of the *Estonia* had forgotten that he was supposed to give the "Mayday" call three times, identify his ship by name, give his position, and tell what help was needed.

On hearing the alarm, the *Europa* operator's voice rose in excitement. "*Estonia, Silja Europa.* Are you calling MAYDAY?" At this point, the *Europa* operator lapsed into English, "*Estonia*, what's going on? Can you reply?"

Then, on the bridge of the *Estonia,* a new voice took over the microphone. It was Second Officer Tormi Ainsalu, age thirty-nine, speaking entirely in Finnish. The voice of the captain was not heard.

"This is *Estonia*. Who is there? *Silja Europa? Estonia.*"

"Yes, *Estonia*, this is *Silja Europa.*"

"Good Morning! Do you speak Finnish?" The casual greeting undoubtedly misled anyone listening, implying that the *Estonia's* problem was minor.

"Yes, I speak Finnish."

"Yes, we now have a problem here," said the *Estonia* operator, his voice finally becoming hurried and betraying a deep concern. Still, his words barely reflected the urgency of their plight. "A bad list to the right. I believe about 20-30 degrees. Can you come to the rescue? Could you also ask *Viking Line* to come and help?"

"Yes, *Viking Line* is coming right behind us and surely got the message. Can you give us your location?"

There was a pause. "We have a blackout. I can't right now. ... I could not say."

"Okay. Understood. We'll start at once."

Immediately, the *Europa* operator called to the other nearby passenger ship, the *Mariella*.

"Did you get their location?" asked the *Mariella*. "Are they the ship to the port bow of us?"

"I could not get their location, but they have to be near here. They have a 20-degree list and blackout."

"I think they are on our port bow, about 45 degrees," replied the *Mariella*. On that ship, earlier in the evening steersman, Ingemar Eklund, had seen the lights of the *Estonia* pass his ship. Now he thought he could catch glimpses of the lights far ahead.

"Okay, I'm just waking the captain."

Then another message came from the listing ship. "Are you coming to rescue?" asked Ainsalu, his voice beginning to betray the tension. In the background, the listeners could hear a warning horn.

"Yes we are," replied the *Europa*. "Could you tell us your exact location?"

"I can't say, for we have blackout here."

"Okay. Can you see us?"

Apparently, Ainsalu did not understand. "Yes, I can hear you," he replied.

"Yes, naturally we will come and help, but we have to get your location first," said the *Europa* operator.

The *Mariella* operator then called Helsinki radio, but could not reach them. Then, the *Europa* radioman asked the *Mariella*, "Have you had any visual contact at all with them yet?"

"No, I haven't."

"We have to find them somehow. It's a little difficult to tell. They were unable to give us their location."

Aboard the *Estonia*, the failure of the engines had meant the loss of electrical power for a short time. The ship carried two GPS systems, a satellite orientation system that could tell any crewman where his ship was located within a few yards. The electrical failure, however, had put them out of commission. It took a minute or two before the emergency generators could kick into action, and it was during this blackout time that the *Europa* operator was unable to give their location.

The lights flicked back on as the emergency generators returned a reduced power. Those listening on the two ships speeding toward the *Estonia* could hear in the background control room the voice of Senior Officer Johan Herma advising about their position. Herma, the head steersman, usually slept after leaving Tallinn because his major responsibilities were at the beginning and end of the trip. The second and third officers handled the offshore duties.

Herma was not on the bridge when Linde started back down to check noises a few minutes after midnight. It is likely that as the boat tilted suddenly, he rushed from his cabin to the bridge. His voice was heard in the background of the taped Mayday call.

After the emergency generators returned some power, the *Europa* came back on. "I can tell you our location now."

"Yes, let's hear it."

"Latitude 58 ... just a moment ..." In the background a voice could be heard detailing their position. "22 degrees."

"Okay, 22 degrees. Clear, we'll go there."

"It is latitude 59, and 22 minutes."

"59 degrees, 22 minutes latitude."

"21, 40 east"

"21, 40 east. Okay."

Finally, the urgency came through. "It looks really bad, really bad here," said Ainsalu.

"Yes, it seems bad," said the *Europa* operator. "We are already on our way."

There was a muffled reply, and all those listening on channel 16 heard only rustling noises.

The recordings show that seven minutes elapsed from the first message until contact was lost. It is not clear if the man with the low voice, apparently Tammes, or Ainsalu understood the urgency of their situation. It is possible the *Estonia* operator refused to admit to himself how dire the ship's situation was.

On the *Mariella*, which was only about eleven miles to the south, Captain Jan-tore Thornroos had ordered his steerman, Eklund, to lower the speed of the ship because of the bucking waves. When the Mayday call arrived, Eklund got his captain on the phone in his cabin.

"The *Estonia* is sending out a Mayday call," he said.

Instantly, Thornroos threw on his pants and ran upstairs barefoot. At the same time, Eklund continued trying to raise the *Europa* on the radio again. There was only silence.

Then, one minute later they could hear on the radio the wail of the tyfon sirens in a distant echo on the *Europa*. They understood its meaning.

The location given indicated the that *Estonia* was about twenty minutes south of Uto, the Finnish outpost island. A thousand years earlier, Uto was used as a Viking route to the east and still boasted one of Finland's oldest lighthouses. It was a region well known to mariners for its treacherous shoals and rocky coasts. In recent years divers had come upon at least twenty wrecks that had gone to the bottom there over the centuries.

About sixty miles away at the Turku Sea Rescue Center on the Finnish mainland, Ilkka Karppila was the lone officer on duty. As he monitored the radio traffic on the busy Baltic Sea lanes, he could imagine what it must be like out there. It was just after midnight, and the wind was whipping at 56 miles an hour, and the seas were running to twenty feet and higher.

Suddenly the radio cracked with a weak voice in Estonian, then in Finnish. The radio message heard at 12:24 a.m. Swedish time made him gasp, and he jumped to his feet as he realized its importance. The message relayed was short.

"Mayday! *Estonia*. 20-30 list. Blackout." It told him that everything. The engines, power, and lights were shut down on the huge ship. In a storm like the one raging outside his window, he shuddered what this would mean. A helpless ship drifting at the mercy of great waves was a scenario for tragedy.

He heard the *Europa* join in on the frequency. When the position was given as latitude 59:23 and longitude 21:42, he knew the stricken ship was only about 25 miles off the coast of Uto in southwestern Finland. Quickly, Karppila notified the main Finnish rescue unit in Helsinki, and then went to wake up his own helicopter crew. He also called Mikko Montonen, the signal boss at the sea rescue station, who arrived fifteen minutes later to supervise communications.

In the ensuing minutes at the Turku base, Commander Fasi Staff and his men listened to the radio accounts and watched the radar screen helplessly. For exactly eight minutes, they could see the *Estonia* on radar. The ship was not moving. They knew the *Estonia* had become a helpless, wallowing beast, awaiting the *coup de grace* from an angry sea. When the radio went silent, they hardly dared imagine what was happening in those heavy seas.

Then the radar blips disappeared.

9 · LIFE VESTS

When the tall seaman Silver Linde emerged on deck with the group of drivers from below, he knew what to do. He was well trained, authoritative, and confident in his orders. He began to hand out life vests and tried to calm those who emerged panicked and wanted to throw themselves overboard, some without life jackets.

He saw passengers who were mostly young, some middle-aged, but none elderly. To get up from below with the heavy slant, fighting the panicked crowds, was an ordeal not suited for the physically unfit. Few older people and no children under the age of twelve made it out of the ship.

"Skylight one, skylight two!" at last, a voice in English came over the loudspeaker.

The voice, frightened and desperate, signaled for crew members to take their emergency positions. By that time, however, it was unlikely that any of the crew would be able to proceed beyond where they already were.

"Skylight one, skylight two!" repeated the voice, shrill and more urgent now.

Until then, the deck had been lit with bright lights. Now they flickered, dimmed, and went out. After a moment, a few emergency lights flickered back on. But the trauma, the storm and the darkness quashed the hopes of many, and they stood on the deck resigned to their fate without struggling. The night was near-black, the sky was covered with heavy clouds that sent sheets of rain on the wind, and the mountainous seas that towered above the ship reminded the passengers that man did not always rule nature.

As Mikael Oun emerged out onto the slanting deck, Linde recognized him from conversatipon earlier in the evening.

"Don't jump!" Linde was repeating over and over in English, holding up his hands as a deterrent.

Mikael gave a nod of understanding and edged his way upward to the rail. Looking down, he saw that that the port rail was high in the air. Anyone who jumped here would land on the hull of the ship, which at best would result in badly hurting oneself. On the starboard side of the ship awaited a frothy and angry ocean, where the railing was already under water. Why would anyone think of jumping in there, he asked himself. "It is okay," Mikael muttered, "She hasn't sunk yet."

Mikael, the thirty-four-year old engineer, had been in Estonia with a Swedish relief group driving a truckload of clothing for the needy. An Estonian living in Sweden, he was from a suburb of Stockholm, and was part of a large Swedish effort to help the Estonians recover from the poverty brought on by past Communist rule. Waking when the ship began to list heavily, he quickly rose and put his clothes on over his pajamas. For a reason he still doesn't understand, he put his alarm clock into his pocket before stepping out into the narrow hallway.

"There were not that many people in the hallway, but the stairs were crowded," he recalls. His cabin was on the car deck, three decks below the open air.

Mikael was able to run upstairs with the growing crowd. On deck, he found life vests strewn about, where Linde, crewmembers, and volunteers were pulling them from the large steel boxes beneath the rafts.

"It all seemed so unreal," he recalled later, remembering how it felt to stand on the slanting deck. When the lights of the ship went out, plunging everything into darkness, he experienced a moment of panic. As the emergency lights fluttered on, dimmer, but providing light enough to see, he was able to calm himself.

Mikael picked up one of the life vests that lay on the deck, studied it a moment, and tied it on as best he could. The *Estonia* carried ten lifeboats, and Mikael could see people frantically trying to loosen them from the steel davits.

"That's hopeless," he thought. "If they get them loose, this ship is at such an angle the lifeboats won't get into the water." He stood there, not knowing what to do, but reluctant to do anything yet. He could see other people around him unfurling rope ladders. He hung on to a steel pipe against the growing tilt of the ship, watched, and waited.

He looked toward the command bridge on the superstructure of the ship. It was now half under water, barely visible. "This is it," he thought. "But she might float for another hour or so."

Mikael hated the thought of going into the water, and he feared that the waves that crashed over the ship would wash him away. But as the *Estonia* rose to the top of a swell, he could see the lights of two ships approaching. The *Europa* and the *Mariella* were coming to their aid.

Mikael watched them desperately, hoping they would arrive before he had to jump. Around his neck, he carried a camera with a flash. He wanted to attract their attention with a signaled flash.

Grasping the uppermost railing, he held the camera high over his head and flashed it toward the ships. Several times, he repeated this futile maneuver.

Unknowingly, Mikael had immortalized a moment in the tragedy. Without realizing it, the haphazard direction of the camera caught a young man wearing a life jacket who was poised to slide down the hull of the ship into the water. It was a photo that within days was published in newspapers and magazines around the world.

As the ship continued to list more heavily, Mikael watched others leap into the sea. He worked his way forward, clinging to the superstructure as the ship turned first on its side, then began to slide stern-first into the dark waters.

Finally, hanging on to a pipe on the rising bow as the stern settled lower, he found he could no longer keep his grasp. A great wave flushed him from his hold and bounced him down the slippery side of the ship and into the sea. As he broke back to the surface, he realized two things: the pain in his elbow indicated a broken arm, and his life jacket was gone. It had been poorly fastened, and the force of his plunge had torn it off.

But on the surface, he spotted the small lights on three orange life rafts bobbing nearby. With a cry, he tried to swim toward the nearest raft, and was lifted up with several other somber survivors. By now, the waves around them were crowded with struggling swimmers. As those in the raft tried to reach others to pull them in, the small light that shone atop the raft's tent went out.

Inside, in spite of the tent covering, the crashing waves had filled the raft with water to the waists of those who sat there shivering.

The young man in the picture, whom Mikael Oun had inadvertently caught in that desperate moment was 20-year-old Janno Aser from Tallinn, who had been headed for a computer exhibition in Sweden. The photo showed him wearing blue jeans and a dark college sweater, along with a reflection of his body on the wet surface of the ship.

"I couldn't understand who could be taking photos in all that chaos," Janno said later. At the time, the bright flash had blinded him momentarily.

Janno had been sitting in a night club on the fourth deck when the ship turned nearly on its side. At first it didn't seem real to him, but after a few moments it became obvious the ship could not stay afloat. He ran to the outer deck and then sat on the side of the ship, wondering what to do next. He had seen many movies of people jumping from ships into warm water, where they then calmly gathered their thoughts. This was not the case here, he found, as he plunged into the icy waters of the Baltic.

He had no idea that he was part of the photograph that would become famous around the world, the only one that depicted the sinking of the great ship. At the moment, he had only wondered what idiot could possibly be taking pictures at a moment like that. After he was rescued the next morning, he forgot about the flashes in the night.

One of the young people on board that night was Gundega Kampuse, a twnty-one-year-old Latvian student going to visit a friend in Sweden. Even though there weren't many people her age on board, she had been planning to dance and drink and have a good time.

The evening had not gone all that well, however, because the swaying ship made her sleepy and slightly sick. By midnight, she sat with some new friends in a lounge with chairs and a television, trying to sleep and feeling frozen. In order to save money, like many of the other young people there, she had not rented a cabin.

When the heavy sounds shook the ship and it lurched to the side, she came to her feet and stared out the window. They were on the starboard side, and she gasped to see the sea rising to lap at their window and remaining there. For Gundega, there was no hesitation. Instantly she realized the grave danger. "We've got to get out of here!" she shouted, hurrying toward the exit. The others looked shocked, but as they ran to the window to check, they also turned and raced for the doors.

Gundega succeeded in struggling up the steps to deck seven and outside. On the deck, she saw only the black sea with the furious, towering waves. She saw no rescue ships, no lifeboats yet launched. She was devastated.

"Oh, my God," she wailed into the night. "I am only twenty-one years old! Why? Why? What have I done that is so bad that I must die?"

As she spoke, she saw a raft below her. She paused only for a second and then jumped. After what seemed an eternity of sinking, she bobbed to the surface and tried to swim away from the wreck. But others were plunging into the water around her and grasping at her legs and arms. As she swam, someone was clinging to her back. In addition, she realized that other swimmers around her were being flung by the waves into the steel hull of the ship. One after another, she was bumped by other swimmers. Someone grabbed hold of her and dragged her under. Each time she fought her way upward to the surface, and those who had been hanging on lost their grip and sank beneath the waves. At last, she had little strength left.

Calling on her last strength, she was able to fight her way upward to float and get quick gasping breaths.

In the cabins below deck, the sounds and the sudden tilting of the ship had awakened many passengers, causing fear and hysteria. These feelings were made worse by the sickening smell of vomit that emanated from the communal bathrooms on the lower decks, caused by the evening's seasickness.

As the rolling of the ship had become worse, Rolf Sorman, a thirty-five-year-old Swede on a pleasure jaunt, and three of his co-workers remained seated on the high bar stools in the pub. His watch read shortly past twelve when the ship suddenly careened to the starboard and sent empty bottles to the floor in a shower of glass. He managed to catch his beer and frowned at the thought that the helmsman had changed course so suddenly.

Rolf was an experienced seaman, and when the ship rolled so heavily a second time, he got up. "It is time to get to the lifeboats," he announced to his friends.

"You're talking nonsense," they laughed.

But when the ship lurched toward the side a third time and stayed, sending the sounds of crashing and breaking glass from the duty-free shop nearby, the mood changed. People were falling near them, and some were smashed against the wall. "All right," the others agreed, "To the lifeboats." There was a race for the doors.

For those trying to escape the lower decks that night, the major enemy, apart from being in the wrong place at the wrong time, was panic. In most crises, panic is the enemy of survival. It robs people of judgment and causes them to either freeze or do nothing when they should be acting. Sometimes it forces them to do something foolish, something that dooms them.

Aboard the *Estonia* that night, there was little time for calm consideration. After the ship listed and the Mayday message was sent, it stayed afloat for only twenty-four minutes. Those who were fortunate to be in the right place and who acted with good judgment were the ones with the best chance of survival.

Others had already made themselves incapable of surviving an emergency. It was not uncommon on such trips for passengers to indulge in large amounts of liquor at bargain prices. Crewmen later reported that there are always passengers who become falling-down drunk and who wander the ship looking for a taxi. These had no chance.

For those who reached the deck and kept their heads, their chances of living through the night were increased. As the ship sank lower in the water and turned more and more on her side, many bided their time. The calm ones often did not know what to do, but they realized that leaping into the sea without having access to one of the orange rafts was foolhardy.

Among those watching the struggle to get the lifeboats loose was Hannu Seppanen, a thirty-one-year-old businessman from Sweden. Earlier, he had asked a crewman what to do and had received no answer. Now, he looked around at the frantic activity on the slanting deck and decided it was hopeless.

Hannu was confused. In the dim light, he could see people running around in their underwear, making their way onto the hull of the ship as it became nearly level. After getting on a life jacket, he went out with them and sat down next to a porthole. "Should I jump or wait?" he asked himself.

He watched one man go running with his life jacket held over his head and leap downward headfirst. "He's going to kill himself doing that," Hannu thought. On the side of the ship, Hannu could see smudges of blood where people had leapt and struck the hull. Even when people jumped into the water, the huge waves sometimes smashed them back against the steel hull. Watching, Hannu decided to stay a while longer. He did, however, take his shoes off so he could swim better, when he did get into the water. He was concerned about getting far enough away from the ship, so that as it went down, it would not suck him down with it.

In the turmoil on deck, another officer, besides Silver Linde, stood passing out life jackets. Einar Kukk, the visiting second mate from the *Mare Balticum*, had made his way to the seventh deck and struggled to get his life jacket on. The jacket straps were too short to reach around his 200-pound frame and the leather jacket he was wearing.

When he finally got his life vest on amid some cursing, Kukk ran to one of the cabinets that held the life jackets and began throwing them down to terrified passengers, who were trapped in the last hallway and unable to get up the nearly vertical stairs. This became difficult because nearby passengers kept snatching the extra vests he carried. Over and over the thought pounded at him: "It's just not possible for this large and modern a ship to sink! It's not possible."

In another minute, the *Estonia* was completely on its side, and Kukk worked his way along the hull toward the stern. But as the stern dipped he turned around and went back toward the center of the ship, walking on the port side, which was by then as flat as a floor. Kukk later testified that when he reached amidships, he heard Captain Andresson use the alarm siren to give one last signal to abandon ship.

The emergency generators kept the lights on in most parts of the ship, until the last minute when it sank beneath the waves. In the moonlight, Kukk could make out the stern already under water. The bow was beginning to lift into the sky. He glanced at his watch.

It was 12:35 a.m.

He could see the smokestacks disappear completely. The tyfon siren continued to sound beneath the water, until it went silent in darkness.

Wearing his life jacket, Kukk scooted down the side of the ship. When he plunged into the water, he nearly lost his vest in the waves as their force almost pulled it over his head. When he emerged to the surface, he tugged on the life-vest string that was attached to a whistle, which a survivor was supposed to blow in an emergency. As he blew it, a weak, sputtering sound erupted from the metal whistle. It was a sound lost even a few yards away in the howl of the wind, the crashing of the sea and the screams of women. He cursed the fact that the life vests bore no lights. Lights would have made it possible to spot a survivor in the dark waters.

At about that time, one of the waitresses from the Poseidon Restaurant, Sirje Johansson, emerged on deck when the ship was lying nearly on its side and obviously going down. She looked up and recognized a man standing near her as Captain Avo Piht, shouting something and throwing lifejackets to the people in the water. Shortly after, the waitress was washed into the sea. It was the last confirmed report of anyone recognizing Captain Piht that night.

The giant ship had begun a slow turn to the left, back toward Tallinn, when the engines failed. Perhaps the second officer or the captain had thought this maneuver might help alleviate some of the list by turning to head directly into the wind. It would have been more logical, however, to turn to the right so that centrifugal force might have helped straighten the ship slightly by pushing the water inside the ship to the port side. Nevertheless, at that point, it was probably too late for any maneuver to make a difference in the fate of the doomed ship.

Silver Linde, meanwhile, knew from the changing angle of the deck that the ship was sinking fast. Above the wind and the screams for help, the wail of the siren sounded louder, signaling every person that the ship was going down and that each was on his own. Farther down the deck, Linde saw fellow crewmen Hannes Kadak and Henrik Sillaste.

The two crewmen had emerged from climbing up through the smokestacks and were at the railing deciding whether to jump. They turned and recognized Tormi Ainsalu, the second officer, who had sent the final words on the Mayday call: "It looks really bad here." By the time the ship was on its side, he was standing on the hull, shaking his head at the magnitude of the disaster. It was the last account of Ainsalu.

Kadak and Sillaste were furiously working to get one of the rubber life rafts launched over the side of the ship. But as they struggled, a huge wave washed over the hull, throwing several panicked survivors into the water. The two crewmen gave up the effort and jumped down the now near-horizontal hull, holding tight to their life vests. Silver Linde also knew it was time. He crawled over the hull and bounced down into the water.

By now, the water was full of people fighting for anything that floated.

It was as the lost ship began to slip under the waters stern first, its bow lifting into the sky, that the clouds skittered away and the moon shone brightly down on the scene. The wind died suddenly, and a hush seemed to fall over the area in spite of the human dramas being played out on the sea below.

At this point, the ship itself seemed to shake like a beast undergoing the shudders of a death throe. Great rumbling sounds emanated from within the ship as the sinking portholes burst from the pressure, sending water gushing through corridors and cabins and pushing everything loose. That which would not move, or became stuck, was smashed. Any life that remained within the bowels of the *Estonia* was snuffed out in an instant as the great pressures built and crashed through the ship. It went lower into the water and pushed a torrent of air before it. When the blast of air reached the doors, where the last fleeing passenger was struggling to get out, it caught Georg Sorensen with the force of a tornado, lifted him, and propelled him out into the sea.

Muffled explosions, the groaning of crushing walls and gurgles of water rose in the stillness that had fallen momentarily over the scene. Like a great, mortally stricken beast, the ship was sharing its death spasms.

10 · IT'S A HURRICANE!

Mikael Oun, the engineer who had taken the photograph on the hull, thought he was extremely lucky as he sat shivering inside the covered life raft with the eleven others there. Even though he had lost his life vest in his plunge into the sea, he had come up between two of the rafts that had popped to the surface and was able to climb into this one.

A moment later, Christer Eklof had surfaced with his poorly fitted life vest also torn away, but also right next to the same raft. He was able to grab hold of the rope near the raft entrance. He stuck his arm up toward the opening, and it was Mikael Oun who took hold of his arm and pulled him in. The two truck drivers already knew each other.

"What! Are you here?" exclaimed Christer with joy.

Mikael nodded, but at the same time he was hit with a wave of nausea. The bouncing, swaying raft had set his stomach churning, and now he lay with his head outside the entrance and retched into the sea.

After a time, Mikael felt better, and he turned to his friend. "We have to find new life vests," he told Christer. "They could make the difference between life and death."

They leaned out through the doorway. Around them, the sea

was littered with life vests. Christer grabbed one, and reached to pull another toward them with a person inside. He felt for a pulse in the lifeless arm, and then shook his head. "Dead," he said. He released the man's arm. In a short time, however, he was able to snag an empty vest. Later, back in Sweden, he wondered who it was that he had in his grasp and then released back to the sea.

They saw others who lived. At least two of the long life boats, which some survivors struggled so desperately to unloose, eventually broke away from the ship as it sank. But they were damaged or overturned. Christer and Mikael watched one man who hung onto a damaged boat, obviously near exhaustion and about to lose his grip. In a stroke of fortune, their life raft drifted so close to the overturned boat that they simply had to reach out of the raft opening and pull the man inside the raft tent with them.

It was Georg Sorenson, a German businessman, and the man who had been blown through the doorway of the *Estonia* and into the sea by a blast of air. He was the final one to join their raft, making twelve aboard. Ten of them would survive.

Earlier that evening, the brother and sister, Wanda and Holger Wachmeister, had gone their separate ways after accidentally meeting at the information desk. Neither had known the other was aboard. About 11:30 p.m., she went to her cabin high up on the sixth deck, while he descended to his cabin on the first deck.

Holger went to sleep immediately, but something woke him, and he was startled to hear that the ship's engines had stopped. Swiftly he leaped from his bed, realizing that something was dreadfully wrong.

"Up and out!" he said aloud to himself. Barefoot, wearing only pants and a shirt, he bounded up the stairs past people who were standing trying to figure out what was going on.

When he reached the outer deck, he had no time to find a life vest, for a wave hit him instantly and flung him overboard. Holger was a large man, weighing 220 pounds. When he thrashed his way to the surface sputtering water, he found a raft only a few feet away. It was an upright raft with the tent up. He grabbed the rope that ran around the side and held on but was unable to climb up over the side even with one of the men inside extending a helping hand. After several attempts, he fell back into the water.

Behind him, however, he spotted another raft, this one overturned. He released the raft with the tent and grabbed onto the overturned one. There he hung in the water a few minutes. He saw another raft and worked his way around the overturned one until he could reach this third raft. From it, several hands reached to help him inside. Once on board the raft, he felt saved. There were fourteen other people. With those on that raft huddled together, he even dared to go to sleep.

All those on that raft were saved. At daybreak, their raft was spotted by a helicopter. One by one in an operation that involved several helicopters, they were taken up to safety.

Wanda, on the other hand, never went to sleep. A natural worrier, she lay awake listening to the sounds of the ship straining against the storm. When the bow visor tore away, she recognized that the loud sound signaled catastrophe. She jumped into a pair of pants and shoes with rubber soles. She was wearing a red-and-white-striped pajama top. Unlike the tortuous route that her brother followed up from the first deck, her cabin on the sixth deck was only one floor below the magical seventh deck and open air. When she ran out into the night, she paused at the railing long enough to put on a life vest. She glanced at her watch, which read 12:15 a.m.

Wanda Wachmeister did not panic. She had told herself that to survive this crisis she must remain calm and think clearly. She decided to jump. But before she could swing over, she too was washed off the ship.

The waves carried her away. Suddenly, she drifted in front of a large rubber raft, and people reached to help her inside. Only once did she turn to look back. It was that strange time of calm when the wind quieted for a few minutes, the moon and the stars came out, and she could see the white hull of the ship against the dark sea. Then it was gone.

Wanda settled back into the raft with Mikael Oun and Christer Eklof and the others. With her usual pessimism, she was sure that her brother was dead by now. Never a passive person, she and Christer took it upon themselves to serve as guardians of those on their raft, keeping eye contact, calling out encouragement and reminding everyone that they must stay awake to fight off hypothermia. When someone looked to be falling asleep, Wanda would sidle over and shake them awake. They worked to keep spirits high. Christer had grown up on an island in Sweden, and he knew the sea. He busied himself by shooting off emergency flares he had found on the raft, and then in lying through the doorway and paddling. He had found a couple of pieces of plastic to use as paddles. With this maneuver, he guided the raft to minimize the wave action that smashed against it and sent cold water through the doorways.

At times, he and Wanda would sit hand in hand and discuss the storm. "Damn, it's blowing," he said as the wind increased. "It is no longer a storm; it is a hurricane."

Wanda, the constant pessimist, recounted other shipwrecks she had heard of in the region.

"But we will survive," Christer chided her. "This raft is safe."

Mikael watched with concern as he saw that one of the men on their raft clad only in underwear was beginning to hallucinate because of hypothermia and shock. The man was shaking uncontrollably and insisted on standing in the middle of the raft. To Mikael, it seemed incompressible that after escaping the ship and coming this far that the man would now die.

The engineer reached and pulled the man to him, holding him tight as he leaned back against the edge of the raft. The man did not resist. They were both sitting in water to their waists. After an interminable time, he could not feel the man breathing any longer. He did not know when he stopped breathing. But his own arms ached, and when he at last had no more strength to hold the man, he let go. The man slid into the water in the raft without moving and remained there.

Mikael had tried to help and failed. He felt himself shaking and coughing. Now, he wanted nothing more than to sleep.

"How are you doing?" came the voice of Christer.

With a start, Mikael awoke. "I ... I'm okay."

"Are you sure?"

"It's okay," Mikael answered with a sigh. But he kept dozing off, and each time, Christer shook him awake to keep him in touch with life.

The young blond Estonian, Hannes Kadak, had made it through the smokestack onto the ship's deck, over the side, and was swimming in the sea. He ignored his burned hands, and when he saw a raft before him he used the last of his strength to climb up over the side and inside. After a few moments' rest, however, he turned his attention to the cries near the raft. Several people were hanging onto the rope around the edge. Among them, he recognized his friends from the crew, Henrik Sillaste and Silver Linde. When he reached to pull Linde up, the tall seaman fell back into the sea, but on the second attempt Kadak was able to pull him onto the raft. Soon the three crewmen were busy pulling people aboard, one by one.

Gundega Kampuse, the student from Latvia, was struggling in the water nearby. Others who had jumped at the same time had pulled her under several times, and now she was desperate. She knew she could not go under again or she would not come up.

"Please help me!" she called out. "Please somebody help me!" By then, her voice was so weakened that it was drowned in the furor of the wind. She was going to surrender to the sea when a strong hand reached down, grabbed her arm and pulled her up. She let out a little moan of relief, as she slid into the crowded raft. As she looked around she saw with alarm how jammed the raft was.

But only a few yards away she could see another raft in the reflected lights of the *Estonia*. Three people were in it, and several others were swimming toward it. She called out, and those in the new raft motioned for her to come over. Few people would have risked going back into the sea, but Gundega slipped over the side of her raft back into the water, and stroked to the new raft. There the crewman Silver Linde reached down and pulled her up into this new haven. As she caught her breath, she felt a calm assurance.

"If I have made it this far," she told herself, "I can't just die."

Margus Treu, an engineer and third crewman, escaped the engine room by crawling up through the smokestack, and struggled to start the emergency generator on the eighth deck. He knew the ship was going down quickly, and he carefully worked his way along its side sternward toward a raft, where he recognized fellow crewmen Elmar Siegel and Paul Andersson. They were trying to get a raft down the side of the ship, but the weight of those inside made it nearly impossible to move.

Before he could reach them, however, a wave smashed over the ship and carried Treu out into the froth of the sea. He had not even had time to put on a life jacket.

Among those on the raft of Linde Kadak and Sillaste was a twelve-year-old Norwegian named Mats Finnanger, who would become the youngest survivor of the *Estonia* disaster. The boy ended up on this raft with fifteen others, barefoot and in a T-shirt and jeans. A young Swedish woman, Mia Fagerston, who was with the Stockholm police union group, took him under her wing. He sat close to her all through the night. Their two languages were similar enough that he could understand her encouraging chatter, but he never spoke a word. When she went to take her turn bailing water from the raft, he followed at her side.

Somewhere in the surrounding sea, Mats knew, were his parents and brothers. The last time he had seen them was as they all ran out of their cabin on deck one and had got up the first stairway. The numbness of his own shock and the fear of what had happened to his family kept him silent through the night.

Mia was wearing a skirt and blouse and was carrying a little purse, but she noticed that several in the raft had on only their underwear. Mia recognized Mihai Turdean, a drummer from one of the bands on board, from the night before. They took turns at trying to shovel the water from the raft out the doorway.

"Why are you and I the only ones bailing?" she asked Turdean. She stared angrily at the others, who were sitting watching. She glared at two crewmen in uniform. "Surely, you are stronger than I am. Do something, then."

One girl moved to help for a time, but the crewmen did not move, and Mia kept working, letting her resentment simmer inside her. Undoubtedly, Linde and the other crewmen saw the futility of bailing water out one end of the raft, when it was likely to be flooded at the next wave through the other. They were conserving energy.

But to Mia Fagerston, it was doing something useful. "You can't just give up," she told herself.

Linde rose from time to time and reminded those huddled there, "No one must fall asleep! Sit close together for warmth."

Sillaste, one of the three who had escaped through the smoke-stack, nodded in agreement. "This raft is strong and safe. We will all survive this," he promised.

After an hour, a surge of excitement ran through those huddled on the bobbing rafts when they could make out through the spray and the towering waves the bright lights of the two nearby ships coming to their aid. When the *Mariella* and the *Europa* drew near the scattered rafts and the giant ships slowed and fought to keep their positions in the wind, Mia's hopes soared. The ships were so close that those on the rafts could see the people on board staring out their cabin windows. Turdean was standing waving his arms. Then the ships sailed on.

"They just can't do this," Mia wailed. "They can't leave us. They have seen us!"

Then, in her utter frustration, Mia prayed to God for the only time that night: "Just let us get home."

Einar Kukk, the visiting second mate who had been floundering in the water, felt his strength waning. At what seemed to be the last possible moment, he was able to catch hold of the side rope of an overturned life raft that drifted close. Even then, he felt his hands weakening. But within a moment, a man looked over the edge, extended his hand, and pulled Kukk up into the raft. It was a young Estonian. He did not even seem tired.

"Hi," he said. "My name is Kikas, Ulo Kikas."

Kukk took the hand and gave it a limp squeeze. There was another Estonian in the raft, a passenger like Ulo, and he was completely naked. His only article of clothing had been torn off by the waves when he was plunged into the water. Kukk nodded a greeting to him. As he sat exhausted, trying to regain some strength, Kukk felt a thumping against his leg, coming from beneath the raft. With a gasp, he drew away. Ulo pointed toward the bottom of the raft and gave a grave nod.

Someone was alive, trapped under the raft. For Kukk, it was incomprehensible that a man was still alive beneath them. He knocked back and felt an answering knock. When he was a little rested, Kukk leaned up over the edge of the raft. It was two feet to the water. They discussed how they might get the trapped man out from under the raft, but Ulo said they had already tried, but it was impossible.

After a half-hour, from beneath the raft, they could hear the man shouting. It was in Swedish. The words were muffled and difficult to understand over the wind. Kukk had spent four years working in Sweden and knew the language. He shouted back. Beneath the raft in the enclosed darkness, Anders Ericson called to ask if any rescuers were in sight yet. Kukk shouted back that they could see some lights but didn't know yet what they were.

For the three men atop the overturned raft, the night was filled with terror. Again and again waves washed over them, sending them sprawling over the edge of the raft and into the water. Only by hanging onto the ropes were they able to pull themselves back onto the raft to safety. Because Jaan Stern was without clothes and near to freezing, the other two wrapped themselves around him to provide warmth and some protection from the bitter wind. Kukk was fully clothed. He had taken time to dress in trousers, boots and a coat before leaving the ship. On the other hand, Jaan was shaking uncontrollably. Einar and Ulo massaged the naked man's body and feet to help him keep alive.

When Kukk was not massaging his countryman, he thought of what he must do to survive. A tall and sturdy man, he was determined he would not die. He knew he must live through this. At home there were his wife, Tiina, and an eight-year-old son, Rainier, as well as a four-year-old daughter, Kaitlin. The seaman had a vivacious, optimistic personality, and he would not allow himself to think of drowning like so many others around them in the sea. He had graduated from the Tallinn Naval School in 1984, and had worked at sea since then.

Even when he was washed from the raft time after time, Kukk did not think that he might run out of strength and not be able to make it back into the haven of the raft. Unlike many of the others, he did not turn to God. He had been raised under the Soviet system and had not learned to pray or turn to a supreme being. Instead, he now filled his mind with the thought that he must *survive*. He took pride in courting challenges, and now he reminded himself that this was one more challenge that he could win. Sometimes at home, he went out to sea in his small motorboat in times of high seas, as if daring them to swamp him. He felt exhilarated when standing on the edge, and this night, faced with a sea that seemed determined to sweep them from the raft and pull them into the depths forever, he had determined he would survive once more.

Anders Ericson, the Swedish man trapped beneath the overturned raft, was in a far worse situation. He was hanging onto a rope in total darkness in a tiny air space as the wind whirled and scooted the raft before it.

Anders was an electronics engineer from Karlskoga who had been invited on the trip by a friend as a weekend jaunt. On the return trip, Anders had been awakened by the pounding of the sea and the crashing sounds from the ship. Worried, he got up, took the time to dress, and ran up to the outer deck. As he ran through the foyer, a soft drink machine came crashing down next to him. It was then he realized something was seriously wrong. As he emerged into the open air, he found the deck in such a slope that it was obvious the ship was sinking. He grabbed a life jacket and put it on. He and another man took time to throw life vests to others and help some get up on deck. Then he stood at the railing wondering what to do.

"I thought this is all going to hell. I heard a siren," he said later. "Then I jumped into the water. I was washed away by a wave and ended up lying on my back in a life raft. I saw a hand stick up out of the water and tried to reach it, but it disappeared in a wave."

An instant later, a great wave washed him off the raft and deep into the sea. When he came up, he found himself trapped under an upside-down raft, probably the one he had been aboard before the wave overturned it. A rope was hanging down from what was now the ceiling above him, and he grabbed this rope. He could see nothing. Terrified by the blackness around him and the sloshing water that lapped at his face, he clung with all his might to the lifeline from the raft.

As each burst of wind thrust the raft along the tops of the waves, he hung on desperately. Before long, he felt three others crawl aboard the raft above him. He considered trying to swim out to join them on top, but the raft was tossed about so much by the waves that he was afraid he would never catch up to it and that would mean death.

It was better to try to hang on to this life-saving rope, even though his arms were cramping and he was shaking with cold. Determined to survive, he hung on, freezing cold, with his head barely out of the water. At first, he was afraid he would run out of air, but when each giant wave came it lifted the edge of the raft and brought a surge of bitter-cold new air.

From time to time, he knocked on the bottom of the raft, and felt a reassurance when the knock was answered. It was difficult to make out the words, but he could hear Einar Kukk tell him when some ships arrived. In the blackness, he could not understand why ships did not mean immediate rescue. Every few minutes, he shouted to know if any rescuers were in sight yet.

As the minutes dragged by, he felt himself going numb from cold, and he tried to think of other things.

11 · IT MAKES YOU FEEL LIKE SLEEPING

As a member of the *Estonia* crew, thirty-year-old Aulis Lee got five free tickets a year for passage on the ship. On this trip, he had brought his wife, Aina. He was in a cabin with her on the fourth deck, rather than in his usual crew's quarters on deck seven. His ship watch had ended when they had left the port of Tallinn, and they had gone to bed early. They were planning a busy day tomorrow seeing Stockholm, which would be their first time together there.

Before turning in, Aina stared out the window at the stormy sea and noticed the illuminated sign on their cabin door that told how to put on a life jacket. She asked her husband how to do it properly.

"Go to sleep," he said grumpily.

Just after midnight, Aulis awoke with a start as their cabin table crashed against the door. Quickly, he woke up his wife.

"Get dressed," he said. "There's a problem." He knew that with the ship listing so badly, water had already entered.

His wife looked at him sleepily. "I'm not going out into the corridors of this ship in the middle of the night," she replied.

The urgency of his look at her and the tone of his voice, however, convinced her. Quickly, she put on her trousers, a polo shirt, and shoes and grabbed her handbag containing her passport and other documents. She had just gotten her driver's license, and the thought came that it would be too much trouble to pass a new driving test.

In the corridor, they did not see anyone. All the doors were closed, with the occupants obviously still asleep. Already, the ship was at such a tilt that they had to run with one foot on the floor, the other on the wall.

"Don't step on the doors," Aulis warned. He knew they might give way and send them sprawling.

When they reached the lobby, people were milling around, confused and shocked. Many just stood and held to the wall, immobilized by fear.

They were able to get up the stairs and push their way outside onto the deck. A sailor on watch handed them life jackets. Aina struggled with the straps and was unable to fasten it correctly. Together, they ran hand in hand toward the stern. Over the howl of the wind, they could hear the terrified shrieks of people on deck and those still inside the ship. Aina noticed a woman who was half naked, and a man wearing underwear with one seam coming unstitched. In her dazed state, she allowed herself to wonder why these people hadn't bothered to dress themselves properly. She even felt sorry that she hadn't had time to fix her hair.

Nearby on the stern, Aulis recognized two fellow crew members struggling to loosen one of the inflatable life rafts. The couple ran to one of the steel containers and Aulis helped the other crew members get two of them loosened and inflated. Because so many other people crowded around the raft, Aulis pulled Aina back.

"We have to get in," she protested. "I can't swim."

In answer, he thrust a rope from the raft into her hand. "Hold on," he ordered. "Don't let go, whatever happens."

He took a turn of the rope around his hand, and at the same time slipped the strap of her handbag around his neck.

They stood on the stern of the ship, with the tumultuous sounds of panic and despair around them. They did not jump. Instead the stern slowly began to sink, and a wave swirled the raft overboard, pulling them with it.

Aina did not let go of the rope. She felt herself pulled deep into the cold sea. As she gasped and swallowed water, the thought came that she was going to drown. She tried to swim to pull herself to the surface, but was helpless. When she finally emerged sputtering and caught her breath, a wave caught her and pulled her under again.

Aulis was carried by the wave off the ship. When he came up, he saw a life raft thirty yards away. Two people were sitting on its roof. Another wave caught him and he felt that he was under the raft. When he emerged, a fellow crew member, Arne Koppel, was leaning out of the entrance and reached to help him into it.

His wife, meanwhile, floundered helplessly, but in another moment she felt herself pulled by the rope to the edge of the raft, and then Koppel lifted her into the entrance. Gasping, she lay in the pitch blackness inside the enclosure.

The sagging roof reminded them that two people were perched on top. The two crewmen called out to them and helped them come inside.

Inside the raft, it was totally dark. Aina could not see anyone but could feel the presence of other people and hear the sobs of some of them. The water inside the raft was waist-deep and bitter cold. Then she heard Aulis's voice. With a little whimper of joy, she leaped toward him and they hugged tight without letting go, each grateful for the life of the other, and grateful for the warmth they brought each other.

Once inside the raft, Aina and Aulis, the only married couple to survive together, held each other tightly for as much warmth and comfort as possible. The raft was half filled with icy water, and the waves kept pounding away, each one adding more cold water into the raft. Aina tried to think of her children, but each new wave took her thoughts to the little raft bobbing in the middle of increasingly angry waves. She did not cry.

In the raft were fifteen people, all sick and miserably cold. In fact, they were so cold that they were intolerably sleepy. Aulis had to keep reminding Aina that they must stay awake so as to fight hypothermia.

"This raft won't sink," he assured her and the others over and over. "It's built to stand up to heavy seas."

As the hours wore on, the storm, instead of abating, got worse. The faint sound of chattering teeth could be heard just below the wail of the storm and the chop of the waves against the raft.

Once, a polite voice interrupted the sounds of the storm. "Please, would you get off my leg," the man's voice said. "I have a broken bone."

In an emergency pocket on board the raft, they located a supply of signal skyrockets. Aulis and Arne fired off some of these. Through the open doorway of the raft tent, they could see the lights of nearby ships that had come to the rescue. With the heavy seas, however, the crewmen recognized that these ships could do little but drop overboard more life rafts, and stand back to await a calmer surface. It seemed that every minute the rain increased in intensity.

Another crewman, twenty-four-year-old Risto Ojassaar, had been drinking a beer next to a window in the bar and staring at the storm shortly after 11 p.m. Tall and slender, with reddish-brown hair and a closely cropped beard, he was a soft-spoken man, who was poised on the edge of a dream. The evening had gone well for him. A professional dancer, he was performing with a nine-member dance troupe aboard the *Estonia*. The luxury ship with its discos, restaurants and the indoor pool was to his liking. Their performance that evening had been a newly choreographed modern dance, which ended in late evening to enthusiastic applause. It was their debut on the ship. He and the others in the troupe looked forward to their three-month engagement. It was their big break.

Ojassar pressed his nose against the window to better experience the drama of the angry sea outside. Ojassaar had always loved sea storms. It was one of his passions to stroll the beach near his home in Tallinn to watch the storms. Later, Ojassaar recalled the waves pounding against the ship that night: "Boom! Boom! Boom! The huge waves were amazing."

He was thrilled by the excitement of the ship against the sea. Even though the *Estonia* was as tall as an eight-story building, the swells seemed to tower above it as they swept toward the bow.

He sat admiring its power, watching the wind-whipped spray splash against the window where he sat.

Shortly before midnight, Ojassaar went to his cabin, kicked off his shoes and settled back to read the day's newspaper. As he drifted to sleep, he barely gave the storm a second thought. Suddenly, he jolted awake to find his legs above his head. His wall was now his ceiling. He knew the ship was in a deep list.

"Okay, now the ship will tilt back," he told himself.

But the list did not change. He rolled out of bed, crawled out into the hallway, and assessed the situation. In the hall, people were bolting for the main stairs, men, women and children, many clad only in their underwear.

Later, Ojassar learned that the main stairs meant almost certain death. Fortunately, the manager of the dance troupe had emerged from the next cabin and grabbed him as he started to follow the others.

"No! This way," she commanded. She had been on the *Estonia* on other trips and understood that with the ship lying on its side, the main stairwell would be an almost impossible way out of the ship.

Quickly, she showed him to the side stairs, steep now and treacherous. Desperately, they helped each other ascend. Once, Ajossaar slipped back onto a glass door. He lay for an instant, trying to understand what he was seeing. Through the glass, he could make out water from below rushing up at him. Like an electric shock, he realized that he was battling for his life.

When they emerged onto the side of the ship, Ojassaar and his manager stood for a moment trying to decide what to do. Around them all was confusion, with people leaping into the sea. From every side echoed the screams of those in the water.

Before they could even move to grab a life jacket, however, a mammoth wave smashed against the foundering ship and knocked them into the sea.

When Ojassaar felt the icy water close over him, he seemed to sink so deep that he was sure he would never come back up. He fought to reach the surface until his strength all seemed to have drained away.

"I don't have any more air," he told himself. "I'm going to give up now. I'm going to die." He could feel his fingers and arms growing numb and stiff from the cold. Then, he felt a new surge of strength.

When he finally popped to the surface, he struggled to stay afloat, gasping for air. Around him dozens of empty life jackets floated. He pulled one to his chest and held on.

In what seemed a miracle, suddenly an inflatable life raft popped to the surface directly in front of him. He was able to crawl inside it, and two other men joined him almost immediately. The raft was waterlogged, but its roof was intact and it did not leak. Although the raft floated, it quickly filled with water from the waves that crashed over it with regularity.

Ojassar and two others on his raft stood up, holding the sagging canvas roof. The knee-deep water, in which they stood, was cold and numbing. If they sat in it, they would die.

"Cold water makes you feel so numb and comfortable that you feel like sleeping," Ojassaar explained later. "That's the feeling you get right before you die."

So in a way, as they fought for life in the frigid sea, the storm became their ally.

12 · RAFTS IN THE WATER

It was almost 12:30 a.m. when Morten Boje reached the life raft, the last one to join the group that included Paul Barney, Kent Harstedt, Sara Hedrenius, Paul Andersson and Elmar Siegel. The raft was designed for thirty-five people, but already it was becoming crowded. The night was pitch black, and they could not make out others across the raft, but everyone seemed to be stepping or lying on someone else. No one knows how many there were — Kent Harstedt estimates at least 20 — but by morning eight remained alive, with several bodies floating in the water. For Morten, like the others, to climb aboard the raft took all his strength, and he sat in the darkness without speaking. He did not learn until morning that his friend Kent was only a few feet away.

Fifteen minutes after he struggled aboard, a strange calm fell over the scene as the *Estonia* lifted its bow into the sky and began to slip stern-first into the depths. Above the shriek of the wind and the thunder of the waves, the catastrophe had filled the night with screams and shouts and the eerie sound of the "tyfon" siren echoing from the ship.

Now a serenity descended over the sea. The sky cleared, and the stars and moon cast eerie reflections through the red glow of flares and the tinkling of the red lights atop some of the rafts. The wind and the storm itself seemed to die as if in recognition of what disaster they had wrought. It seemed to Morten that even the screams and shouting stopped.

Silently those on the raft turned their eyes toward the *Estonia*, where its bow was lifting majestically into the air. The front half of the ship stood out in silhouette against the moon. Those on the raft could make out the contours of the now-darkened superstructure. The whole unforgettable sight seemed to be outlined in bright red steam. After a moment they realized that the strange red glow was the smoke from the rockets some of the rafts were sending arcing into the windy sky. In a surrealistic scene, the moonlight glistened on the wet hull, the sea shone like silver lace, and the contours of the ship stood etched sharply against the moon.

It was both magnificent and horrible. The ship seemed to twist slightly as it ever-so-slowly slid beneath the sea. The great animal was going to its grave.

The mechanic Elmar Siegel could see that the bow visor was entirely gone, torn off by the storm. For him, that explained what had happened to the ship. But he did not speak.

There was an eerie silence. The screams, even the wind seemed to fade away as if in tribute to a dying ship.

"Look!" A bright voice said in accented English, "How beautiful!" In the ensuing hours, it was a voice they came to know only as "Mr. Positive."

Sara was appalled, and she reminded the optimistic speaker how thoughtless such a comment was. Paul Andersson added his own disapproval.

Yet later each admitted that in the light of the red glow, there was something unreal and awe-inspiring, as if it were a movie they were watching, something that didn't involve them. Nothing at that moment seemed as painful as it had been minutes earlier. Kent re-counted later that as the ship went down, in his exhausted state he had no thought of fellow passengers perishing with it. Somehow it had seemed to him that everyone had by now escaped onto the rafts.

But most passengers were trapped in the ship, either awakened too late by the siren and the list of the ship or simply unable to make their way out. Those with cabins on the starboard or sinking side of the ship had little chance to work their way out with the list so deadly. Some lay with broken legs or other injuries that made them unable to find their way upstairs to the outer decks.

The last sound, the ship's tyfon siren warning, died away as the sea closed over the last projections of the bow, leaving a smooth and desolate spot on the water filled with flotsam.

It had seemed hours since the first lurch sent passengers scram-bling to get out of the doomed ship. Yet when the ship went down before their eyes, they were shocked when someone said they had been on the raft only fifteen minutes.

The relief from the dreaded storm was short-lived. When the *Estonia* disappeared, the waves rose again and the wind howled with renewed fury. In the near distance where the red lights of the other rafts danced, an emergency rocket occasionally lit up the sky. When that happened, those on this raft cheered. But it was a precarious sit-uation. On the rafts that had overturned — as this one — survivors were desperately hunkered down and clinging to stay atop the over-turned bottoms. On the raft of Kent and Sara, anyone who watched those rafts that were upright did so with a sense of gnawing envy.

All on the raft expected rescue to come at any minute. Before the emergency, they had seen the lights of the other ships on the same route. Now each time their raft rose high on a swell, they scanned the sea for those lights coming to their aid. With the *Estonia* gone, and only a flotsam-ridden sea remaining, the lonely terror grew even worse as the minutes dragged on. The wind tore at them, and the rain came in sheets. Without the stricken ship in sight, the sea seemed wider, more empty and more threatening than ever. As time passed, a loss of hope seemed to creep around the raft. Now for each of them the longest night's journey had begun. People began to moan and to complain about aches. Kent's legs began to feel numb, and he feared that his back injury would paralyze his legs. Also, there was a constant fear that their raft was losing air and would sink. It had doubled in the middle and was taking on the shape of a taco shell.

Yet they were not entirely alone, for when they rose high on a swell they could see the little red lights atop the other rafts. The sight gave them a sense of togetherness, of hope. They could not know, however, that many of those rafts with the tents up and lights shining on top were empty.

From their voices, Paul Andersson of the crew recognized his friend the disc jockey opposite him on the raft, along with a girl who was a waitress and the young Russian manager of kitchen storage.

"Take off your shoes and start bailing the raft," Andersson had called after the first large wave hit them. "We need to get the water out."

A few on the raft did as was suggested, but Paul Barney only stared. "What a waste of energy," the Englishman told himself.

Kent had only his right shoe remaining, and after using it for a few minutes to bail he passed it to others to use. It was obvious that even if they did manage to remove a little water — which the wind flung back in their faces — that the next large wave more than replaced it.

Paul Andersson stood next to Elmar Siegel, and they finally realized that both were crewmen. They had never met, probably because Siegel was from the engine room and Andersson from the bar.

"Do you think we'll make it?" Andersson asked quietly. "The raft isn't inflated properly. It was probably damaged when we pulled it off the ship."

Siegel didn't answer. He had convinced himself that to survive he needed to do two things — keep himself in the raft and not go numb. He did this by trying to shut out all that was going on around him. His Balkan personality kept him inside himself. He had decided to look only at the sea beyond the raft until dawn.

As a young man, Siegel had graduated from the naval school in Tallinn and had been at sea as a diesel engineer for twenty-eight years. His home was on the Estonian peninsula of Noarootsi, surrounded by the sea. As a child he had grown up with its sound in his ears, and it had become a part of him.

Standing next to Elmar Siegel, Morten Boje tried to talk to him. Siegel wore a coat with a hood pulled close about his face. When Morten made efforts to communicate, he was met only with two dark eyes staring from the hood, and no answer.

When a particularly large wave washed over them, at times someone was washed off the raft. Sometimes they struggled back — sometimes they were not seen again. Some panicked and screamed constantly for help, with their cries lost on the wind or blending with the wails from the surrounding rafts. Others stayed calm, huddling together for warmth.

Kent and Sara huddled and talked to keep up each other's spirits.

But the experienced seaman Elmar Siegel felt that the best strategy to survive was to pull within himself, sit quietly and stay as warm as possible with his own heat. He watched with sullen disdain those who jumped up and down in the center of the raft to try to stay warm. He had wrapped a thin rope from the raft around his wrist and held it tightly.

By now the water in the raft had risen to the chests of those who sat. The cold began to take its toll. The grim rhythm of teeth chattering could be heard as body heat drained away. No one spoke it, but each thought: how long can I last like this? Will help come in time? Where are those rescue ships?

Most of those who perished after gaining the outer deck of the *Estonia* probably died by drowning. Their number will never be known. But even those fortunate enough to make it up from below faced daunting odds. Unless they found shelter in a covered raft, even healthy, strong persons would normally survive only a short time in such conditions. The water temperature, the gale winds and freezing rain, the incessant waves washing over the rafts made for a deadly combination.

The human body is a wonderful machine and at times can take almost unimaginable punishment. But fifty-degree water is only a few degrees above freezing. The sea that night off the coast of Finland was terrible in the chances it offered for those who leaped into or were thrown into the waves.

Heavy clothing can provide some insulation, trapping body heat against the onslaught of the chill water. But most of those who managed to get off the sinking ship had no time to dress warmly, and some even believed that heavy clothes would drag them down and so avoided them. A majority apparently fled their cabins in their underwear or wearing only their night clothes. Others had their loose clothes torn off by the water in their plunge from the ship.

It is well to remember that the Baltic Sea where the *Estonia* went down is at the same latitude north as Hudson's Bay in Canada or the Bering Sea between Alaska and Russia. In such seas, by the end of September the icy thrust of winter hurtles down from the Arctic with a fury most of us can only imagine.

For those at the mercy of bitter winds, drenching waves and cold temperatures, first would come deep chilling, then a numbing hypothermia. Water drains heat from the body twenty-five times as fast as cold air. Without protective clothes or heavy fat tissue, within an hour the body temperature begins to drop. After only a few degrees' loss of temperature, the brain becomes numbed and coordination is lost. It becomes difficult to speak or even think. The will to fight and survive begins to wane.

When the body temperature lowers to around 30 degrees C. one loses consciousness. Even the heart begins to lose rhythm. During World War II the U.S. Navy learned that many survivors who ended up in the water died when they were picked up. Their hearts could not take the strain. Sometimes rescue, then death.

For those on the raft, they had all felt that help was very close, but as the time dragged interminably a greater sense of despair set in. Only the optimistic voice seemed hopeful. "Don't worry. We'll be okay," he constantly assured in heavily accented English.

A flare suddenly lit the sky near them; then another. In the light they could see other rafts, and life jackets bobbing on the waves.

"Hooray! They can see us now," shouted Mr. Positive. "They'll be here soon. We'll be saved!"

He had become a cheerleader for them, shouting encouragement at each hopeful sign.

The flares excited a great flush of optimism on the raft, even though there was no sign of rescuers. At least signals were being sent. Rescue had to be on the way. Surely those who fired them had seen something.

But when the blackness descended after the flares and in the ensuing minutes nothing happened, a surge of dismay fell over the group. That was when a new movement occurred on the raft. Those huddled standing in the middle began jumping up and down in unison. In their frustration they were trying to do something to warm themselves and to show their impatience. It did not last long, but the jumping would become a deadly pattern through the night.

Another flare erupted into a blaze of light. Again Mr. Positive cheered and reassured them that their worries were nearly over.

Paul Barney noticed that he was caught up in the excitement with the others each time a rocket flashed across the sky. He decided then that he needed to save his emotions in case this lasted until morning, for the disappointment that came with the darkness after each rocket was devastating. Before long, the others did not have the strength to shout or show excitement.

After a time it seemed that the water in the raft had warmed a bit. Sara told Kent that something warm was behind her back, and asked him to look. It was a body. Yet Sara let it remain there for the heat it offered. But when another wave washed over them, it brought an unbelievable chill as it poured in frigid new water. It also dashed any rising hopes.

Such large breaking waves seemed to come from time to time, preceded by an unbelievable roar. After a while the group caught on and called a warning each time such a massive wave was imminent.

This allowed them to brace themselves, and those around the edge could hang on to a rope.

All this time Paul Barney had been holding desperately on to the Estonian girl he had helped pull into the raft, trying to protect her from the icy wind. By the raft's movements he knew the weather was worsening again, and a glance up told him that the moon that had shone on them a few minutes earlier was covered with clouds again. Somehow the sight of the moon and stars shining down on them had brought a calm assurance. Barney spoke soothingly to the girl, telling her that all would be well, even though he was not sure she could understand him.

Then came the voice of the optimist again, "It's okay. Take it easy. We'll be okay." He said it in a loud voice to everyone on the raft. "We'll be safe in two hours."

It was a refrain that for several hours burst from "Mr. Positive" at every possible hopeful sign — a rocket, a helicopter light, the lights of a ship drawing closer. He was incurable in his cheerfulness.

Nevertheless, before long they drifted away from the lights of the other rafts. Only when they were lifted high by a swell could they catch a few glimmers in the distance. Finally even those were out of sight. The waves continued to wash over the raft, and most of the people were standing to avoid the waist-deep water that had collected in the bottom. A sense of despair, of doom, slowly grew over the raft.

Those fighting for their lives in the raft spoke little. They became absorbed with the struggle to stay on the raft and not be swept away. Most of the waves were gentle, and the raft rode these. But periodically an angry wave cascaded over them, taking away what little precious warmth they were each nursing. Sometimes when they felt such a wave coming, they tried to lift the edge of the raft so as not to be inundated. And always they hung tight to the ropes around the raft, so tightly that their arms and hands ached unmercifully.

The moon was visible through the clouds like a blurry tennis ball, but it cast little light. The night was now so black they couldn't tell how many were in the raft. Some lay on top of each other for warmth.

Kent and Sara kept up their conversation, partly to keep awake, partly to keep their spirits up. But the roar of the waves made it so that he had to speak right into her ear to be heard. He warned her that he was going to be sick and that she should turn, but before she could move he vomited into her hair and on her clothes. In another minute, though, a wave cascaded over them once more, and she said it thoroughly cleaned her, so there was no worry. Others in the raft also were sick from the motion of the raft, made worse by the sea water they had swallowed.

There was little communication among those hunched over in the raft to conserve their warmth. The fight for individual surviv-al was so intense there was little room for anything else. The wind picked up and like a lash stung their faces time after time. Everyone was so plagued by fatigue and fear that nobody had the strength to talk — except that Kent and Sara would not let each other fall into that stupor. They sat close against each other. But each person's world had shrunk, and was dominated by thoughts of what the next wave would bring.

13 · THEY CAN SEE US NOW

Almost everyone on Kent Harstedt's raft saw the ship at the same time. The bright lights, looking like a moving hotel, appeared through the rain. The ship seemed to be stopped, but the raft was drifting directly toward it. A palpable wave of hope swept over the raft, and a wild cheer went up. Soon, they could see the lights of two other ships close by. Around the ships, searchlights played on the water, probing for survivors. Some of the distant rafts sent up rockets.

Mr. Positive was shouting, "Yes, yes! They can see us now!"

Several of the survivors in the raft began to use the shrill whistles that were attached to their life preservers. The whistles and the shouts were lost on the wind. Two people tore off their life vests to flail the air with them as a signal. Mr. Positive was ecstatic, reassuring the others that it was finally over. Even the waves seemed to diminish. Surely, it was now only a matter of minutes until they would be hauled aboard, filled with hot soup and given warm beds. The mood was almost jovial. There was a great release of tension, and a unified sigh of relief seemed to go up from all of them. The yawning abyss of death that had been so close seemed to have been defeated.

A half-hour passed, and the ships seemed to be doing nothing. They could see some of the ships' spotlights centered on rafts that were nearby, but nothing was being done to rescue those caught in the lights.

At last they drifted close enough to read the closest ship's name, the *Mariella*, shining in neon on the superstructure. On her bridge, Captain Jan-Tore Thornroos scanned the water before the ship, but the black overturned raft on the dark sea was not visible.

When they drew abreast, the raft turned into pandemonium as the shouting grew to screams and pleas. The survivors bobbing on their tiny craft could see people staring out of portholes and the broad restaurant windows. They seemed only a stone's throw away. Yet there was no reaction from those on the ship. After a time, the brightly lit ship was drawing away, and the lights grew dim as they were almost lost in the rain and the waves.

The shouts of exultation turned to despair, then anger. The ship had passed them. The *Mariella*, with its lighted windows and warm and safe passengers staring with curiosity or snuggled in their warm beds, was gone. It had missed them. The survivors could not understand. They had made it through shipwreck and drowning in a stormy sea, and now the rescuers had come and were doing nothing. The two Russians stood shaking their fists in anger, swearing at the ship that was disappearing through the rain.

In addition, Paul Andersson realized that they were now drifting away from the other rafts. They were moving out of the circle of ships.

The raft was thrown into absolute silence. From the height of hope, of the great promise of rescue, came the descent into dejection and despair as the lights of the ship faded in the darkness.

"Now, we are out of the search area," Paul Andersson admitted to himself.

The sight of the lights and the passengers on the ship staring out had unnerved many of those on the raft. The raft was back in total darkness. There was now only silence from Mr. Positive.

As if in reaction to the disappointment, those standing in the middle of the raft began the jumping again, this time more furiously than ever. Morten watched a man stop jumping and simply settle down into the water without protest, face down. It occurred to the Dane that the dance itself was a prelude to death. It was obvious the huge disappointment of the warm ship passing them had plunged spirits into despair and pushed some struggling survivors over the edge into the acceptance of a waiting death.

Morten decided that those about to die turned white in the face, mumbled deliriously, and stared apathetically. Watching those who were jumping in the center of the raft, he began to realize that the jumping was a last effort to ward off death, to keep some semblance of circulation going and provide some warmth. He knew that it also used precious energy. When their strength and their will were used up, they began a low moan. That sound took on a somber meaning, for it preceded a final surrender. It was a sound that would come intermittently through the night.

At first Kent and Sara did not understand the sinister meaning of the jumping and moaning, but as they discussed it in the darkness they worked to keep each other optimistic. They agreed that the arrival of the ships, even if they could not help much in the face of such heavy seas, surely meant that other rescue efforts were under way.

After another few minutes, it appeared that fewer jumpers were continuing their dance. It became apparent that in the deep water of the raft several bodies were floating. Some were washed over as the waves periodically flushed over them.

Those standing along the edge of the raft stared silently into the darkness, where the ship had disappeared. The ones who screamed the loudest, whose hopes rose the highest, were now the most dejected.

"It is the ones who cry and show a lot of emotions who die among us," Elmar Siegel thought. "The ones who sit quiet and up straight at the edge, they are still alive." Afterwards, those who survived agreed that it was the ones who turned their energy inward who survived.

After the disappointment of the *Mariella* passing them, Kent told himself and Sara that they had to keep their spirits up. They knew they had something the others did not have. Of those on the raft, they alone had their pact, their promise to help each other make it through.

To do this, even as the weather got worse again, they prodded and teased and joked and reminded each other of their coming date. When a huge wave washed over the raft once again, bringing near-freezing water over them, Kent joked "I may be an Aquarius, but wasn't that a little too much?"

"Well, I'm a Virgo," Sara shot back.

In addition, he teased her about being so careless as to lose her glasses when they had leaped into the water. His own glasses were tucked safely in his pocket where he had put them just before jumping.

It was exactly the right thing to do. Survival experts say that in such a crisis, keeping up spirits is as important as keeping body heat. The stronger the determination and the optimism, the stronger will be the survival instinct. When the mind is without hope and gives up, it notifies the body to begin shutting down. The stronger someone's spirits are, the greater protection against panic and the ultimate defeat of sliding gently into death. Hope helps build an iron-clad shield against destruction.

After a time, someone on the raft pointed to a stabbing light that danced in the sky in the distance. It was a helicopter, probing the waves for survivors. They watched with restrained excitement, for it was far away, and shortly it disappeared in the other direction.

As Kent and Sara were desperately trying to stay alive, they hugged each other tight and tried to make tents out of the extra life jackets on board. The wind stung at their exposed skin, tearing at them with gale force, winds strong enough to topple trees on land. To counter the unending misery, they kept up their needling and teasing in an effort to stay alert.

They took turns sitting as a windbreak for the other. At times, the wind tore at their faces so much that it was difficult to breathe. After two hours, they began to talk about what actions they could take to survive. Some in the raft continued jumping and doing exercises to keep warm, moving their arms and legs to increase circulation. Sara explained to Kent that they needed to huddle and conserve their body heat.

"How do you know that?" he prodded.

She explained that she had seen a television program about how to avoid hypothermia. He agreed she was right, and they hunkered down out of the wind, while still keeping out of the chest-deep, sloshing water in the raft.

Kent was reminded of his own military training in Sweden, where all healthy young men serve a year in their country's service. His platoon leader instructed the men in how to save themselves from extreme cold, advising them that body heat was conserved most in the armpits and between the thighs. On some terribly cold nights, the soldiers had taken turns lying atop one another, with the hands thrust beneath the other's armpits. Somewhat shamefacedly Kent told her of these recommendations for dealing with life-threatening cold. Even in their dire circumstances, he felt embarrassed because she was an attractive girl.

Her response was enthusiastic, however. So they lay with their legs entwined, Kent on top and his arms under hers holding on to the ropes. This gave added protection from being washed off the raft. Sara still had no vest. When the one on top grew too cold, they exchanged positions.

For mental survival, they encouraged, cajoled, teased, and joked. Even though they had little contact in the darkness with the other survivors on the raft, they knew they were not alone. Their pact and their constant communication kept them alert and hopeful.

In the distance, they could see some of the small lights from the other rafts once more. Perhaps the seas had calmed slightly so that they could be seen more easily, or perhaps they had drifted closer to the other rafts.

14 · THE ENVY OF A PEACEFUL EXIT

The Englishman Paul Barney shrank from the wind, desperately holding the Estonian girl he had helped pull from the sea. After the calm, he felt the raft begin to rise and fall and lean once more. As if on cue, the storm had resumed with greater fury after the sinking of the great ship. The stars and the moon that had been so bright earlier had been replaced by darkness and slashing rain.

Earlier, they had found comfort in seeing the small red emergency lights bouncing around them atop the other rafts. Without speaking it, they had envied those rafts that were upright, which had tents atop them to keep out the waves and give protection from the wind. The little colony of red lights gave them a sense of community.

After a time, however, they saw that they had drifted away from the others. The reassuring glow of the flares and little lights from the rafts was gone. In the dark expanse of churning sea, the rafts had separated. Once more, darkness had grown close all around them.

In the raft, Kent and Sara sat facing inward in the water at the edge, holding tight to the ropes so they would not be thrown out. They bundled together, not only for warmth, but for shared company. At this moment, not to be alone was worth everything. In the center of the raft, a dozen people stood pressed close for warmth.

Each time one of the giant waves came with a roar, they braced for the onslaught before it broke over the raft. It was a sound they dreaded, and they called a warning as these approached.

Whenever a wave dashed over them, it took away the precious bit of warmth each had accumulated from the person next to them or from a warm garment. As the minutes went on, it became obvious that there was more room. Those who were washed off disappeared in a torrent of water, usually without a sound. It was as if some dark beast hovered just beyond the next wave, waiting to drag one silently away, as a lion sometimes takes a victim during the night from a jungle camp. But in the sea, there were no tracks left as evidence.

After a while, Morten pointed, and they could see one of the white wooden lifeboats that those on the deck of the sinking ship had tried so hard to get loose from its davits. It was overturned, dipping on the waves only a stone's throw from them. It had apparently come loose as the ship went down, as the angle changed on the davits that held the boat. They watched five or six people desperately trying to stay on top of it. Horrified, they saw a wave wash one, then another of them off. When they drifted out of sight, only one or two pitiful figures remained clinging atop the lifeboat.

By then, Sara and Kent had found a rope and tied themselves to the edge of the raft. Now that there was more room, they lay with their heads against the bulge of the raft. The girl had grown more concerned because the water where they sat was rising, and the raft seemed to be folding in the middle from losing air. Also, the raft was not as firm as it had been.

"These rafts are unsinkable," Kent reassured her. "I know they're unsinkable." He tried to sound convincing, but he did not know if the rafts could sink or not. He pushed aside the image of a raft doubling around the people standing in it and sinking into the sea. He knew that such devastating thoughts can lead to despair and surrender. On the ship and in the sea around them, they had seen what happened to those who lost hope and slipped into shock and apathy. He was grateful that he and Sara had made their solemn vow not to surrender.

Paul Barney, who sat with the young Estonian woman enfolded in his arms against his chest for warmth, felt his heart race each time a flare went off. He had decided not to be swayed by Mr. Positive's emotional outbursts. Paul had convinced himself that to survive he needed to control his emotions and his strength. If we make it through until dawn, he told himself, there would be time enough to become hopeful.

In the darkness, the despair seemed to grow after each flare died. Barney also noticed that the uncomfortable movement of the raft from those jumping in the middle seemed to increase following each flare.

"Don't worry. Take it easy," sounded the reassuring voice of Mr. Positive again. "We'll be safe within two hours." It was the same cheerful promise he had been making for nearly three hours.

Meanwhile Morten Boje, the Dane, felt an older man squeeze between his arms. Morten was standing at the edge of the raft holding onto the rope which circled it. The other man was small and thin-haired, and he snuggled a place between Morten's chest and the edge of the raft. When the waves came they shared each other's warmth. Morten noticed that the man had only underwear on, so he started to rub the man's thighs to help his circulation and to become warm from the exertion. They did not speak.

The water in the raft in which they sat or stood had grown slightly warmer from all the bodies in it. Then several waves came crashing in again, once more making the water frigid.

Those standing in the middle of the raft once more began jumping more furiously than ever. In Morten's arms, the small man lapsed into panic. He began crying uncontrollably. When Morten tried to console him, he broke away. Morten understood that his tears were not from fear, but because of sorrow from losing a family member.

Morten watched him, irritated. He knew that to lose control was to be on the edge of the precipice. The man could have stayed, gotten warm, and maintain control of himself. Instead, he pulled away and joined those in the center of the raft.

Nearby, Paul Barney was suddenly lifted by a wave and thrown from the raft. His life jacket was torn off by the force of the water, and he lost his grip on the Estonian girl. Earlier, when he had found the life jacket floating in the sea, he had been unable to fasten it on properly. Fortunately, he still clutched the rope in his hand.

As the raft scooted along propelled by the giant wave, Paul was dragged along by the rope that he now clung to desperately. He swallowed sea water, until his stomach churned, and he vomited over and over as he tried to hold on. He was too weak to call out.

Amazingly, as he was dragged through waves, hanging by a thin thread of life, he had a vision of a boyhood scene he had experienced when his family lived in a big house in Wales. He had climbed to the top of a ceiling-high window, had opened the upper part and was hanging on it, expecting the counterweight to lower him gently. Instead, the whole window came crashing down over him, shattering and covering him with glass. He had been in a state of shock and was unable to move for minutes. Now in the icy sea, he felt the same shock.

But Paul Barney had traveled the world and had come in contact with yoga and the principles of controlling one's emotions. "Calm breathing revokes the shock. Calm breathing," he told himself. Concentrating, he began to will his arms to move. Inch by inch, he began to pull himself through the waves toward the raft.

At the same time, the Estonian girl was thrown from the raft. She also had retained hold on a rope. Morten and Elmar Siegel had seen the girl go flying over their heads into the sea. When they saw that she was struggling to pull back into the raft by the rope, they helped haul her back aboard. She still did not speak, but was trembling uncontrollably.

Paul Barney then made it back into the raft, shaking and coughing up water. The Estonian girl had moved into the center of the raft by then to take a place with those standing huddled there. Barney looked for her, and then shrugged. Trying to gain control of himself, he buried his head in his arms.

Paul noticed that their situation had grown more desperate. Nearly three hours had passed in the raft, and he could sense that those around him were losing hope. There were no visible signs of rescue. Those standing in the middle of the raft had seen that it was getting harder to stand; the water was deeper now and getting colder all the time. The waves were still pounding the raft and sending it whirling like a toy. In the center, the water was as high as the chest of a standing man. Everyone struggled to be at the edge where they could hold their upper body out of the water.

The two Russian men in the center raised their arms and once more began shouting obscenities into the sky. Elmar and Paul Andersson, being Estonian, understood their words. One of the Russians was a crew member who was the head of kitchen storage. These violent emotions and obscenities sent a further shock of panic among those who had despaired, and the jumping in the center of the raft increased.

At the same time, Paul Andersson felt himself pushed and pulled by those surging toward the edge of the raft, where there were ropes that one could hold on to. The pressure against the bartender made it difficult to breathe, and he felt something give within him.

"One of my ribs is broken," he thought. He began a prayer and repeated it over and over. "God, let your will be done, not mine."

Andersson was used to hardship. As an Estonian under Russian rule, he was only eighteen when he was sent to Russia for military duty. During his two years of service, he was unable to return home for a visit even once. "It was a hard school, a terrible school," he recalls. "It was two years without one single happy day." Now he told himself that, hardened by such an experience, he could endure this terrible challenge.

After another half hour, the storm grew even worse, and a new sense of desperation seemed to fall over the raft. Sara felt someone pulling her away from the edge, insistent and demanding. The person began to pull at her hair, not aggressively but as if to simply have something to hold to. It was as if someone was sinking into the deep water lapping at their chests, and needed something to hang onto to preserve a life.

Finally Sara was able to pull herself loose.

When he got back in the raft, Paul Barney had come to two conclusions: he needed another life vest, and he needed to tie himself to the raft. He had narrowly escaped death by being thrown out, and he vowed it would not happen again.

But his hands were stiff and numb. He doubted that he could even tie a knot. He told himself that he was still in shock, and that the yoga breathing exercises would help him control himself. The deep breathing would not only help the symptoms of shock, but would eventually carry blood to his numbed hands and fingers to make them function again.

It is a matter of self-control and patience, he assured himself as he began to inhale deeply.

Later, he wasn't sure when, as he had lost track of time, his hands and fingers responded. He was able to tie one of the raft ropes around him.

In the middle of the raft, the situation had grown worse. People there were tumbling around, and Barney felt people pushing at him. Something heavy was pounding at his leg under the water. When he reached down, he saw that it was the body of the 50-year old man who had been sitting next to him, now hitting his leg by the motion of the raft.

Barney did nothing, did not push him away or show signs of despair. They were still comrades in a desperate situation, riding the same raft on a cold and determined sea. He refused to be devastated by the man's death.

Kent Harstedt, meanwhile, became aware that the jumping in the center of the raft had slowed down. Unlike the others who peered out over the edge, he and Sara had decided to stay low, curled up and sharing warmth. They talked quietly of cheerful matters, still debating at which restaurant they would keep their date.

Morten Boje was feeling his own situation getting worse. His legs and his arms were becoming numb. Facing the sea, he felt someone grab at him from behind. The close body brought some warmth so Morten did not object. But this was followed by a tug on his hair, and then a kick. Slowly, Morten turned and saw face of the thin-haired man, who earlier had provided some warmth by wriggling between him and the raft.

The man was stretched prone, with his face up and feet toward the middle of the raft. Morten watched almost dispassionately, as the man, whose face was only inches away, exhaled a huge breath and lay with his mouth open.

When little waves washed into the man's mouth and he did not move, Morten knew that he was dead.

It was strange, but Morten almost envied the man's peaceful exit. For this thin-haired man, this fellow voyager, the horror was over. It was as if he had decided that since life itself was over, he would slip away easily and without fuss.

A moment of desperation rose in Morten. Though they had not spoken, they had shared warmth, an unspoken camaraderie. It was as if a friend had gone from his life. Yet on the man's face the fear and the pain were gone. He looked to be sleeping peacefully.

"His death was gentle," Morten told himself. He glanced around at the others still standing, dark silhouettes against a still-dark sky. At that instant, he was filled with a need to be with live people. To one side, he could make out the form of a man in blue overalls, Elmar Siegel, where he had been standing. Earlier Morten had spoken to the machinist, but had received no reply. Now he sought warmth, so he put his arms on Siegel's shoulders. The machinist, however, distrustful and fearing that Morten might panic and pull him from the raft, pushed him away. On Morten's third try, Siegel saw that he was calm and let him put his arms around him and hug his back for warmth.

Slowly it became apparent that Mr. Positive would not be heard from again. There were no more cheers or encouraging outbursts. After a time, it was obvious that he was one of those face down in the water. Nobody remembers his face, but all who made it from this raft cannot forget his enthusiasm, his optimism, his cheerfulness that he shared with them for a time.

15 · A TANGLED FOOT

Earlier that night, Tom Johnsson, the 33-year-old member of the police officers union from Stockholm, had been brushing his teeth just after midnight when he felt the ship roll uncomfortably. Luckily, his cabin was next to the lobby near one of the stairways on deck four. When the ship heaved to the side, he knew he had to get out as soon as possible. Dressed only in his shirt and underwear, he pushed through his door and rushed up the stairs past others, who were struggling upwards toward deck seven that led outside.

When he came to the lobby on deck six, it was filled with desperate, confused passengers, trying to communicate with each other in different languages. He watched a large man climb over others to try to get out. And there came to his nose the stench of panic and death, the overpowering odor of urine and feces — the result of some of the passengers losing bodily control in the grip of pure terror. Some people sat or stood in resigned shock, watching dumbfounded or with their faces buried in their arms. Some leaned against the walls sobbing. Others were calm and were trying to cooperate to climb upwards, but many were panicked and flailing in their efforts to pull others down to climb over them.

Tom was able to pull himself up to the seventh deck, where a man was standing holding the door up for others to pass. When he emerged, Tom could see a hundred passengers helping each other don life vests. He took one, got it on, and joined a small group, a man in his forties and three girls. All were wearing life vests.

The next thing he remembered was that he was in the water, most likely flung there by a wave that washed over the ship. When he emerged coughing up water, he could make out the lights of several rafts floating nearby. He tried to swim toward them but could not get close. As a big wave came, he rode to the crest of it and spotted atop a swell one of the big wooden lifeboats from the ship. It was one of those that people had struggled so hard to launch, but the angle of the ship had made it impossible. He could see that it was partially smashed and filled with water. In the next moment, he saw an upside-down raft drift towards him. Two girls and an Estonian crewman helped him up onto the raft. All were wearing life jackets. The Estonian was a large, strong man. To keep warm they lay huddled together, with Tom on bottom because he had on the least clothes. One of the girls had bare legs, so she intertwined them with his. The Estonian, a man about 40 years old, was on Tom's right, and the girls were to the left of him.

Tom noticed that their raft was drifting away from the *Estonia*. Overhead, as the sky cleared briefly, he could make out the moon and the stars that made the night bright. In the distance, they could see their ship sinking. It seemed as if they had been on the raft for hours. In reality, it had been only a few minutes.

The storm began again, and each time a giant wave came and washed over them, it brought new cold, new fear. As the minutes went by, they desperately tried to keep warm, to offer and receive body heat from the others. Worst of all, they were washed off the raft by the waves time and time again. For security, they tried to hold on to the loose ends of the raft's ropes so that they could crawl back on when they were washed off.

The cold and the constant strain left them drained and exhausted, barely able to move. Finally, one of the girls could not find the strength to pull back to the raft and disappeared with a moan into the sea. A short time later, the other girl followed. The men had lost the power to help them.

The two men lay close on the bottom of the raft, trying to hang on and not give up. It had been raining the whole night, except for the brief respite when the sky cleared. The cold had reached unbearably deep into Tom's bones. To combat the hypothermia, he tried to imagine himself warm and basking in the sun. But each time another giant wave washed over them, it dashed him back to reality.

For them, hope rose and waned. To keep his mind busy, Tom focused on his children and his wife. But his thoughts kept drifting to his own father, who died when Tom was only 12 years old. Would his own children now be cheated of a father by the sea? Was this how it would end? There amid the dark waves, he refused to accept that possibility.

Finally, they could see the spotlights from the other ships that had arrived. Tom could feel himself going numb. He became vaguely aware that one of the spotlights was trained on his and the Estonian's overturned raft. A surge of hope flooded over the two men. "We will make it after all!" Somebody shouted. But the ships passed them by.

Alone now, Johnsson and the Estonian hugged the bottom of the raft, straining to hold to the ropes so they would not be washed away. The storm grew worse again, and they were flushed from the raft several more times. Each time, it was more difficult to get back. Through the long hours, they shared the Estonian's windbreaker, with it pulled over Tom's head.

To endure the cold, Tom tried again to imagine himself basking in the sun in the warm places he had known during his life. It seemed to help, as if his mind willed his body to stay warm. But the damnable waves came again and again, and would not let him remain in the sunny paradise of his mind. The rain continued through the night.

At last the light of day broke through the clouds. Through the windbreaker, Tom could hear the sound of helicopters circling, coming closer and closer.

"If I made it this far, I'll make it to be rescued," Tom told himself.

Three helicopters were circling them by then, and the men waved with frozen hands and arms. Then another giant wave covered them, and they were once more washed into the sea. Tom felt his foot catch in one of the raft's ropes, and he could not get back into the raft, with his foot caught and holding him in an awkward position. He was left floundering in the water, trying to stay afloat. He struggled in panic, his foot still caught. Was he to endure so much, to then lose the battle at the last moment? Was he to leave his son fatherless, after all?

Suddenly, he could see a figure descending from the sky on what looked like a spider web. It was a rescuer from the helicopter. The figure splashed into the water right behind Tom, and he felt the man's arms around him, getting his tangled foot loose and then supporting him and working the harness around him. With a whoosh, he felt himself lifted upward, and in a few seconds felt the strong hands of the crewmen pulling him inside the helicopter, where they immediately put him on a stretcher. "The feeling was incredibly nice, even heavenly," he remembers.

His whole body was shaking, as he was transported with the Estonian to the crisis center on the Finnish island of Uto. His body temperature was only 31 C — which is 87.8 degrees Fahrenheit, a full 10.8 degrees below normal body temperature. There, he and the other survivors were given warm fruit juice, warm blankets and intravenous fluids.

Aulis and Aina Lee, the married couple, hugged together for warmth as the hours wore on. Through cold-numbed lips, Aulis told Aina all would be well and they would return to their children. At least, they told each other, they were together. The darkness, the storm, the horror seemed endless.

But after six hours, when a gray drizzling dawn had crept slowly over the eastern sea, the huddled survivors heard the sound of a helicopter. Amid cheers, the women were taken up first. It was, Aina would say later, the worst part of the ordeal. "You had only one strap around you, nowhere to hold on to and you did not know how long they were going to let you swing up there in the air." Once she got inside the helicopter, and only then, did she begin to cry.

The helicopter took them to the *Silja Europa*, the ship that had first received the Mayday message. They were given a luxurious cabin and a maid. As they warmed, Aina watched the news on television. When they began talking about a disaster at sea, at first she did not realize they were talking about the *Estonia*. Later that day the *Europa* proceeded to Stockholm, where the couple was taken to a hospital.

16 · THE LONGEST NIGHT

Incredibly, when it seemed that the storm could get no worse, hail began to fall with the rain. The sting of it on the wind increased the misery and despair, but for some on the raft in their numbed state it did not matter.

For Sara and Kent this meant the pact they had made was even more important than ever. At this time of darkness, of bone-chilling cold, of death all around them, their mutual covenant sustained them, providing hope and human dignity. They were aware of the surrender of those a few feet away who fought and then gave up, or who simply slipped silently down into the water of the raft. Each felt keenly aware of their inability to do anything to help the others. They knew it was beyond their power to decide which of the others lived and died. Kent and Sara knew only that they could help each other. So they hugged tight and provided comments and small bits of cheer and hope that kept their humanity intact in the face of an insufferable situation.

They had seen that the first sign of hypothermia was the slurring of words, then the slipping away into delirium before the body shut down entirely. As they heard more death cries around them in the darkness, they knew it was more and more important to talk. At times they fell silent. Then either Kent or Sara would ask a question of the other to see if they were still alert. After a time they began to wonder if they were the only clear-headed ones left in the group.

As the endless hours wore on, Kent began to falter in his resolve. He began to admit to himself that perhaps it really was too much for them. His thoughts went to a friend named John Andersson in his home city of Helsengborg. Andersson was a politician whose duties included attending the funerals of local people. They had worked together in city government, and Kent now wondered if Andersson would be a speaker at his funeral. But each time he admitted such misgivings, Sara chided him.

"We must hold out till the light comes," she reminded him over and over. "Because then they are going to find us."

For Kent, the coming of daylight seemed so far away as to be impossible. To counteract such pessimism, they began to joke again about their dinner date in Stockholm. He teased her that she would have to fix her hair, which was plastered against her head, before he would be seen with her.

After a while even the jumping in the center of the raft stopped. Almost all communication ended. It was a situation almost beyond endurance. For some, their final struggle for life was desperately furious, resulting in wild thrashing and grasping of others. In their final minutes they would leap and crawl around in the raft, involving everyone aboard. Barely conscious, they hit and pulled and kicked anyone within reach, tugging them into the tumult in the middle of the raft. Those hanging on to the ropes around the edge could only protect themselves as much as possible. Several times Kent was kicked in the back, and handfuls of Sara's hair were torn out.

The weather let up a little, but after a short respite began to worsen once more, and the black night seemed darker than ever. On the raft Kent and Sara directed all their strength to hanging on to the ropes to remain inside.

"That one was too much!" Kent exclaimed after a large wave hit him from behind and pushed him under the water in the raft. He had come up sputtering and spitting.

"Too much," she echoed in agreement. It became a buzzword for them through the night, to make a joke of the whole experience. Indeed, it had become surreal; the jolt of the ship, the plunge into the water, the red glow from the flares on the wild sea, and a raft that threatened to escort them to a frigid death.

"Too much!" Kent called after another wave washed over them. His mind grappled with the situation. "What the hell am I doing here?" he thought. "Can this really be me, or is it not real that I am lying here fighting? All I was going to do was to go up to karaoke bar, listen to some music, and here I am fighting for my life in the middle of the Baltic. This can't be reality. This is too much."

Then, when the waves seemed at their worst, the rain turned to hail again, this time pounding hard. It struck against their arms and faces like flung gravel. They tried to cover up, but it found vulnerable spots. With little gasps and shouts they reacted to the painful attack of the hailstones. Kent wondered if hell itself could be worse than what they were experiencing. The low moans from those who were losing the fight increased after the hail. They were calling for help in three languages, "Help! *Hjelp*! *Appi, Appi*!"

Listening to them, Kent and Sara discussed if there was anything they could do. They agreed hanging on and fighting for their own survival seemed the only possible course. Through the long hours the horrible guttural sounds of people crying out with their last breath rose above the wind.

A young man dressed only in a T-shirt edged over and talked briefly with Paul Andersson, who had had the foresight to dress in a warm crewman jacket before leaving the ship. The young man was a waiter from the ship and had known Andersson there.

Morten still hung on to his place at the edge of the raft, even when someone hit or pulled at him from behind. If they pulled his hair, he shook them loose, but if they simply wanted to hold him for warmth, he let them.

Paul Barney, after being able to get back on the raft after being washed off, had lost track of the Estonian girl he helped. He had found no one else to share warmth with, so he concentrated on breathing deeply to save energy. As he noticed others around the raft sitting as if in stone, he realized they were all in shock.

Barney reached to touch one of the men standing next to him, but the man was stiff and showed no response. With a shrug, he returned to his spot and lost himself in his meditation. His mind went back to the pretty girl he had seen sleeping on the couch in the cafeteria. He wondered if she had got off the ship, and was somewhere on the sea. He had no idea that Sara was curled up against the edge of the same raft only ten feet away.

For Kent and Sara, this was the most critical time of all. They knew that some of those around them were dying from hypothermia and shock. The water, the cold, and the darkness had all taken a horrible toll on every side of them. To renew their strength and resolve, they watched for the moon, which occasionally peeked through the clouds. It helped to focus on the clouds scudding across the moon's face or anything that was normal in the world rather than the horror around them. Time seemed no longer to exist. Even while splashed with water, while hanging on to the ropes with aching fingers, they found themselves drifting into a half-sleep. Several times Kent got cramps in his arms from clinging so tightly to the raft. When that happened, Sara responded by rubbing them briskly to ease the pain.

Just when despair seemed about to take them all, the swooping searchlight of a helicopter stabbed through the darkness a half mile away from them. Someone pointed and shouted "Helicopters!" But this time there was no Mr. Positive to lead a cheer.

A new feeling of hope caught them. A couple of those sitting stood, and some began to heave their arms in great waving motions. They waited as other helicopter lights became visible through the rain, darting, pausing, hanging in the air in the distance, then moving on. They could not hear the helicopters over the howl of the rain and the wind.

Beyond them they could catch glimpses of what looked like a wartime battle scene. Through the thick darkness they could see the lights of ships gathering and above the ships the sweep of helicopters' spotlights probing the sea. Occasionally above the wind they could make out the sound of the ships' horns, sounding now for encouragement. The effect was a dismal one, however, for those on the raft realized the big ships were helpless to rescue them. Twice, circling helicopters came near, each time bringing less enthusiastic waves from those still alive in the raft.

"It's because the raft is overturned," Paul Andersson said glumly. "It's black. They can't see us."

His pronouncement was met by a heavy silence. Kent hugged Sara tighter and tried to think of something cheerful to say. The helicopters had gone. He knew that most of the others had given up hope. He felt himself falter. He could see the outline of the dead floating inside the raft, and nearby in the sea he could make out others.

Kent looked to an older man sitting near him. The man's features reminded him of a close family friend back in his home town. The man was obviously in the last stages of his struggle for life.

For a time Kent began to feel sorry for himself. "It is a shame that I should die when we are so close to being rescued," he thought. "I am grateful to be alive, but at the same time it is hard to think about all those who didn't make it in the raft."

The Russian, whom Paul Andersson recognized as the storeroom manager from the kitchen, shook his fist at the ships and the helicopters in the distance, swore at them heartily, and then slumped back down.

As if matters couldn't get worse the hail came again. To endure the added misery, all of them covered their faces with their arms until it ended a few minutes later and settled into a steady rain.

17 · RESCUE BEGINS

Six minutes after receiving the Mayday call, the image of the *Estonia* disappeared from radar screen of the Viking Line's *Mariella*. When Captain Jan-tore Thornroos of the *Mariella* was awakened and told the *Estonia* had a 30-degree list and a blackout, he threw on pants and a shirt and ran to the bridge barefoot. They were about ten miles away from the sinking ship.

"At first we got visual contact," he said later. "Then after ten minutes the lights went out, and after another ten minutes we lost her on radar. So we figured the worst."

It was forty-five minutes after the alarm that the *Mariella* arrived at the scene where the *Estonia* had gone down. In the beams of the searchlights the crew could see rafts dipping on the waves and people fighting for their lives in the water.

"It looked like Christmas lights bobbing there," said Thornroos.

Away from the small circle of light of the rescue ship, the small raft lights were all that was visible on the dark sea. The newly arrived ship stopped its engines to avoid running down survivors.

On the decks of the *Mariella*, the crew began throwing over life rafts and life vests. Above the crescendo of the rain and the wind, they could hear screams coming from the water.

On arriving, a *Mariella* crewman radioed, "We have got our lifeboats in the water, and we're picking people up as fast as we can. It's so dark out there, all we can see are a few lights from lifeboats and emergency flares."

Unfortunately, the radioman was wrong. The seas were so high and treacherous that the huge passenger ferries that arrived could do little to help. Most captains would not risk their crews by putting them into such danger. The sea was simply too wild.

Captain Esa Makela of the *Silja Europa* was one of those who received the original radio message from the *Estonia*. There is some disagreement about how quickly the *Europa* responded, but at 1:30 a.m., almost one hour after the sinking, his ship reached the site and found the sea covered with people fighting for their lives. At first the captain was worried about striking wreckage or running aground, but when he learned that they were in 300 feet of water, they were able to maneuver freely.

The scene was unreal, with flares going off and little red lights twinkling everywhere. Like the crew of the *Mariella*, Captain Makela's men could make out dozens of people in life vests, some of them waving and pleading, others who floated face down. His crew put over additional rafts, hoping that those who were floating there could find them and get inside. The winds whistling around them and the huge waves kept them from doing more.

Eventually some lives were saved by the ships, but generally all the crews could do was throw over life rafts, wait, and watch as the helicopters arrived and began to pluck people from the sea by dropping rescuers down on cables.

An American, Harry Whipple, publisher of the *Cincinnati Enquirer* in Ohio, was on board another passenger ferry bound for Helsinki, the *Symphony*, as it received the distress call and hurried toward the sinking *Estonia*. He was asleep after 1 a.m. when his wife woke him. She was sitting looking out the window of their cabin at the thirty-foot waves.

"Come look out the window, Harry!" she called, her voice excited. "There's something going on!"

As he reached the window, he could see red flares lighting up the sky. Hundreds of life jackets were floating in the sea around them, and the *Symphony* crew was throwing dozens more into the water to those struggling there. Bright-orange life rafts dipped and swung on the huge waves on every side of their ship.

With a newsman's instinct, Whipple quickly dressed and went on deck. What met him was like a movie scene from World War II. Flares lit up the sky, tent-topped rafts dipped and rose on the waves, and bodies floated in life jackets, the ship's crew fighting the sea to get close enough to those alive to help them.

"I could see life rafts all over the place," he said. "I counted about thirty, and almost half of them had capsized. I couldn't tell if anyone alive was in them or not."

The first survivor that Whipple saw brought aboard by a helicopter was a forty-something Estonian musician. Between 2 a.m. and 3 a.m., about ten people were brought to the *Symphony* by helicopter, said Whipple. Four people, a kitchen helper, another orchestra member and two passengers arrived about 3 a.m., and six more came by helicopter around 6 a.m.

It was a helpless, almost guilty, feeling watching those in the water who were screaming and pleading. The high seas prevented almost any rescue efforts. Even if they had not been incapacitated by sitting up to their waists in the cold water, these survivors had no means of moving their rafts, no oars or sails. They were driven only by the wind and the waves, making it dangerous for them to come near a ship. A raft carried on a wave's crest might smash against the side of the ship, crushing some of those inside and no doubt spilling all those aboard into the sea.

Frustrated by their inability to help, the officers of the *Mariella* finally consented to lower one of its own rafts. A few of the desperate people floating there were able to drift within reach. This enabled some to crawl aboard the tethered raft to be hoisted to safety. Some reached it but were so frozen they were unable to climb from their sinking raft, and they waited while courageous crewmen from above slid down a rope to help them move into the new raft. In addition, on the side of the ship just above the waterline was a doorway that opened to the sea. Now, this door was opened and a few survivors were taken in, although the raging sea made it nearly impossible. In an odd stroke of luck, a group of doctors were on the *Mariella* for a sea-going conference, making quick medical help available onboard for those who reached it. The ship's conference room was converted into a hospital where warm blankets and hot food were furnished.

More helicopters came an hour after the initial Finnish ones, joining the search and sending their spotlights playing over the rough seas. Whipple, the American publisher, watched and admired the helicopter crews swinging on the wind to descend here and there on cables, going into covered rafts caught in a spotlight, only to find them empty or those in it already dead.

The crew kept working to take on survivors till midmorning. By midafternoon it was obvious that there were no more alive. Through the day the *Mariella* took on seventeen survivors through crew efforts, and the helicopters delivered nine more to its deck. In midafternoon the Finnish Sea Rescue officers in charge of the operation gave permission for the *Mariella* to depart with the twenty-six survivors for Stockholm, where ambulances were waiting.

Much more dramatic rescue efforts took place aboard the *Isabella* of the Viking Line, where the crew took great risks in order to pull survivors from the sea.

Henning Eriksson, a Finn from near Abo who had been a bartender on the ship for fifteen years, helped pull up seventeen people. Later he recalled arriving at the wreckage scene a little more than an hour after the *Estonia* went down. He was appalled at the sight there: bodies of naked men floating in life vests, along with some children and those waiting helplessly in rafts or life jackets.

Two crewmen of the *Isabella* spotted a man waving his arm. They quickly ran to reach over from the engine room door as far as they could to pull him up and ended plunging into the sea themselves. In a short time a helicopter appeared and pulled them up, along with the man who had been waving, who died a short time later.

Quickly the *Isabella*'s captain ordered life rafts to be lowered, keeping them tethered to his ship. Two persons struggled up into the devices and were safe. But most others were too exhausted by then to struggle up the high sides. For them, the crew rigged "the slider," which was normally used to allow passengers to slide down into life rafts in an emergency. It was much like the inflatable slides used by airliners for emergency evacuations, except that the ship's slider ended in a large float. With that lowered into the sea, a crewman volunteered and slid down into the water to help those who could make it to him. He tied a rope around them, and Henning Eriksson and a dozen other crewmen hauled them to the safety of the ship. They saved seventeen people who would probably have died otherwise.

Eriksson saw tragedies as well as rescues. One man waved to him near the stern, and he threw him a life-buoy, but the man was sucked into the churning ship's propellers. Two others struggling in the water were near the crewman at the end of the slider, but they were too weak to reach him in time, and sank beneath the waves, out of his outstretched grip.

A little less than two hours after the *Estonia* disappeared from radar, Second Engineer Peter Tuur was still floating in his life vest when the *Isabella* crew spotted him waving from the water. A raft was lowered with two volunteers in it, and they pulled Tuur aboard and the raft was raised back to the ship. It was 2:48 a.m. He was one of the first to be pulled from the water, and one of the very few who survived without getting into a raft.

The main Coast Guard rescue station at Abo was where the major decisions regarding the *Estonia* were made. A temporary command station was set up aboard the *Europa*, where five men were working and Captain Esa Makela of the *Europa* was helping direct the rescue operation with the help of Finnish naval officials. At 3:10 a.m. his ship took aboard the first four survivors brought to them by a helicopter. They were surprisingly alert, probably because they had been in the water less than two hours. Then a half-hour later the lookouts spotted a young man alone in a raft directly ahead, frantically waving his arms. It was Marek Kaasik.

A few of those struggling in the tumultuous sea in those first desperate hours were fortunate enough to drift in exactly the right positions to be helped by the large ships. Marek had been one of the young people chatting in the lounge with Gundela Kampuse when the ship lurched to its side. Frantically, he had stampeded up the stairs with the others. When he reached the deck, the ship was tilting badly and it was obvious that the *Estonia* was doomed. In the rain, he began working to get a lifeboat lowered from where it hung on its davits. After a minute of frantic struggle, he saw that the angle was so great the boats could not be loosed. After donning a life jacket, Marek stood at the sinking railing wondering what to do. A wave washed him into the sea. Shortly he had found himself floating among the frothing waves, alone and able to see nothing around him. With the crests washing over him, choking him, and leaving him sputtering, he was after a time ready to give up and accept death.

He was startled from his impending surrender by a loud scream that was astonishingly close. He turned and saw not one, but two life rafts were bearing down on him. One was upside down, and the other had a tent raised with a little light above it. He chose the raft with the shelter and swam to it, but found that he could not climb over the high sides to get in. His strength was nearly gone. He hung to the rope and tried to gather all his will and might, calling out for help. He breathed deeply in an effort to calm himself. Then, inch-by-inch, he pulled himself up and over into the raft. It was empty, but he was out of the sea, and now lay wheezing for breath. He was alone, terrified and exhausted.

After what seemed hours, Marek sat up and analyzed his situation. He was so cold he could not make his fingers work well enough to open the packet of emergency flares he had found in the raft. He gasped for joy when he saw the large ships approaching. His hands were shaking, but by using his teeth he at last got the package open and managed to fire off two flares. For the first time since the ship had listed, he began to feel as if he would live through this.

"Here! Over here!" he shouted in excitement as one of the ships turned toward him and shone its searchlights over the surface. But the bright beam of light flicked past him and the ship continued on. In another minute he was once again enshrouded in darkness.

Alone on the raft, he was devastated for several minutes. He then saw the *Europa* bearing toward him, and again frantically waved his arms. Holding his breath, he watched the ship ease toward him, barely moving to avoid overrunning any survivors. He shouted wild-

ly as it grew closer, its bright lights looming high above him. Soon
he could see crewmen leaning over the rail, actually shouting to him.
They had seen him. They were gesturing to the side of the ship where
a door swung open and a rope ladder flopped down toward the sea.

Marek had no way to move the raft. The ship was still moving
slightly, and he was afraid he would be carried by the wind away
from this imminent rescue. Life was only a few yards away. In desperation, he dived into the water and began to swim toward the ladder. At last he was able to grab onto the lowest rung, and he began
to pull himself toward the hatch. When he reached it, he fell inside
and fainted. When he awoke, he was lying in bed, tucked in beneath
a heavy layer of blankets. Lying next to him, holding him close for
warmth, was a woman speaking in a calm voice in Finnish. Never
had he felt a more beautiful sensation.

Another fortunate raft of four men had a comparatively easy escape from the grasp of the sea. Thure Palmgren, a retired Swedish
sailor, had come on the trip at the urging of his wife, Clary. He had
escaped to the deck with her, and in the pushing and confusion they
had become separated. He searched desperately for her, even clipping
a spare life vest to his own to use if he found her in the water.

When he was washed into the sea he found a raft with three other men, Daniel Svensson, one of the Bible college students, Eckard
Klug, and Veljo Juuse. For them, good fortune was riding on their
shoulders, for they were washed directly toward the lighted hull of the
Mariella as soon as it arrived at the wreckage site. Because they were
in the perfect spot to be seen, they were sighted and their raft was
lifted up. They were on the water only slightly more than an hour, but
they already were seriously chilled. Thure's temperature had fallen to
34 degrees from the normal 37 degrees Celsius, and all were shocked

to learn that Eckard's body heat had fallen to a critical 28 degrees. Without the stroke of luck of drifting directly into the ship's path, they would not have endured the long night.

Captain Modig of the *Symphony* said his ship picked up twenty survivors in the early morning, mostly delivered by rescue helicopters.

"It felt hard, very hard, the helplessness of watching those that remained," Captain Modig said.

Only two women were among the twenty taken aboard. The ship delivered them all to Helsinki hospitals or hotels, where they were out of reach of the world press, who were frenzied to get firsthand accounts from survivors. At 7:57 a.m., helicopters delivered the last eleven of those they had plucked from the water to the *Europa*. One was dead.

By 9 a.m., the searchers were convinced that no one else was left alive on the still-stormy surface of the sea. It had been more than eight hours since the *Estonia* sank.

"We are one hundred percent certain there is no one left in the water alive," announced Pekka Kiviniemi, commander of the Finnish Coast Guard at Aland. "The whole area was searched thoroughly by helicopters and ships. The frogmen have gone down and searched all the rafts, and have found no one else. This catastrophe is like none other in this part of the world."

In spite of the weather, the search continued throughout the day. Because only larger ships could survive such high seas and gale winds, the Coast Guard searchers could not comb the sea in their small craft for anyone who might still be alive. Later in the day, as the seas calmed somewhat, the hunt continued with smaller boats after the large passenger ships left. They found only a few bodies.

When darkness came after a day of searching, most of the ships left. Two Finnish and two Estonian ships continued to search the area for survivors through the night, but none were found. No one was found alive past mid-morning.

18 · THE HELICOPTERS

Turku, Finland, 12:24 a.m.

When the Mayday message arrived at the Finnish Coast Guard base of Turku, Lieutenant Karppila had relayed the distress call to the main Sea Rescue Base in Helsinki. Tragically, a trick of fate intervened. As with the tragic sea disaster of the *Titanic* more than seventy years earlier, a massive communications blunder kept aid from coming to the stricken *Estonia* as quickly as it should have. The alarm of a sinking passenger ship should have flashed across the Baltic states instantly, alerting sea rescue units and launching them in a critical race against time to pull survivors from a merciless and bitterly cold sea.

The radio connection itself was a major cause of delays. The Finnish coastal radio in Helsinki, the most important and powerful in the area, didn't get the original signal from the *Estonia,* but a relay of the sinking ship message. The operator at Helsinki Radio who received the message either didn't understand its importance or simply made an error in judgment. Instead of the Helsinki operator sending out a widespread alarm to alert the whole Baltic region, he sent out what is called a "Pan-pan" message, a low-priority alarm reserved for minor warnings such as ships maneuvering or standing still when someone falls overboard. Little attention is paid to pan-pan warnings, as they are local and minor in nature.

Undoubtedly, this low priority of the alarm delayed the reaction of other rescue units. To compound the matter, the radio signal from the *Estonia* was very weak. Its regular radio should have reached beyond Turku and nearby ships to Stockholm and other stations, but that was not the case. No one knows, but there is speculation that the ship's usual radio was out of commission and the weak signal was caused by sending the Mayday alert on a small, ill-powered portable radio the ship carried. The assumption of Lieutenant Karppila and others who heard the *Estonia* message was that other rescue units had also received it. They had not. In fact, the spread of the alarm about the sinking under way was backwards. Some accounts say Swedish sea-watchers were alerted only when a truck driver using a short wave radio called Stockholm to ask what was going on in the Baltic Sea emergency.

At 12:55 a.m. the Swedish Coast guard station in Stockholm received a call from their counterpart in Mariehamn, Finland, asking if they knew anything about the *Estonia* having problems. "On this side we had heard nothing," said Orjana Thor, the sea rescue leader in Stockholm.

Two minutes later the Stockholm station called the Finnish coast guard at Helsinki and Turku to verify that something was wrong. The Finns had assumed that Stockholm Radio had received the signal. Shocked on learning what was happening, Stockholm offered whatever help was needed. Only then did the message spread out to Swedish rescue units. By that time, survivors had been struggling in the water for almost half an hour. Tragically, that delay meant death for dozens, possibly hundreds in the chill waters.

There was a more general cause of the slow reaction: no established procedures for a giant rescue operation in the area. Emergency efforts had always been local. None of the Baltic states were used to cooperating in rescue efforts in the East Sea, as the area is known there.

At the sea rescue unit in Stockholm, there was already feverish activity when the news of the *Estonia* arrived. A fishing boat had sunk in the storm off Aland Island, and the Stockholm unit was monitoring the rescue of two men in the water by a helicopter. That helicopter received orders to return to its base to gas up and then head for the *Estonia* site as quickly as possible. In the next fifteen minutes the Air Force bases at Soderhamn and Gotenberg were alerted and asked for additional help. At 1:42 a.m. a Danish air rescue station called the Arlanda base in Stockholm and asked if Danish rescue help would be needed. The Arlanda officers immediately answered yes, and by 1:48 a.m. two Danish helicopters were headed toward the disaster area.

Arild Winge, forty-three, was working that night at the sea rescue base in Stockholm. He had been on duty a year earlier when the *Jan Heweliusz* had sunk, and as he learned of the predicament of the *Estonia* he immediately felt it was headed for the same fate. When the *Mariella* arrived and radioed that it had found only debris, survivors in rafts, and bodies, that feeling was confirmed.

Tragically, when Swedish helicopters headed to the area they were dogged by communication problems and equipment that did not function well. The helicopter crews could not communicate with the flight commanders in Arlanda, the international airport near Stockholm with extensive radar control, because its short wave radio was not working at the time. They had little guidance in finding the accident site, and only a vague knowledge of where the *Estonia* had gone down. Those who found the wreckage had to guide the later helicopters there.

A Swedish rescue search plane, equipped with radar to search areas of the sea, did not leave until 6:30 a.m. to aid in finding survivors. The first two Swedish marine helicopters that attempted to rescue survivors from the rafts had problems with the winches and had to return to base, leaving behind those in the rafts, stunned with anger and shock. The winches were old models, and were replaced in the ensuing weeks with newer versions.

Other snafus contributed to the slow reaction that without doubt cost scores of lives. The *Estonia* was equipped with EPIRB: automatic emergency beacons. When a ship sinks, these buoy-enclosed transmitters are supposed to pop to the surface and transmit the ship's position. At times this takes a few minutes until the proper satellite that initiates the message is in position. On this night, the emergency beacons aboard the *Estonia* did not work — for reasons that are not entirely clear. The crew did possess the capability to activate the EPIRB manually, but they were probably proceeding under the assumption that the devices would automatically release once they were submerged, as they had been designed to do. Had this system operated, the rescue helicopters would have found the wreckage site much faster.

As the word of the disaster taking place flashed across the world, it became the center of international attention. At the Coast Guard station in Turku, Finland, the office was besieged with calls from far-flung news organizations.

"Yes, there was a blackout on the *Estonia,* and the ferry is sinking," Lieutenant Karppila told them. "There's a whole lot of people and all kinds of stuff in the sea."

When Reuters News out of Britain reached the Finnish Sea Rescue Center at 3:25 a.m., the duty officer told them, "The *Estonia* has sunk. Rescue operations are in full swing. The conditions are terrible." He added that even though additional helicopters and ships were rushing to help, efforts were being hampered by the sea conditions.

One hour after the sinking, the first Finnish helicopters were on the scene. To get there, they battled 60 mph winds, pitch-black darkness and, waiting below, heaving seas. When the first Finnish Super Puma arrived, it found chaos.

"The sky was at times lit up by emergency flares, but the darkness made it nearly impossible to see who was alive," the pilot later said. "My surface rescuer asked with desperation if we were the only helicopter in place. It almost felt that way in the beginning."

Additional helicopters began arriving shortly after. Some came from Swedish bases at Berg, Visby, and Ronneby. The first Swedish helicopter arrived at the disaster area at 2:35 a.m. after a one-hour flight from the Swedish Visby base. Another took off from the Berg base at 2:02 a.m. By morning 26 helicopters had scrambled from bases in Finland, Sweden, and Denmark to search for survivors.

The Finnish Super Puma, the first helicopter to arrive, was especially effective, partly because it carried professional surface rescuers, and partly because the crews were trained to land on the ships' helicopter decks to unload the survivors they had picked up. This saved the helicopter from having to return to land, unload the survivors, and return to the search. Swedish helicopter pilots had little experience with landing on ships, and so usually flew their survivors to hospitals on land. At first there was consternation among the helicopter pilots because so many rafts with tents covering them were empty and there was no way of knowing which ones had already been checked. The problem was solved when the frogmen rescuers began marking those rafts they entered.

The helicopter work was grueling and dangerous. One Swedish helicopter piloted by Captain Ronny Larsen spotted six people hanging onto a raft at about 4 a.m. During a long chase, the helicopter crew tried to keep a spotlight on the frail craft dancing among the whitecaps. Finally the rescuers took turns descending, swaying in the wind and fighting the seas, the gale, and the spray. One by one they began to winch the six near-frozen survivors up from the sea to safety. The passengers were unresponsive, almost totally frozen, in shock, and apathetic to what was going on around them. Often the rescuers didn't know if those they pulled from the water, having pried their grips loose from the raft ropes, were alive or dead. Even Captain Larsen's experienced crew was shaken by the winds, the black waves, the bodies in the sea, the horrible feeling of dangling on a cable while the wind tossed them back and forth. They barely spoke.

Hour after hour, the grisly work continued. One helicopter pilot brought up one person in a life jacket who showed signs of life but was dead by the time they got him into the helicopter. They chased another person on a raft, but the darkness, the wind and the waves made it so difficult that they could never catch up.

Stefan Olsson was pilot of helicopter Y74, the first to leave the Swedish base of Berga. Shortly before 2 a.m., he swept low over the sea at the site of the accident. "The circumstances were terrible: fog, rain, twenty-seven-foot waves, and gale winds of sixty miles an hour," he reported. They could make out fifteen or twenty rafts and dozens of life vests dipping on the waves.

As the helicopter swung in the wind, twenty-eight-year-old Patrik Rydell hooked himself into a harness and was lowered toward the surface. Twice he descended to rafts, skittering across the wave tops to reach them, only to find them empty. The canvas tops on the life rafts preventing rescurs from knowing if anyone was inside or not without precariously descending on a cable, chasing the raft in the troughs and wave crests, and then tumbling inside to investigate. Sometimes it was too late, with only stark-white bodies waiting as evidence of the fatal power of hypothermia. In the third raft Rydell found three survivors. He was able to get them fitted with a harness and lifted to safety aboard the helicopter.

"Everywhere in the water were people who had tied themselves to their life vests," Lars Tiren, the navigator of Y74, lamented. "Obviously they had not had time to put them on correctly. They had simply taken what they could find. Every one of them was dead."

Just before 9 a.m. the helicopter Y74 returned to Sweden, carrying the six people they had plucked from the sea. Along with those they rescued, two of the rescuers had to be admitted to the hospital.

For the sea rescuers and the crews, such work was a harrowing, traumatic experience. Conditions of the wind and the sea could hardly have been worse. Each of them knew they were risking their own lives hovering just above the wave tops, and those who descended on cables and plunged into the sea to rescue a floundering survivor were especially vulnerable. The very act of bringing up so many bodies was traumatic in itself. The contact with the bodies had a psychological effect that could lead to long-lasting problems if not somehow defused. Trauma Specialists advise that involvement in such haunting scenes — unless resolved — can affect a person for a lifetime.

Psychologists set up debriefing sessions for the helicopter crews in which they were encouraged to discuss their experiences. Even before these sessions, however, the rescuers went through a process called "defusing," which involved conversations immediately after a rescue. Those who had experienced a traumatizing situation were called together immediately to discuss and bring to the surface those emotions that otherwise might lie smoldering. Reliving the experience with others who were there helped to unload the tensions and mitigate the emotional damage. The Swedish Air Force had a crisis group working with the rescue crews as soon as a group arrived from the scene. Following that, the groups met every day for a month in debriefing sessions that sometimes went on for four hours.

"We had a group conversation where everyone had the chance to systematically tell about their experience and how they felt about it," said Tom Lundin, a dean of psychiatry who worked with survivors, families and rescue crews alike. The sessions were mandatory for the crew. Such debriefings usually enable those exposed to mind-shattering traumas to continue in rescue work, while without it some might abandon such work in the future. Afterwards, almost everyone involved expressed relief to have been able to talk about their part in the accident.

Twenty-year-old helicopter crewman Johan Steene was involved in one of the most incredible incidents of the rescue efforts carried out that night and morning. Just before 2 a.m., he had been awakened at the Soderhamn military base in Sweden with the news that the *Estonia* had gone down. Five minutes later he stood dressed by the SuperPuma helicopter hurriedly getting the aircraft ready to fly. Because there were no after-hours personnel there to pack the rescue gear, it was an hour before the helicopter was in the air. The crew landed at the Berga Navy Base near Stockholm to load blankets and rescue equipment, then headed into the storm.

Shortly after dawn they arrived at the wreckage site. As the designated rescuer on board, Steene had changed into a frogman's wet suit as they flew. A grim sight met them in the growing light: the ocean was filled with life vests, rafts, and flotsam from the sunken ship. The rescue work was being directed by radio from the *Silja Europa*, and the newly arrived helicopter was sent to check on a report of survi-

vors on a distant raft. Johan sat in the open door with his feet dangling out, peering through the rain. He knew the helicopter itself was
in jeopardy, skimming the waves and fighting the violent turbulence
over the heaving sea. They could make out numerous bodies floating
in life jackets or showing eerily white against the dark water inside
the overturned rafts. They could also see people leaning out of one
raft, waving. Johan felt the mechanic behind him give a pat on the
head as the helicopter hovered and the pilot tried to steady it in the
howling wind. Such precision is difficult even in calm weather, but
given the conditions it was nearly impossible to remain stable over
the raft, with it dipping and scooting on the waves.

Beneath the raft, the electronics engineer Anders Ericson had
hung on to the rope during the night through the long hours of
despair, horror, and hopelessness. He was grateful he was not totally
alone. Sometimes he knocked on the bottom of the raft and one of
the Estonians would answer. Sometimes he shouted, his voice echoing hollow and unreal in the enclosed space, with the water lapping
at his chin. Einar Kukk would reply, informing him that a ship had
passed by and left them, or that helicopters were in the distance but
none had come near. In the terrible darkness he kept wondering if he
would even realize when daylight had come in his dark entrapment.
Through the hours he felt a numb devastation, but he was determined not to let go of the rope, but to hang on in order to survive.
When it grew light in the water around the raft, he felt his spirits
rise. Morning had come. His hands and arms had gone numb, and
he did not know how much longer he could last. After another long
hour, he heard the roar of a helicopter passing above them, but when
it grew quiet again he knew their raft had not been spotted.

After another long while the welcome sound of more helicopters
grew louder than before. Beneath the floor, Ericson banged on the

bottom of the raft and screamed to the others above him that they should signal the aircraft. By this time, Einar Kukk and the other two Estonians were already waving wildly.

As Johan Steene descended from his helicopter on a thin cable, swaying and bouncing in the wind, he felt an overwhelming surge of satisfaction. He could see mingled joy and relief on the faces of the three men on the raft as he splashed into the water nearby. The three Estonians, Ulo Kikas, Jan Stern, and Einar Kukk, joyfully greeted him. The visiting officer from another ship on the *Estonia* for training, Kukk was the only officer on the bridge that night to survive. One by one, Johan slipped the harness around them and signaled to lift the cable up to the waiting arms of the crew in the SuperPuma. Kukk was the last of the three, but when the frogman slipped the harness over him and was about to lift him from the raft, Kukk gestured urgently.

"There is one more!" he shouted in Swedish over the roar of the helicopter.

Confused, Steene looked all around but saw no one. A short distance away he could see a dead body floating in an orange vest. Eager to get the rescue finished, he shook his head and motioned to the helicopter. But Kukk emphatically pointed downward.

Steene heard a noise and a thumping from under the raft, along with a muffled shout. With a shock he realized that another survivor was trapped in the water beneath the raft. His first instinct was to dive under himself and guide the person out, but the sobering thought came that it would be too risky, that he might become disoriented under the large raft. He screamed with all his strength that he would have to ascend to the helicopter and bring back a knife. He hesitated to leave, realizing that the survivor might think he was being abandoned.

Anders Ericson could hear the loud roar and feel the vibration of the helicopter poised above as Johan Steene descended to the raft, and began to lift up the Estonians. Down in the air space below, the trapped man shouted and banged on the floor with all his remaining strength as he heard the Estonians taken up one by one.

Terrified that nobody realized his predicament, Ericson screamed louder as no one moved on the raft above. His shouts were not answered, lost in the scream of the helicopter's motors racing to steady in the wind. Now nothing moved except the rhythmic swaying of the raft, vibrating in the downdraft. The specter of a lonely and dark death beneath the raft loomed over Eriscon as he told himself that in all the confusion and the storm he might have been forgotten. His horror grew as he felt the swaying of the raft and the lapping of the waves over the roar of the helicopter above. Barely able to breathe in his anxiety, Ericson listened, dreading to hear the sound of the rescue craft fade into the distance. In a few minutes, however, he felt a thump on the raft ceiling above him. He nearly wept with joy, and sent a huge shout and several gigantic thumps in answer.

On the raft, Steene moved his hand across the raft bottom, and felt Ericson's hand follow it. Then, he led Ericson to the edge of the raft. Then, away from the trapped man, with his diver's knife, Steene carefully thrust it through the raft and began to cut. He was then able to peer beneath the raft and discovered Anders Ericson reaching for his hand.

"Come here," Steene said. "It's okay now."

The fresh air and the sky above, even filled with clouds and rain, had never looked sweeter. Ericson had been in the water six hours.

Anders Ericson's ordeal of surviving after being trapped beneath the raft during the entire horror-filled night stands as probably the most dramatic example of courage and determination of the *Estonia* catastrophe. On that night, however, his was only one of the remarkable examples of strength and fortitude.

After taking Ericson and the three Estonians aboard The Swedish SuperPuma, Steene's crew continued their search. Shortly, they located another raft with two survivors. One was hanging outside the raft, with his right hand cramped around the gas bottle that inflates the raft. With his other hand he was holding the other survivor, whose foot was tangled in the sea anchor line. The man with the stuck foot was Tom Johnsson, from the Swedish Police Officials union. He had been flushed from the raft by a wave as they grew excited about the approaching helicopter, and had fallen in and become tangled.

Steene first cut the rope that had snared Tom, then fitted the large man into the harness and sent him aloft. With some effort, he then released the cramped fingers of the man who had been holding the gas mechanism. When both of those were winched aboard the helicopter, they had a full load, so they headed for Finnish Uto and delivered the survivors to the hospital there. After refueling, they returned to the search area.

It was painstaking, miserable work, but Johan Steene had found great exhilaration in helping to rescue and winch up six people from the two rafts. On returning to the search, however, the magnitude of the tragedy became sobering. They had hoped to find more survivors. Instead, only bodies awaited them. All the rafts they found then were either empty or had bodies sloshing in knee-deep water inside. In these cases, they moved on to look for more survivors. After searching two more hours, they began to bring up the bodies. It was a grim task.

"The giant waves rolled over you, and you were completely alone," Steene explained. "It was difficult to fasten the harness around the lifeless, stiff bodies. When I tried to save the survivors, at least I had someone to bond with."

By noon, the Finnish Coast Guard officer who was directing rescue efforts told the press that the search was continuing, but he was pessimistic. "In the past few hours we have found only dead bodies," he said. "There is very little hope of finding anyone else alive."

With only a couple of exceptions, the only ones found alive were in the life rafts.

One young Swedish Doctor, Ulrik Linforss, was involved in a remarkable rescue when he went with a helicopter crew from Huddinge, near Stockholm, to search for survivors. They only knew that a ship had sunk but they had no idea of the extent of the catastrophe. After a 55-minute flight they arrived just as dawn was breaking. Among the debris on the sea they saw a person floating in a life jacket. With the wind making the descent unstable, one of the rescuers was lowered by winch down to the surface, grasped the floating man and fastened a harness around him and raised him along with the rescuer into the helicopter. When they got him inside, no one spoke. He was dead.

But soon they spotted an overturned raft with two women huddled on top. The doctor watched as the rescuer approached from above, and he breathed a sigh of relief as he saw the women were still alive. Then they pointed to the side of the raft. A middle-aged man was in the water, holding on to the raft with a grim look of resignation on his face. After taking up the two women, the rescuer jumped in alongside the man and tried to get him to let go of the rope that encircled the raft.

"Let go," he commanded.

The man did not respond, but only stared at his hands.

"Let go, I've got you now," insisted the officer. "You'll be all right."

A wave washed over the raft, and, sputtering with sea water, the officer tugged at the Swede to get him to come. Finally, the man looked at him.

"I can't. I tried hours ago. My hands are frozen around the rope." During the night, the situation had seemed hopeless. Numb and in shock, the Swede had decided to quit struggling and simply sink into the sea as so many others around him had done. He had been able to escape the sinking ship and to get into a life raft with many others. But like so many of the others, his raft tipped and spilled them into the sea. He was able to hang on to the rope that circled it, but did not have the strength to crawl back on top, nor were the others able to help him.

After the first hour his arms went numb. Only his head, shoulders and hands were out of the water. He expected help would arrive any minute. It was a lucky thing, he told himself, for he was sure he could not last much longer this way. The darkness, the screams that filled the night around him, the paralyzing cold that splashed over him each time a wave came all combined to build to a sense of growing hopelessness.

After a few more minutes the despair was replaced by a feeling of peace. The struggle was over. A feeling of warmth, of well-being came over him and he decided to simply let go of the rope and slip downward into that blessed state of the abyss that waited. He wanted to be released from the pain and struggle. With an effort he tried to open his fingers from the rope. They did not move. Again he tried, concentrating on his cramped right hand. The hands were frozen in position. They had gripped so tightly for so long that he could not move them. He gave a supreme effort but nothing moved.

He felt like crying. Instead, he stared at the black rubberized canvas of the raft before his face and tried to think of other things.

His hands and arms and whole body had ceased to ache; they were numb. As the minutes turned to hours, his mind shared that numbness, and he swayed in the water with the waves, attached to the raft only by stubborn, cramped hands that would not let him find peace. Now he stared up uncomprehendingly into the eyes of the frogman who had descended into the sea for his sake.

Shocked by the Swede's apathy, the officer looked from the man's face to his hands. With a grim nod he began to pry at the fingers, one by one, until he loosed the strange death-like grip that had saved the man's life. He waved to the crew above and the two of them swung in the wind and the spray together in the twin harness as they rose to the safety of the helicopter. The Swede had surrendered, and yet had survived. Had he been able to let go of the rope on the raft, he would have sunk into the sea with so many others that night. He was saved by his frozen hands that would not let go of the rope.

19 · THOSE WHO WAITED

At dawn, Elmar Oun, sixty-four, had hurried to the dock of the Estline shipping building in Stockholm where 200 other relatives and friends of the *Estonia*'s passengers had gathered to await word. He had heard of the disaster on the 5:30 a.m. news and rushed to the wharf where the ship was due to dock. As he arrived, a wind was whipping the water in the bay and driving dust before it in the parking lot.

His thirty-four-year-old son, Mikael, had driven his truck aboard the *Estonia* in Tallinn the evening before, returning from a relief aid mission to the Estonian people. His truck had been loaded with clothing and food for people whose lives had never been easy, and who were now struggling to gain self-sufficiency.

The father's first thought was, "He's dead." He was among the first of the somber group milling there, waiting for word. During the early morning nothing happened to offer hope. Mikael's name was not on the first lists of survivors released by the Estline company.

At first the news was hopeful for those keeping vigil on the docks. The early radio accounts said that only a few had lost their lives, and most of the passengers had been rescued. Before long, however, the immensity of the tragedy became clear. Many Swedes simply wandered around in a daze. Sweden, particularly, had little frame of reference about disaster in general. The country had not taken part in either of the twentieth century's world wars, and nature has spared this nation the agony of frequent natural disasters. Most did not know how to cope, and the misery was both wide and deep. Even the Swedish prime minister, Carl Bildt, had several acquaintances among the passengers. The incoming prime minister, Ingmar Carlsson, lost a boyhood friend aboard the ship.

Through the morning a growing crowd of Swedish relatives and friends of the more than 500 Swedish passengers assembled in stony silence. They milled around the terminal, frightened and confused, smoking, barely talking, waiting for the list of survivors. A couple in their sixties, walking hand in hand, obviously devastated, said their son had worked on the ship for a year. A crisis group of social workers, priests and psychologists soon arrived to help ease the grief of those waiting. These teams moved among them, offering hot coffee and encouragement.

Confusing information began to arrive, was posted on the walls, then was changed. Only eighty people of the more than one thousand aboard had been saved, said the first posting. A half hour later that figure was revised downward to twenty-six survivors. Next the figure rose to ninety, then to 126. Frustrated and afraid, those keeping the vigil at the terminal could only hope and wait.

A Red Cross helicopter circled and landed in the terminal parking lot, its blades whistling in the wind and raising a swirl of dust. Over it all there was a surreal quality, like a dream sequence in a Bergman movie. People crowded around the helicopter, expecting that survivors might be arriving, hoping against hope that it might be carrying someone they loved. Instead, the pilots unloaded piles of gray woolen blankets. By 1:30 p.m. a list of fifty-six identified survivors arrived from Finland, along with some of the names of the dead.

Knut Isaksson and his wife rushed in a taxi to the terminal in Stockholm after calling to find out about their son, a crewman aboard the sunken ship. Confused and frightened, they sat stoically on a bench and waited as one list of survivors was posted after another. His name was not among them.

By noon the Red Cross workers found themselves almost glassy-eyed themselves as they moved among the trauma-stricken relatives of the *Estonia* victims. The enormity of the tragedies they were trying to soothe was almost too much for some of them. One volunteer described the wrenching feeling of watching an eleven-year-old boy realize that his father would not be coming home from his trip. One middle-aged man began to weep, turned away, and slowly made his way through the terminal toward the door. His friend's name had just been posted as one of the victims whose body had been found by the helicopters.

For a few, there was good news. But even when new lists of survivors arrived and were posted, there was uncertainty about how accurate they were. For instance, when Peeter Barassinki, thirty-nine, got word on that fatal morning that the *Estonia* had gone down, he rushed to the terminal to await word on the survivors. His wife, Carita, worked on the ship. At midmorning he emerged from the terminal beaming and shouted to bystanders, "I have just received the most beautiful news of my life. My wife is alive!" Later in the day, he was to learn that the report had been mistaken. His wife was among the missing.

In Sweden in the industrial city of Norkopping, south of Stockholm, the town hall became a crisis center where relatives waited for word of survivors. A group of fifty-six pensioners from the city had taken advantage of the cheap group booking rates to the newly opened countries that had been behind the Iron Curtain on the other side of the Baltic Sea. None returned. Those in the town hall waited with a faint hope, because word had already arrived from survivors that few of the elderly aboard had been able to climb the steep listing stairways, or to survive the cold waters even if they had reached the decks.

Across the turbulent Baltic Sea, in the tiny, close-knit country of Estonia, people wondered not if they knew any of the victims, but how many they knew. Throughout this nation of 1.6 million people, families and friends gathered around television sets to watch in stunned silence as updated lists of survivors and passengers were flashed throughout the day. In Tallinn, people crowded around the terminal to check names of passengers and survivors as they were posted on a handwritten list.

Only a month earlier Estonia had celebrated its newly won independence with the departure of the last Russian troops from its soil. The troops left Aug. 31, an event marked by speeches, rock concerts and parties in the capital. This tragedy came on the heels of that joyful celebration. With news of the *Estonia* disaster, people wept openly on the streets of Tallinn. Bars, restaurants and cinemas closed down, and theaters canceled performances. Inside the terminal building, people lit candles and strewed red roses around the floor. After a few hours of suspense, those who had gathered at the terminal at dawn were told to go home and await more information on the radio.

"I'm staying till I find out," one young man who had driven from Lithuania said grimly. "My parents were on the boat."

"Remember, this is a tough business," another added.

On the waterfront at the Estline docks, one woman stood weeping and clutching a teddy bear to her chest. "My husband and son were on their way to Sweden," she sobbed. "My son left his teddy bear behind."

Nearby, Kaja Kaljurand was waiting for word of her niece, Katlin, a twenty-two-year-old ship waitress making her last scheduled voyage on the *Estonia*. "She was such a pretty girl," the elderly woman told any who would listen. "She planned to leave the ship and work at a beauty salon."

Among the missing from the *Estonia* were the mayor and entire city council of the small town of Voru.

In Parnu near the capital city of Estonia, Torbjorn Hedrenius received a call at dawn from his wife, Maria. "There has been a catastrophe," she said in a shaken voice. "*Estonia* has gone down. Sara ..." Then the line went dead. Frantically he tried to place a call again, but the lines were jammed.

Torbjorn stood stunned, certain that his daughter was dead. In his sorrow he relived those joyful hours two days earlier when he and Sara had ridden horseback along the beaches of Parnu. He cherished the closeness they had felt.

It was impossible to get a call through to Sweden for several hours, and then the information was sparse. Finally the word came: Sara was safe! So Torbjorn Hedrenius caught a plane to Mariehamn in Finland, where his daughter and the other five survivors of her raft had been taken.

Sigrid Tammes, the wife of Third Officer Andres Tammes, who was heard on the Mayday message, was listening to the 6 a.m. news in Tallinn as she prepared to go to work. When she heard of the catastrophe on the Baltic, she rushed to work to await further word. She was notified that her husband was missing, but after a few days someone told her that a fax had arrived with the description of an officer who had survived that matched her husband. But it was a phantom document that could not be found. For some strange reason, it was not until weeks later that Sigrid was informed by Finnish authorities that her husband's body had been located September 29, the day after the sinking. Tammes's body was sent home to Tallinn October 20, and he was buried two days later.

For the Estonians, it was a tragedy reminiscent of the events of World War II. For the Swedes, it was a blow unlike anything during the past century.

20 · THE SEA IS THE ENEMY

One of the popular dancers of the variety show aboard the *Estonia* was a slender, pretty girl with light brown hair and bee-stung lips that Hollywood would call "pouty." Marge Rull knew that the dance troupe she performed with that evening on the ship had been a smashing success. In spite of the swaying of the floor, there was a jovial spirit and the audience joined in by clapping with the rhythm of the music. The leader, Ester Hellermaa, afterwards told the group it was the best she had ever seen them perform.

After the performance, as the weather got worse most of the troupe was sick, and went to their cabins without eating the smorgasbord of food they were offered. By the time Marge entered the cabin she shared with another Estonian girl, Heddi Manniste, she was already frightened. The other dancers had teased her that night for her apprehensions about the storm and the swaying ship.

Instead of preparing for bed, Marge put on a T-shirt and trousers. When Heidi asked why she put so many clothes on, she explained that she had recently seen the movie *Titanic* and in her dreams she had seen herself drowning. She no sooner explained that, when they heard the gigantic crash that signaled the beginning of the end for the ship. It was the metal-on-metal sound that alarmed many of those who were awake.

"I'm going to run!" she exclaimed as she bolted out the door. Heddi started to get dressed.

As Marge Rull fled down the corridor, she pounded on the doors of other dancers that she passed. In one door, slouched casually against the doorframe, an old woman watched all the frantic activity. She made no effort to join them. It was a sight that would remain forever etched in Marge Rull's memory. As she reached the foyer, the dancer slipped and fell on the floor, which was wet with water sloshing in. Already the ship was at such a slant that the floor acted like a water slide, and she slid down and slammed against the wall, breaking her foot. As she picked herself up, she saw that another woman who had smashed into the wall head-first lay still, her face covered in blood. The woman appeared to be dead.

The dancer struggled to the staircase and heaved herself upwards by grasping the banister, hand over hand. Glancing back, she saw Heddi slide down the foyer floor and hit the wall. That was the last time she saw her friend. When she reached the deck and got outside into the rain, she knew she must get upward to the port railing high out of the water. Holding on to first one piece of ship, then another, she worked her way to the railing. Those around her who could not hold on fell into the sea. Above the confusion she could hear the voice of another dance troupe member shouting for a friend, "Hannely," in a loud voice.

By then the ship was nearly lying on its side. Marge clung to the railing, with her back against a steel box. Terrified, she listened to the screams of women and children coming from inside the ship. She didn't know what to do. The ship was sinking fast. She knew she must do something or she would stay clinging to the railing forever. The thought of her young daughter back in Estonia came to her. What would the girl do without her? With that thought spurring her on, she determined that she would survive.

When she saw one of the life rafts stuck on the hull, she crawled on all fours toward it, and got inside. But the men who were trying to get it launched shouted that she must get out or it wouldn't move. She got out and then stayed close as the men bounced the raft down toward the water. She cringed as a wave washed over them, but she managed to hold onto the back of a man who was clinging to its side rope. As they plunged deep beneath the waves, she let go of the man and struggled upward toward the surface. Yet she felt herself pulled back beneath the waves by someone grasping her foot. She fought to get loose, but could not. Finally, in desperation, she managed to kick her foot loose and get back to the surface. She called then for the men in the raft to help her inside. Silver Linde, the crewman who had first reported the trouble on board, reached down and pulled her into the raft.

The moon had emerged from the clouds, and in its light they could see the great propellers of the ship, silent and still now as the ship lay on its side. Their raft was upright, with the tent overhead for protection from the wind and waves. Nevertheless, water poured in through the doorways each time a large wave washed over them. There were sixteen people inside. Along with two of the young men, the dancer tried to shovel out the water with plastic bags. When that appeared useless, she tried to exercise her muscles to help her circulation and keep warm. She told herself that she had made it this far, and for her daughter she would do whatever was necessary to endure until rescuers arrived.

The night grew inky black again as the moon hid beneath the clouds once more, and a grim depression spread over the raft as the minutes dragged by. Then after another hour, they saw distant lights of helicopters moving over the area. They shouted; at first they believed they would be immediately picked up, but then they noticed the helicopters were picking up those in lifejackets struggling in the water. Once they were caught in a spotlight from a helicopter, but it swept on beyond them. During the night, the only other helicopters they saw were in the distance.

As the hours passed, the water sloshed around them like the inside of a washing machine. They were unable to close the entrances to the rafts to keep the waves out, because in the darkness they could not figure out how they worked. Only when daylight came could they see that they had to unhook the rope ladders, dangle them overboard so that a struggling swimmer might crawl aboard using them, and then the entrances could be closed. Almost all the survivors who made it to the upright rafts reported how difficult the struggle was to get up over the high sides of the rafts and inside. In the darkness and tossing waves, almost none of the rafts had the ladders lowered. In general, those who could get into the upright rafts with the protective tents were saved. One galling aspect of the tragedy was that many of those struggling in the water reached the rafts, but were unable to climb aboard because of the high sides and thus perished.

During the first hours, Marge Rull feared she was going to die. It didn't seem fair to her. She had a daughter waiting who depended on her. Later, in the face of the relentless cold and the water sloshing about her almost to her shoulders, all her strength seemed gone. It seemed so easy to just give up and die. Once she drifted off into a dreamy state. In her mind everything was bright and warm. She no longer cared where she was. Then a wave washed over her through the door and snapped her back to her grim reality. With a start she regretfully recognized she had left the warm place she had been enjoying during her dream.

About daybreak, they noticed the water was growing deeper in the raft, apparently from a leak. By then they had no energy left to try bailing the water out. In a state of total exhaustion, with body temperatures lowered to the danger point, they were apathetic and sleepy. Within a few minutes after daylight, however, the welcome roar of a Finnish helicopter hovering overhead pierced their stupor. In another few seconds a knife blade cut through the roof of their tent and a rescue worker thrust his arm through. He called to them that they were all right now. He explained that they would be taken up two at a time. Because of the protection the tent offered, all sixteen were still alive. Marge Rull was one of the first taken up. As she swung in the wind, at first she closed her eyes. Then she realized that after all she had been through, there was little else to fear. So she opened her eyes and watched as she was pulled into the helicopter. When all but four men were taken up, the rescuer signaled that these would have to wait for the next helicopter. Later she learned that the men had been saved also, but that they had been in water up to their necks by the time other rescuers arrived.

Being in prime physical condition was itself no guarantee that one would be able to battle up the stairways onto the deck of the *Estonia*, onto a raft, and make it through the night. A group of Estonian world-class tri-athletes were on the ship bound for Germany to compete in a track meet there. Of the five athletes, two survived. The coach of the team, Urmas Randma, was scheduled to go with his wife along with the team, but he had some urgent business to attend to, so the couple remained behind, planning to catch up later.

The team's minibus was the last to enter the ship and thus was parked near the ramp, where the water entered when the bow visor tore off. Since the bus had a bed in it, Jaan Pehk decided to save money by sleeping there instead of getting a cabin, a decision that cost him his life. The four others shared a large cabin. Ulle Karu, a female tri-athlete, was nervous because of the storm and could not sleep. When the ship heeled over so hard, she woke the others. When she did, they could hear women screaming and crashing sounds, as if a metal object had hit the ferry. Ain-Alar Juhanson, the youngest of the group at only seventeen, quickly put on his jeans and a shirt and sprinted for the hallway until he realized that his friend was not with him.

Anti Arak had gone back to sleep, and Ain-Alar came back to rouse him out while Kristjan Raiend and Ulle went ahead. Anti Arak, who was twenty-three, finally came wide-awake when he could hear the screams of women and children. Along with Ain-Alar, he rushed up the stairs to the upper decks.

In the sinking of the *Estonia*, good fortune was one of the major elements of survival. Two of the athletes who died, Kristjan Raiend and Ulle Karu — the heart of the team, according to the coach — left the cabin before the ones who survived. The coach is convinced that Kristjan would have made it had he been alone, but that he chose to remain with his female teammate.

With Ain-Alar, Anti Arak rushed up the stairs amid the terror and confusion. As they passed through the lounge of the fifth deck he could see elderly people clinging to the stairway, unable to move further. When he glanced into the side casino, he could see people where they lay crushed by the slot machines. Anti Arak had not tied his shoes, and as he bumped into someone they came off. He found that it was easier to climb the banisters barefoot.

At the exit on the seventh deck, the door was almost overhead, a distance of about six feet. They had to reach up, grab onto the railing, and pull themselves up through the door. For athletes in prime condition it was not difficult. For others, it was nearly impossible. Those who missed fell back against a far wall with a sickening thump.

When Anti Arak and Ain-Alar emerged onto the seventh deck, the ship was leaning heavily. They each grabbed a life jacket that two crew members were handing out, but in the chaos they had lost contact with Ulle and Kristjan. Anti Arak noticed a Swedish girl sitting crying, and he tried to comfort her. He found his mouth so dry from shock that he could barely speak. The girl jumped to her feet and pointed out to him that his life jacket was not fastened properly, so he took time to fix it. As the incline grew greater, they could feel the panic begin to spread around them. Anti Arak and Ain-Alar climbed to the highest railing, grabbing onto anything possible to keep from getting washed down into the sea by the waves that were breaking over the hull. They decided to remain on the ship as long as possible. The ship still seemed a link with life, and the sea was the enemy.

As the bow began to rise, they worked their way forward. There they saw with astonishment that the bow was gone, torn away by the storm. Around them some others could not hold their grip as the deck turned nearly vertical, and fell to their death as they smashed against parts of the ship or caromed into the water without life jackets.

The two athletes knew they must jump into the water from a height of thirty feet. They jumped together, then swam quickly away from the ship so as not to be dragged down with it. As tri-athletes they were strong swimmers. They saw no others around them, and a raft not far away. They swam furiously toward it, but it was pushed by the wind faster than they could swim, and scooted away from them. They then saw a white wooden cupboard floating nearby, and they were able to float for a time holding onto it until it began to sink. After another few minutes, as they floated in their life vests and fought the waves, an empty life raft drifted by and they succeeded in climbing inside.

Twice during the night they saw how helicopters caught them in their spotlights, tried to steady in the wind above them, but were unable. Finally, in early morning, one of the helicopters hovered near their raft, and a frogman splashed down from the cable and started swimming toward them. Anti Arak caught his collar and pulled him into the raft.

"What now?" Anti Arak asked.

The frogman pointed to the straps he carried and showed the Estonian athletes how to put them on. Then he signaled and Anti Arak was hoisted into the air, but immediately a large wave hit him and he was once more under water. He held on to the straps, however, and an instant later was jerked into the air again and lifted to safety.

One of the most interesting groups aboard the *Estonia* was made up of nineteen students and three teachers from a Pentecostal Bible college at Torhamm, near Stockholm. They had been in Estonia for six days, singing in churches and schools. They had even learned some songs in Estonian for the occasion. Twenty-year-old Daniel Svensson had begun at the college a month earlier. When the *Estonia* lurched on its side, he was lying on his bunk on the lowest deck, the spot where there was the least chance of escaping to the open air of deck seven. The nausea of seasickness kept him wide awake and fully clothed lying on his bunk. Two of his cabin mates were in the karaoke bar. The other, eighteen-year-old Yasmina Weidinger, was in the cabin with him.

When the ship heeled over so abruptly, immediately he said, "The ship is going to sink now." Yasmina didn't agree, but when Daniel bolted out into the corridor, she followed. Only a month and a half earlier Daniel had finished his mandatory military service, in training with the Swedish Board of Civil Aviation. As well as keeping him fit physically, that service had included training for emergency situations.

"I owe my survival to God and the Swedish Board of Civil Aviation," he said later.

From his cabin he ran through water that was flowing down the stairs. Looking back, he believes he made it up the six flights of stairs in around ten seconds. Out on the deck, he saw people falling unconscious as they were slammed into parts of the ship by the heavy slant. Quickly he put on a life vest, climbed over the railing, and leaped sixty feet into the water, where the force of his fall ripped off his life jacket. As he swam, an overturned raft suddenly appeared before him on one of the giant waves. He was able to pull himself up onto the raft, where he was alone, then noted with alarm that it was drifting toward the ship. He gasped at the thought that his raft would be sucked down with the ship when it sank. Fortunately the wind then switched and pushed the raft away from the ship. Then Daniel paused to watch the *Estonia* turn bow-up and sink into the waves.

A moment later he spotted fellow Swedes Thure Palmgren and Eckard Klug struggling in the water. He hauled them up. Then they pulled an Estonian up with them. Yasmina, the other Bible College student in the cabin who followed Daniel, also survived. Because the Swedes were wearing only underwear, the other two lay on each side of them to help keep them warm. As the storm raged around them, they settled down to pit their endurance against the horrors of the night.

Courage and the determination to live obviously played a major part in the survival of those who were able to get to the outer decks, get into a life vest, and then into a raft. But the good or bad fortune of what part of the ship one was on when the *Estonia* turned on its side was perhaps the major factor of whether one was trapped below decks or was able to escape the ship and begin to fight the sea for survival. Amid all the tragic tales of those aboard the doomed ship, it is clear that luck or providence played a major part in deciding who lived and who went to a watery grave in the dark Baltic Sea that fatal night.

One truck driver in Tallinn was supposed to take a load of furniture to Stockholm aboard the *Estonia*. He was running late, and when the traffic control radar caught him, a traffic policeman pulled him over. The trucker had been driving so fast that the officer took his driver's license and gave him a set of temporary papers instead. With those papers he was not allowed to board the ship, and he and his truck were both left standing on the dock as the *Estonia* pulled away that stormy evening. Two days later he walked into the Tallinn police station to thank them for saving his life.

21 · AM I GOING TO DIE NOW?

The decisions of those who stood on the deck of the doomed *Estonia* as it slipped into the angry sea that night were critical ones. Those who panicked upon emerging from the chaos below decks and leaped over the dipping rail without life vests usually perished. Some who were frozen by fear and only stared at the deck and their feet as it dipped lower toward the water met their fate in resignation, barely fighting. Others who were more calm analyzed the situation, weighed the possibilities, and placed themselves in the most favorable circumstances for survival. They had the best chance.

Thomas Grunde, the oil company executive who had stopped to light a cigarette on deck and to size up the situation, knew that he must now get into the water, for the ship was going down. He went toward the stern, which was slowly settling into the rough seas, and there he hung onto a scaffold used to lower lifeboats. Using this as a support, he was able to get over the side. There, he inched down the slick hull of the ship on his stomach. Halfway down he was able to grasp the rope of a life raft, but he didn't have the strength to hold on, and plunged on into the sea. His life vest was not fastened correctly, and in the drop it became stuck between his legs. Struggling in the water to pull it up, he felt it come loose and slide over his head. He hung on and by pulling it to his chest was able to keep his head above the choppy surface.

He remembered then that he must get some distance from the sinking giant. With all his might he swam, but the frigid water drained his strength. Briefly he wondered if it was worth the struggle to continue. Then he spotted a yellow raft ahead, swinging on the waves. He grabbed a trailing rope, shouted for help, and waved one hand. A man leaned out of the raft and took a firm grip of his hand, and held him.

"Someone help me!" shouted the man who was holding his hand. "I don't have the strength to hold on much longer."

At that, Thomas, perhaps unwisely, grew angry and shouted, "Hold on, damn you!"

Another hand reached down then and grabbed Thomas's shirt, pulling him toward the raft. The shirt caught tightly across Thomas's throat, and he thought he would be strangled.

"My belt! Grab my belt," he pleaded. At last the two men were able to pull him onto the raft, where he lay gasping and exhausted.

The winds rose, catching the raft atop a crest, and sent it flying down the wave like a surfboard. The motion sent those on the raft tumbling, but no one cried or screamed. Nor did those on the raft talk to each other. The cold, the terror, and the trauma of the surreal experience had put most of them into shock. Through the hours people became sick from the tossing of the raft. Only the wind kept the smell of the vomit from overwhelming them.

Finally, when it seemed that daybreak was long overdue, someone asked what time it was. "It is three-thirty," came the answer. It filled them all with dread, for it had been only three hours. Already it seemed interminable, and they were not yet halfway until dawn. Given the conditions, most of those hunched there silently questioned how much longer they could last.

When dawn finally came, they could see the *Mariella* only a few hundred yards away. But the ship seemed to be doing nothing.

"Why aren't they doing something?" someone shouted angrily. "They must have seen us."

Now that it was light, Thomas could see there were ten people on the raft, two women and eight men. All were pale and listless and wet. Some were splattered with vomit, but none of them cared.

In the distance they saw a helicopter grow close, turn, and then leave. In a few minutes, another helicopter swept down out of the sky toward them, and hovered overhead. Those on the raft cheered and waved lustily.

From the helicopter a wet-suited rescuer dipped toward them on a steel cable, swinging in the wind as the pilot tried to maneuver to put him next to the raft. He splashed into the sea, swam to them, and Thomaas and the others helped him onto the raft. The women were taken up first. Thomas Grunde was one of the last to be hoisted aboard the helicopter and deposited onto the deck of the *Mariella*.

On board the ship, Thomas slipped and fell in his leather-soled dancing shoes. Then he and the others from the raft were rushed into a teleconference room, where doctors and nurses who had been at the shipboard medical conference attended to them. Of the fifteen people at Thomas's oil company excursion, only three survived. Margareta, the woman who left the party because of seasickness and went to her cabin, was not one of them. She had two little boys at home.

Mikael Oun, the Stockholm engineer on the mercy mission who had taken the photograph on the hull of the *Estonia* as a futile signal to the oncoming ships, had spent the night yearning to be able to get back to his wife and three daughters. They absorbed his thoughts and lessened the pain. But always he was brought back to the reality of their tiny raft bouncing on an endless sea. Nevertheless, when daylight came, a helicopter spotted them and hovered overhead while a rescuer was lowered on a cable. Then Mikael knew that he would see his family again. Fitted with a harness, he was lifted above the sea to the helicopter, and later put aboard the *Symphony*. That ship continued its rescue operations for another two hours, then turned toward Helsinki to deliver to hospitals those who had been taken aboard. Oun tried to phone home, but all the lines were tied up. At the ship terminal in Stockholm, his father waited for word, devastated that his son's name was not on the list of survivors already released by the Estline Company. When Mikael Oun had left his cabin, for some forgotten reason he had stuck his alarm clock in his pocket. At the hospital he pulled it out and saw that it had stopped at 12:45 a.m.

On that raft with Mikael, the pessimist Wanda Wachmeister had talked with Christer Eklof and grimly waited for the dawn, half expecting it not to come. Their raft eventually had twelve people in it, fighting the 55 mph winds, rain, and cold. Two died before morning.

At 7:10 a.m., Wanda was plucked from the sea with the other survivors in the raft. Through the long night, Wanda and her brother Holger each knew nothing of the other. Holger was convinced that Wanda had survived. As a worrier, Wanda was sure that her brother had perished but could not bear to think of it. It was not until at the end of the day as they made contact with family did the news come to them both by relatives yelling over the phone, "Wanda has survived! Holger has survived!"

Another survivor, Vilho Itaranta, a Finn who lived in Sweden, had gone to Estonia with his friend Raimo Auvinen as part of a retired club excursion. At over sixty years old, Vilho had been a sailor in his younger days. When the ship began listing, his table and luggage in his cabin crashed against the wall. Immediately he recognized the danger.

"Quickly, out!" he cried to his friends in the cabin. In spite of the heavy list, they were able to run upstairs to the slanting outer deck. There they climbed up the deck as the ship continued to dip to starboard. Once in the open air, he did not panic, but put on a life vest, then stopped to help other frantic people with their vests. In the turmoil he lost track of his friends. He made his way to a rope ladder someone had put over the side, and began to work his way down the slanting hull until he could let go and jump into the water.

He floated near the ship, considering which way to go when a wave surprised him, pulled him into the depths, and bashed him into the steel hull. His back and his head were injured, yet the shock of the cold water revived him. He could feel that his legs were not broken, something he had feared. In the plunge the life vest had worked up over his head, but he hung onto it as he sank down. At last he bobbed up, and saw two life rafts before him. He swam to them, and found himself wedged between the rafts and unable to move.

"Am I going to die now?" Vilho asked himself. Struggling, he was able to work himself out from between the rafts. He got an arm over the edge of one raft, but was unable to pull himself up. A new wave washed over the raft then, bringing some survivors tumbling along with it. He could see others floundering in the water nearby. He felt himself pulled downward by someone under the water hanging onto both of his legs. In addition, someone else in the water behind him was grasping at his face, and found a hold in his mouth.

Vilho managed to grasp onto a trailing rope. He tried once more to pull into the raft, but it was too high. A young woman reached down and grabbed his hand and tried to pull him up, but she did not have the strength because of the two men in the water who were hanging on to him. At last the others let go, and a strong man reached down and heaved him up inside. He did not look back to see what had happened to the men who had been hanging on to him.

In the raft was a young woman and three other men, all sitting up to their waists in the near-freezing water sloshed in by the waves. They were able to get the roof up, which, although torn, offered some protection. One of the men soon died.

The girl who had reached to pull Vilho Itaranta into the raft died after five hours, only one hour before the welcome sound of a helicopter grew louder and then hung in the sky above them. The men were taken up into the helicopter to a hospital. Later Vilho calculated that he could not have lasted more than another half-hour himself.

In the meantime, the young Estonian duty-free store worker Timmo Vosa, who had trained as an orchestra conductor, had been making his peace with God as he clung to the railing of the sinking ship. When an enormous dark wave engulfed him, he felt himself tumbled farther and farther into the depths. A wonderful feeling came over him.

"Now it is coming," he told himself. "Death. I only feel sorry I cannot say farewell to anyone."

He had thought of death before — where he should go and what it would be like. Now he found the thought peaceful, quiet and dark, not a sound. And reassuring. He felt himself running out of air, and he began to think of surviving. "Is He not here with me?" he asked. "I am not a great sinner. I have not sinned much!" He made a promise not to drink a drop of vodka again.

In a moment he popped to the surface, with freezing water lapping at his face. He managed to take a deep breath just before another wave buried him again. When he came to the surface again, his life jacket had slipped over his eyes. Then he saw that a life raft was nearby. Vosa caught hold of a trailing rope and managed to climb in as it dipped and rose in the waves.

He found that he had lost his trousers, one shoe and, worst of all, his eyeglasses in the water. Everything around him appeared fuzzy. By now the bone-chilling cold had reached deep within him and he could not feel his legs.

After a minute he saw that a girl was struggling in the water nearby, and he recognized her as Hele Motus, a fellow worker in the duty-free store. He helped her and a Swedish woman into the raft. Another swimmer, a heavy-bodied Swedish man who was very drunk, had caught hold of the raft, but was unable to help himself as others reached to pull him in. Vosa and the others tried to help him up, but were unable to lift him. He muttered in Swedish for a while as he clung to the ropes, then slowly disappeared into the dark waters.

Suddenly a wave threw their raft against the side of the sinking ship, and Vosa felt panic as the raft made a creaking sound against the metal. He knew that sharp metal pieces of the ship could rip their raft apart. Again and again, the waves threw them up against the ship. Finally they were able to push themselves away from the stricken *Estonia* until they felt it posed no further threat. They tried to hug together for protection against the bitter-cold wind. Each wave brought a new spasm of frigid water over them, taking away any little warmth they had been generating. But Vosa found that even his soaked clothes gave warmth.

From their raft, Timmo Vosa watched with awe as the bow of the *Estonia* rose in the moonlight slowly into the night sky when the ship began to slip beneath the waves. It was a sight he would remember all his life.

Twenty-three year-old Hele Mottus had gone to her cabin when her shift in the tax-free shop had ended at 11:30 p.m. She was feeling sick because of the extreme motion of the ship. What was more, she had learned only a few days earlier that she was pregnant. She and her husband, Rene, back in Tallinn had celebrated the news.

But that evening on the ship she had been unable to sleep, partly from a sense of anxiety she felt because of the storm. Along with others of the crew, her cabin was on the eighth deck. As she lay there, she could hear the sounds of laughter in the cabin next to hers where other crew members were celebrating a birthday. Someone knocked on her door and shouted an invitation to come join them, but she declined.

A moment later the ship jerked. At times she had felt such things before as the *Estonia* had hit a large wave, but this time all her things on her counter top went crashing toward the window and onto the floor. That had never happened before. With the light on she could see that the ship was leaning badly toward the starboard. Quickly she put on jeans and sport shoes, pondered briefly whether to put on only a pullover or something warmer. She decided on a leather jacket. By the time she dressed, the cabin was leaning so badly that she had to pull herself to her door by clinging to the bunk and the door handle. At the same time, the sound of the tyfon, the alarm siren echoed through the halls.

"Alert! Alert!" came a female voice in Estonian over the loudspeaker. There was an urgency in the voice that told Hele Mottus that something was very wrong. Further instructions were shouted in Estonian to the crew over the microphone, but by that time panic had seized the passengers. Later many of them insisted that no alarm was given. Obviously most passengers did not understand the meaning of the shouted alert in what was for them a foreign tongue.

When Motus left her cabin she saw other crew members who

were panicked. Some stood shouting, some sat apathetically, resigned. A cabin maid grabbed Motus's arm. "We must get out quickly," she said. Motus nodded, and both of them shouted to the other crew members that they had to get on deck as fast as possible.

The two women darted down the stairway to the open seventh deck, where the lobby was full of people. Many of them were wearing life jackets but seemed unable to move, standing in shock. Outside, the sea and the storm were raging, and some did not want to leave the shelter of the warm lobby. Motus did not recognize any of them as crew members, but most seemed young and she guessed that many were crew members whose cabins were nearby.

Determined not to panic, Motus reminded herself that help could come only from the outer deck. But reaching the door that led to the outside deck was itself difficult because the floor was on such an upward slant and water had sloshed in to make the way slippery. For a short woman like Motus, it was nearly impossible. But as she struggled, a man by the door lay down and allowed her to climb up by hanging on to his clothes to reach the doorway. Most passengers testified that it never grew dark inside the ship. For a few seconds the lights faltered, then came back on dim as the emergency system started to work.

On the outer deck there was total confusion and dismay. Screams rose above the wail of the wind. Near the doorway Motus fell down and felt people stepping over her. But, determined to get out, she regained her feet. As she ran out onto the deck into the rain, a crewman handed her a life jacket and she put it on.

"Is someone coming to rescue us?" she shouted, and then realized it was not a good question.

The cabin maid who had emerged with her turned to look back. "Only God can save us now," answered the cabin maid. Motus was not a religious person, but at that time her thoughts went to the purpose of life. It suddenly seemed so fragile, so quick. Later she learned that the cabin maid died in a life raft.

Hele Motus began to climb higher as the ship sank lower in the water. Soon the white side of the hull was as level as a field. Ahead she could see some sailors loosening a life raft, and she tried to help them. She planned to jump into the raft, but suddenly the force of a great wave from behind her carried her down the side of the ship and into the sea, helpless. While falling, she hit several obstructions on the ship, injuring her neck, back and leg.

In the water she fought the turbulent force of the waves, then popped up right next to a life raft. She grabbed a trailing rope and pulled herself to the entrance, but did not have strength enough to pull herself up into the raft. Then Timmo Vosa, her fellow worker from the ship's store, and a Swedish man pulled her on into the raft.

On the raft together Hele Motus and Timmo Vosa encouraged each other. As the hours wore on he kept falling asleep, numbed by the cold. But each time his friend poked him in the ribs to keep him awake and moving his legs so the circulation would not stop in the cold water. With alarm they noted that their raft seemed to be sinking lower and lower in the water.

Finally someone handed Vosa some Verity emergency flares they had found floating in the raft. He did not know how to handle them and could not read the instructions in the dark. But when Vosa pulled the fuse a rich glow flared up, lighting the sea around them. The new light made them all feel better, not only because it would make them visible to rescue ships but because the warm yellow light brought a new cheerfulness to the somber sights around them. After he had lit four of the flares, he noticed that he had burned his hands without being aware of it. He saved the last Verity light in reserve.

By the time the last flare had burned out, a ship bore down toward them through the heavy swells. Painfully slow, it eased near them so as to put their raft in its lee as protection from the wind and the waves. Above them, crewmen from the ship threw a heavy rope called a hawser toward them as the raft plunged and dipped in the towering waves. Vosa caught the rope. He tried again and again to tie the rope to their raft but failed because of his cold-numbed hands. Finally in despair he threw the hawser back into the water.

Unable to lift them aboard because of the seas, the ship lowered them a new life raft. Nothing had ever seemed so wonderful as a dry life raft. Even though his arms and legs did not obey him, Vosa managed to crawl into the new raft. One after another those on the nearly submerged raft climbed into the new one. One heavy woman could not make it into the dry raft. Vosa tried to take her by the hands and pull her in, but it was no use. Then he caught her by the arms, but they were slippery and she kept sliding out of his grip, whimpering and staring at him with glazed eyes. He began to lose hope of helping her at all. But each of them realized that unless they got her onto the raft, they would not be lifted aboard the ship. Time and time again with his numbed hands Timmo Vosa struggled to pull her onto the life raft. At last, despairing, he gave a lunge and caught hold of her pullover. It was thick and strong, and with the others joining in, they managed to slide the woman up into the raft.

With that done, Vosa stared upward at the ship towering above them, wondering if the swells were going to capsize them as they were lifted. He watched warily as the lines from their dry raft to the ship began to tighten, and then he hung on as the raft was raised from the water and into the air. Hardly daring to believe that the rescue was actually taking place, he held his breath as the raft swung in the wind and then was hoisted onto the bow deck of the *Mariella*.

As the rescuers crowded around them to lend first aid, Vosa felt as if he were experiencing this all through a mist. His legs were bleeding with wounds from deep gouges that had occurred when they were without sensation. His face was covered with blood from a wound he had not realized he had received.

His body temperature at that time was 28 degrees Celsius (which translates to 82.4 Fahrenheit, more than 16 degrees below the normal 98.6 F.) As they carried him to a warm room and covered him with blankets, he nearly screamed from the excruciating pain that swept over him as if his whole body was on fire. His feeling was returning. Even his hair hurt.

Someone asked him for the phone number of his parents, and they were immediately informed that he had survived. His group was taken to Stockholm to the Sodersjukhus hospital. His uncle phoned him from Toronto, Canada, and asked what he could do for him. "First and foremost I need spectacles," Vosa told him. His uncle sent them.

22 · FATHER, GRANDFATHER, SON

One of the miracle events of the rescue efforts was the saga of the Voronin family. Most of the survivors of the *Estonia* were young and in good physical condition. They had to be because of the demands of reaching deck and then getting off the listing ship, finding a raft, and surviving the long bitter-cold night while constantly being drenched with chilly seawater.

The Voronin family had established a business dynasty in northern Estonia in the town of Kotla-Jaarve. On this night the grandfather, Vassili Krjuchkov, the son-in-law, a Russian giant named Alexander Voronin, with a heavy shock of graying hair and beard, and his fifteen-year-old son, Vasya, were on their way to a business meeting in Denmark.

Originally they had planned to go by plane, but they changed plans when warned that due to strong autumn winds there was a good chance the flight would be canceled. On board the ferry, they had dinner, then Vasya, who was the image of his father, went to their cabin on the sixth deck to sleep. Alexander and the grandfather stayed at the bar to watch the show. By the time they left the bar the two men commented that the rolling of the ship had grown worse. They made their way to the cabin and turned in.

They were half asleep when Vasya became seasick from the violent swaying of the ship. "It was like a roller coaster," he said. As the father was trying to help his son, the ship lurched, followed by another jerk, and began to lean so much that both Vasya and his grandfather were thrown from their beds. The table and chair slammed against their cabin wall. They listened for the sound of the ship's engines, and heard only shouting outside. There was no longer a vibration of the engines. And the ship leaned more and more.

"Get dressed, quick!" Vassili ordered. After throwing on trousers and coats, they ran toward the door. In the corridor there was confusion all around them. Fortunately for them, their cabin was on the sixth deck. It was only one stairway up to deck seven and the opening to the sea. However, there was no one to tell them how to find life jackets or how to get outside, and they made the mistake of descending to deck five. As soon as Vassili opened the door to deck five, they felt a strong blow shake the ship. At the same time the ship heaved to the side and the two men and boy went hurtling down the corridor and crashed into the wall there. Alexander, a heavy-shouldered bear of a man in fine physical condition, felt something crush within him and thought he was losing consciousness. Later in the hospital he would learn that his spine was fractured.

Around them Vassili saw people crying and moaning, some covered with blood. Over the ship's loudspeakers they could hear something, but it was in either Finnish or Swedish. First it was a male voice, then a hysterical female voice. They understood neither.

Alexander's son was also injured, and he looked up plaintively. "Father, I think my arm is broken," he said.

By then it was obvious to Alexander that the ship was sinking. He realized that in order to leave the ship, they had to get to the upper deck that led outside. The door that led upwards was above them. The stairs were covered with people, screaming and begging for help. Alexander was racked with excruciating pain in his back and down his legs. The pain was so bad he could barely move without screaming, and he knew his back must be broken. He told his young son that he probably wouldn't be able to make it, that they should leave him.

"I'm not going to abandon you," Vasya told him.

Around them people lay scattered on the stairs, covered with blood, hysterical, crying, begging for help. Alexander, who weighed 245 pounds, grabbed the banister and pulled himself upward as much as he could, using only one leg. He found the pain unbearable, but with his son pushing from behind and his father-in-law pulling him up by the hand, they made their way upward on the stairways and out onto the seventh deck.

On the outside deck they found a crewman passing out life vests. The sea was beating at the stricken ship, and the sound of the wind almost drowned out the sounds of sobbing and cries around them. Older people stood in the darkness staring at the deck, trying to ignore the huge waves that towered at times above the ship. Many could make no decision, and feared to leave the steady deck for the great troughs and peaks of sea that yawned beyond the railing. Fear had immobilized them.

Darkness seemed to close on the three Voronins as the lights went out. Vasya helped his father put on his life jacket. Then the three stood wondering how they were going to get to a lifeboat. Not far away toward the bow they saw a crowd of people gathered around one of the lifeboats, struggling to get it loose. But the boat would not come loose from its steel bindings. Nevertheless, people clung to it as if it would save them. The Voronins hurried to try to help unloose the boat. Just as they reached it a gigantic wave swept over them, carrying them all overboard.

Vassili, Alexander, and Vasya found themselves separated when the wave washed them into the sea just before the *Estonia* went down. When Alexander rose to the surface, he cried out for his son several times. In answer all he could hear was the sound of the sea and the screams around him. He could see an unopened raft floating about fifteen yards away. He wondered if it took some special knowledge to open the rafts. In reality, they were designed to open automatically when a ship sank. After another few minutes Alexander saw that the floating rafts were beginning to open. Each raft carried a little red light, but they were so distant he knew he could not reach them.

In great pain, Alexander had been holding on to a piece of floating plastic. When he spotted another raft only a dozen yards away, he abandoned the floating plastic and tried to swim toward it. But he had misjudged the distance, and it seemed to draw away as he approached it. The waves tossed him and tossed the raft, which tantalizingly dancing away from him each time he drew near. He wondered if he would drown so near to safety. In his struggle he tried to ignore the pain that tore through him. He began to lose hope.

At last he got hold of the rope that circled the raft. He cried for help. Some people looked out of the raft and tried to help him in, but he could barely move. For ten minutes he struggled trying to get a leg up and get pulled into the raft. Finally two men reached down and pulled him up through the doorway.

On the raft were sixteen others. They could hear cries from the water, but as they looked out of the little tent, there was no light to show where the cries came from. There were no emergency rockets on the raft. Alexander lay in the water of the raft, exhausted. The waves had taken all his clothes but his underwear. After a time everyone got violently seasick because of the heaving motion of the raft. Around them in the darkness the cries continued. He could not help but think that one of those cries might be from his 15-year-old son. To add to his misery, as the hours passed the rain turned to vicious hail that pounded at them.After Alexander, nobody else came to the raft.

His son, Vasya, felt himself slammed against a piece of metal as he was thrown from the ship. When he came up, he was by a raft that floated upside down. He held on to it. Nearby he soon saw another raft with people in it. He pushed himself to it and someone helped him inside. In that raft there were flashlights, a first aid kit, and light rockets floating in the water.

After he climbed in the raft, Vasya looked around for his father and grandfather. In the moonlight he could still see about a quarter of the *Estonia* above the surface. Then above the roar of the wind came the wail of the ship's siren, the most lonely, ominous sound he had ever heard. Then everything was gone where the ship had been. Nothing was visible. Only the waves.

The grandfather, Vassili, lost consciousness as he was thrown from the ship but came to as he fought for air in the sea. He had swallowed a great deal of water but managed to get to the surface, where he bumped against a soft blackness. Quickly he realized that he was under a raft. Working furiously, he groped his way out and took a deep breath of fresh air. Nearby was a raft only a few yards away. Those in it helped him crawl aboard when he reached it.

He sat in the raft, water up to his waist. He had lost his shoes, but still had on his left stocking. Somehow his life vest had become tangled around his neck, and the strings seemed to be choking him, so he removed it, but maintained a firm grip on the rope around the raft. Vassili found there were twelve others with him. A man of about thirty was wearing only his underwear. After about three hours, with the wind still whistling and the waves still crashing, this man died. Another man about age forty-five died in only an hour and a half.

With the waves constantly tossing them, Vassili sat thinking that the raft was not going to last much longer. At times he was sure it was sinking. And he thought of how close they were to three countries, Finland, Sweden, and Estonia. Surely one or all of those places was sending help. If only the rescuers would come.

Through the torturously long hours, Vassili told himself that he had to survive. He was not a religious man, and had not prayed before. But sitting in the water with the storm around him, he reminded himself that he had never claimed there was no God. That night several times he prayed for the lives of Alexander and Vasya to be spared. As for himself, he refused to give up the idea that he would survive.

At dawn the ships and helicopters came, and then he understood that they were going to live. But he was shivering uncontrollably, and he did not know if he could hang on long enough for them to reach him in time. All in all, he dared not think that his son-in-law and grandson could be so lucky. The helicopters lifted up Vassili and the others aboard his raft two at a time and took them to the *Silja Europa*. They were landed on board, wrapped in blankets, and given hot coffee. Vassilli's shivering would not stop for another hour.

On the raft of Vasya Voronin, the grandson, after three hours one of the helicopters flew above their heads, its searchlights probing the waves. It passed on, not seeing them. Around them they could see the lights of the *Mariella* and *Europa* and other ships, but none were nearby. They shut one of the entrances to the tent that stretched over the raft, then closed the second entrance and pulled in the ladder. Nevertheless, when the waves washed over the raft, they brought new batches of cold water.

Even when rescue seemed imminent, some did not make it. Fifteen-year-old Vasya found that his raft was fortuitously carried by the wind directly to one of the ships that had joined the rescue efforts, the *Isabella*. The crew lowered a similar raft to them, this one dry. One by one those in the raft scampered into the new raft and the winches of the *Isabella* began to lift them. The raft began to rise, something tore, and it plunged back into the sea, spilling some people out, but they were able to crawl back into the raft. For fifteen minutes the crew tried to lift the raft aboard. Again the raft was lifted, fell again, got loose, and started to sink. Yet those huddled inside were able to stay afloat.

On board the ship, they tried a new tactic, opening the outside door of the engine room. But the waves were too high, smashing those in the raft against the side of the ship time after time. Once more the crew tried to winch the raft aboard. It swung up and down in the wind. Then one man leaped forward and held on to the side of the raft in order to reach toward the ship. Just then a great wave crashed the raft into the ship, crushing him. His body hung tangled in the ropes of the ship. At last Vasya and the other survivors on the raft were lifted aboard the *Isabella*. The crew took him inside, removed his icy clothes and wrapped him in warm blankets and rubbed his feet to restore circulation.

Around 7:30 that morning, the father, Alexander, was rescued. Two or three hours after the sinking those on his raft saw the lights of the rescue ships. Because of the fury of the storm, the ships were unable to get near the rafts. But just the sight of them buoyed the spirits of those waiting for help. Once a helicopter flew above them, and Alexander and the others waved wildly, but the air crews were unable to spot them on the rough sea, and the helicopter's lights disappeared.

Waiting in the darkness for morning, they tried to keep their spirits up. Inside the raft the water seemed to be getting deeper, so they worked at bailing out as much as they could. Alexander used only one hand, because he could barely move the rest of his body. After several hours they discovered there was a hole in the raft. It began to sink and the men in the raft tried to stop the leak. The raft grew lower in the water, but did not sink.

It was light when the helicopter found them, after almost everyone else who was still alive had been plucked from the water. As soon as the helicopter lifted them all up and took them to a ship, Alexander was asked his name and offered a hot sauna. The first thing he did was to ask about Vasya, but no one knew anything. Alexander was put in the hospital at Turku in Finland. Two hours later a police officer came and promised to find out anything he could about his son, Vasya. Alexander hesitated to call his wife back in Estonia because he was afraid of what he must tell her. Then, in an unbelievable and joyous reunion, Vasya called. By the evening Alexander was told that another ship had also rescued his father-in-law, Vassili. They were taken to different hospitals, then brought together at Turku where Alexander was being treated for back injuries. Against great odds, these three members of the Voronin family were able to reunite and celebrate their survival together.

23 · DAWN

At long last, a subtle change grew in the darkness. A slow grayish light began to grow in the east, barely discernible through the rain. When the dawn finally struggled through the gray drizzle, some of those adrift had already been snatched from the sea by helicopters and the crude makeshift methods of the large ships. But many survivors still waited in the rafts, with their life forces waning rapidly. Those in the black-bottomed upside-down rafts had been nearly impossible to spot in the darkness. As the helicopters flitted over the wave tops, searching, it was the deadliest time for those who had survived nearly six hours sitting in the frigid water that sloshed inside the rafts. Some of those who had fought for so long finally had no warmth left even as their rescue helicopter spotted them on the sea troughs below. When daylight came, those on the raft of Kent Harstedt saw for the first time who their companions were.

"Kent?" came a voice that wavered through numbed cheeks. Morten Boje for the first time recognized his friend. "For heaven's sake, is that you, Kent?" Both from the conference, the only two survivors of that group, they had spent the dark night on the same raft without knowing it. They briefly congratulated each other, but it was with restrained joy, for the waves still washed over the raft every few minutes. By then Morten had lapsed into a state of numbness and did not care much. In the darkness all of them had reached beyond the point of talking. During the night the Estonian girl had moved next to Sara. Now she sat doubled there in the fetal position.

Through the night they had seen the lights of numerous helicopters, but all were far away. With the light now on the horizon they had new hope. And with faces to go with voices, there was more discussion. Kent and Sara began to talk of the good things that would come with their rescue: the hot chocolate, the sandwiches, the warm blankets, and the joy of just being warm and safe. In the growing light their spirits picked up from the nightmare they had endured on the dark sea. With the light it did not seem so cold. Yet each time a freezing wave washed over them in the dawn, they were reminded that much lay ahead.

Worst of all, in the light they could also see the bodies that washed about their feet. Until then each had been only a voice or a moan in the night. Now, floating there, each body was starkly white, as if it had been bleached. It was shocking to see that most of the dead were young, in their twenties. The survivors tried not to look at them. In the beginning, at least twenty persons had hunkered on the raft. Now only half were still living.

Suddenly in the growing light they could make out a raft scudding toward them, riding on the waves. It was overturned like theirs, with a man huddling in the bottom, borne on the waves by the wind, moving fast because it was light. With only one person on board, it was not filled with water as theirs was. The man was lying on his stomach with his arms and legs outstretched. He was wearing no life vest, only underwear and a T-shirt. At first they could not hear him because of the wind, but as the raft approached they could make out his desperate pleas.

"*Appi! Appi!*" the man called out for help in Estonian as his raft drew close.

Quickly Morten and Elmar Siegel grabbed hold of the approaching raft. If they could join the man in a relatively dry raft, they knew their chances would be better. Paul Barney and Paul Andersson moved around to try to help turn the new raft around. No one spoke, but it was the first time they had tried to work together. All of them saw a chance to bring the man in with them, turn the dry raft over, raise the tent, and have a better chance of being spotted by the helicopters.

As they struggled to shift the raft, the man lying there screamed louder and louder. They shouted at him in different languages to get him to cooperate and climb over into their raft so that they could turn his upright, but he didn't seem to understand any of them. Paul Barney finally found the man's screaming unbearable, and felt his grip slip. At the same time, a huge wave bore down on them and tore the raft from their grasp. Quickly the raft danced away on the wave toward the graying east. The four men watched it go with dismay. Then it was gone.

Morten settled back and closed his eyes. The thought kept coming to him that he was not concerned about the man on the raft they had lost. He was shocked. "If I had been able I would have turned over the raft just to get into it, no matter what happened to him," he mused. "That was attempted murder." He could not shake the thought.

Slowly as the dawn grew lighter, the tattered horizon began to show through the rain. In the growing light Paul Barney could make out the Estonian girl he had helped aboard. She was thrashing around in the bottom of the raft, delirious and muttering as others had done before losing their battle. Barney himself was barely able to move, numb with cold and exhaustion. He tried to speak to her, but she did not respond. He stretched to take her hand, but he had tethered himself to the raft so as not to be washed overboard. She was just beyond his reach, even though he strained to catch hold of her hand and pull her to him. The young woman stared blankly and turned away from him toward the center of the raft.

"Do something! Do something!" Paul told himself. But there was nothing to do. He felt himself going into deeper chill and shock. He looked at the others. The survivors around the edge sat huddled like statues. With a sigh of dismay, Paul wondered if any of those still alive were going to make it. The ships had come during the night, the helicopters had come and gone, and now their raft had drifted miles from the *Estonia*. He turned to stare out over the sea so that he would not have to see the pretty Estonian girl with the flowing black hair slip into the water at their feet. He remembered her long black hair, but he could not recall her face. He did not turn to search her out to refresh his memory.

Instead of calming with daylight, the waves grew more violent. Each survivor had begun to wonder how many more hours and minutes he or she could endure before they slipped away from reality to join their comrades in the bottom of the raft. For Kent, no matter how much they had saved their strength and kept up their spirits, he admitted to himself that he gave himself another half-hour, an hour at most.

Perhaps most unnerving was the sight of the Estonian girl. For the last hour before daylight she had been sitting next to Sara. Now they could see her floating face downward, with her long dark hair mingled in the water with the blonde hair of Sara. It looked as if some loving fingers had intentionally plaited the locks of the living with the dead. Paul Barney turned away from the sight, and Sara buried her face into Kent's shoulder.

During the dawn, Kent had pondered what he might do to improve his situation. He prided himself on being a man of decision, of action. In the nighttime he had occasionally made a suggestion for them all, but all his recommendations had fallen on deaf ears. For one thing, he had suggested that everyone jump in the water while they turned the raft upright so it could function properly. Or he had proposed that the strongest ones should get in the water and kick their legs to propel the raft where they wanted it to go. Such desperate thoughts were all met with deafening silence.

In the growing light they could see an older man sitting shoulder-deep near Kent, fighting for life. His face and his lips were growing whiter by the minute. He swayed back and forth, struggling to keep his head above water. In his elemental battle, he reached and took hold of Kent. The young Swede helped him hold his head up.

Now the sight of the dead in the raft brought Kent to chastise himself silently for sitting and waiting for his fate. Had he endured so much only to sit here and freeze to death? What irony, he told himself, when he could have slipped to an easy death hours earlier when he had been caught in the rope in the depths of the sea. Had all this suffering of the endless night been for nothing? He determined he was not going to die like the others around him. He wanted to have a hand in his fate, not to sit idly like the others as they slipped away into death.

When he was silent too long in his thoughts, Sara would call out, "Kent, how you doing?" He would do the same for her. It was a ritual that ensured one or the other would not wander away into that barely conscious state that was so deadly. This time when she asked, he sat reasoning with himself that he must do something before his endurance gave out, no matter how unreasonable it seemed. He shared his latest idea with her. He had decided that he had eighty percent of his normal strength left. Nearby, only thirty yards or so away, a raft with a cover over it floated in the same direction they were drifting. He told Sara that he would simply swim over to it. He was determined to do it.

"Get hold of yourself!" she scolded instantly.

He shrugged, realizing that without him she would be even more vulnerable to the cold. After considering a while, he agreed that it was not a good idea to try to swim to the other raft.

In a few minutes a helicopter that had been in the distance swung near them. This brought new excitement over the raft. Even Sara stood up and cheered and waved, each drawing on their last bit of energy. But no one saw them, and the helicopter flew on.

"Take it easy and wait," Sara said. "It is daylight now, and they will find us."

As they sat back down, they saw that the older man lay on his back with his face under the water. His eyes were open. The sight added to the quiet pessimism that now hung over them like a shroud. They knew their black raft was barely visible on the dark sea. Eventually someone was bound to see them, but would help come in time?

The rain stopped intermittently, and the whir of distant helicopters pierced the morning. Other than that faint sound, a brooding silence hung over them, broken only by the chop of the water against the raft. This time there was no cheering. Hardly any of those on the raft bothered to look over the edge.

As daylight crept slowly through the clouds, finally the waves seemed to calm a little, and only the rain brought water into the raft. The eight still alive on the raft had endured the unendurable for more than five hours, and now they hunched in gloomy resignation, beyond numbness and pain. They were poised on the razor's edge of a great abyss that beckoned enticingly. Even in daylight, their plight had begun to look without a glimmer of hope.

Morten felt himself sinking. He well realized the danger of drifting into the state of near-unconsciousness that preceded death. To counteract this, he concentrated on Fredericke, his girlfriend back in Copenhagen. He could feel this tactic begin to work; he was filled with a new resolve to live, a new determination to get back to Fredericke, to see, to feel, and love her once more.

"I will get home," he promised himself over and over. "I will get home." He looked around to see what he might do to bring some warmth. Around his feet was the constant bumping of the bodies. In desperation, he studied them. They were fellow passengers. He had been alone, without anyone to hug against. In that critical hour he made the decision that his fellow passengers could provide warmth and life. He pulled some of the dead against him. They were still warm. With a start he realized that many of them were his own age. The border between where they were and where at that moment he existed was a very fine line, he admitted. It was a frightening admission. He wondered vaguely if he was about to cross that thin line himself in the next hour.

Morten felt a scratching against his thigh. He looked down and saw a dead man's chin chafing against him, with the stubble of a beard irritating his leg. It was the balding man who had hugged him from behind. With a shudder, Morten pushed him away.

Paul Andersson paused to look over their raft in the new light, and was surprised to see that the bottom showed orange from the life vests of those bodies floating there. He realized that all the night he had been without a life vest. But floating not far from him in the raft was an empty life jacket, and he put it on. He did not know whether someone had removed it or if it was an extra. He was surprised at how much warmth the vest brought him.

Then, over the sound of the rain and the slap of the waves against the raft, they heard the rhythmic chop-chop of helicopters approaching. They were not close, but they offered promise of eventual rescue, and once more stirred the hopes of the eight. By then the raft had fallen into complete silence. The gloom of near-surrender hung heavy over them all. Their body temperatures had each fallen by then to around 30 degrees Celsius — at the equivalent to 86 degrees Fahrenheit, a point at which the brain and the body nearly cease to function together.

The rain stopped. Over the sound of the sea they realized that the distant noise of the helicopters was growing closer. But they did not move to peer over the edge of the raft. The eerie sound hung heavily, but no one dared speak, as if they might break the spell.

One of the eight was the young Estonian waiter from the ship. Until then he had been suffering quietly. Now he began to stumble around in the middle of the raft, falling over the dead bodies.

"Dammit, five more minutes," Morten pleaded, partly to himself, partly to the young Estonian.

Paul Barney watched the young man with dismay as the waiter began the last convulsive movements that preceded death. "Oh, my God, he is so young," Barney thought. "This is too much. This, this is where the line has to be drawn. It is light and all, and the helicopters are beginning to come down. This is too much."

He grabbed the young waiter's shoulder, trying to hold him upright. Although he was too tired to try to speak encouragement to him, Paul strained to hold his head out of the water. His muscles ached with the effort, and he held tight as long as was possible. Then he paused to look up as a helicopter circled above them. When he looked back, the young Estonian had sunk down against the edge of the raft, face down. He was gone.

The others turned their eyes toward the helicopter. Hardly daring hope, they watched almost with indifference as it circled overhead. All seven survivors gathered around the edge, facing upward, as the helicopter hovered directly over them. No one cheered. The bitter memory of earlier disappointments weighed too heavily on them for that. But now vibrations shook the raft and the downdraft of the blades sent spray over them.

It was a Finnish helicopter and from inside a rescuer wearing a black rubber body suit stepped out of the doorway, dangling by a cable, he descended toward them. It was a delicate operation, for the raft was scooting along on the wind and the waves, and the swells rose and fell beneath the aircraft. The rescuer swung back and forth on the cable, at times dunking into a wave and then left dangling high as the wave retreated. Finally he splashed into the water a few yards from the raft, which was shaking from the downdraft. He swam to the raft and hung on the rope, saying nothing. In fact, nothing could be heard above the roar of the helicopter and the wind.

It was obvious the young Russian storeroom manager was most in need of immediate aid. He was struggling to stand up. It was he who earlier in the night had stood and cursed their fate. Paul Andersson pointed to him as the frogman rescuer climbed into the raft with the cable in tow. The frogman nodded. He placed the loop around the chest of the Russian and showed him how he must keep his arms at his side. The storeroom manager gave a numbed gesture of assent.

At a signal from the frogman, the winch took up the slack and the Russian began to rise from the raft, quickly at first, then slower. They watched as, halfway to the helicopter, the Russian's head began to roll from side to side. When he was nearly to the open door, his arms began to move upward. When barely out of reach of the helicopter crew reaching for him, the Russian storekeeper's arms shot straight up. He slipped from the loop and fell headlong into the rough sea.

Immediately the frogman leaped into the water, swam to the Russian, and pulled him back to the raft. Holding on to the raft's rope with one arm, he checked the man's pulse with the other. He gave a shake of his head. The storeroom manager was dead.

Inexplicably, then the frogman was winched back up into the helicopter, and it lifted back up toward the clouds. Apparently the rescuers felt they needed a better harness arrangement to haul up survivors in such bad shape. In their dazed state, none of the six understood why the helicopter left. It seemed the cruelest of tricks. Without a sound, some with eyes closed in despair, they sank back against the edge of the raft. Perhaps, in their wariness of the false promises of the night, they were not even surprised.

But almost immediately a large double-ended Swedish Vertol helicopter from the base at Save in southern Sweden swooped down and hovered directly above them. The large blades of the aircraft whipped up the water around them. A man in a military helmet leaned out from the doorway with a camera in his hand and began filming them.

"What the hell are you doing?" shouted Kent Harstedt angrily, shaking his fist.

The helicopter crew was working quickly to ready the winch. All morning the helicopter rescue crews had been having trouble with the winches in trying to bring up survivors from the *Estonia*. Several had to return to base without success because the winches jammed or did not function in some way. The pilot of the helicopter kept it hovering barely over the tops of the waves, just above the raft. Then frogman Torbjorn Olsen, age thirty-one, stepped into the doorway and studied them. This was an operation which he had spent days practicing, but never in conditions like these.

Watching it, Morten Boje was overcome with the fear that he could not last if he was not the first taken aboard. He was under the impression that the craft would take aboard only one person at a time, fly them to safety, and return much later for the others one by one. "I can't wait that long," he thought. "I can't last that long."

At the same time Paul Barney watched the helicopter with suspended judgment, in a state of near apathy. He saw how the rotor blades at times nearly touched the waves. "It will probably spin into the sea," he told himself. "Many helicopters are taken by the waves."

Elmar Siegel, on the other hand, was calm and did not show the elation he felt. In his calm, introverted way, he was the most convinced of all of them that the ordeal was finally nearing an end.

Sara and Kent watched silently, still holding each other. No one spoke because the scream of the helicopter drowned out all other sounds, even the wind. The powerful drafts from the whirling blades splattered water over them, and the raft itself bounced in the downdraft. There was a momentary fear that the raft might be overturned.

Torbjorn Olsen stepped out into the wind and began to swing back and forth as he was lowered on the cable toward them. He studied the mountainous waves, trying to find a time to slip into one of the valleys for his landing by the raft. After splashing in next to the raft, the frogman grabbed a rope and studied the people inside. He was shocked at the bodies floating there. At the same time Morten struggled past the others toward the rescuer with the cable lifeline, nudging and pushing. Morten almost blacked out. Sara, seeing his condition, grabbed him and with his face between her hands, screamed at him to hang on. Then she slapped him hard across the face.

Shocked, Morten gasped, looked around and saw Sara standing before him, commanding him to stay alert. He let the frogman slip the harness around him, then felt himself winched into the air above the raft. Only half-conscious, he felt like a bird swaying in the wind. Eager hands reached out to pull him inside as he reached the cabin. The crew tore at his clothes, laid him on a stretcher, and covered him with blankets. He was the first taken aboard. A woman with a ponytail was leaning over him, tucking him in, rubbing his hands to warm them. For the first time that night, he felt he was in safe hands. And for the first time, he began to sob.

Torbjorn Olsen descended a second time to the raft. He studied each of the survivors carefully to determine their condition. Sara was the second to ascend on the thin cable and be welcomed into the haven of the helicopter cabin and the crew that waited there. Watching her go up, Elmar Siegel marveled at her calm expression and lack of fear. "What a brave girl," he told himself. Following her, Paul Andersson was taken up. Then Kent Harstedt, who seemed surprisingly alert.

"What time is it?" Kent asked the frogman as he slipped on the harness.

"Five thirty," he answered, giving him Finnish time, which was an hour earlier than Swedish time.

Left on the raft were Paul Barney and Elmar Siegel, each of whom motioned for the other to be next to go up the cable. It was an "After you, Alfonse" routine as they pushed the cable harness back and forth between them. Torbjorn Olsen decided the issue by slipping the loop around Siegel. Above them the cameraman was still filming. Then, twenty minutes after Torbjorn Olsen splashed into the sea near them, they were all aboard. Kent Harstedt, half sitting, half lying on the stretcher, waved his hand at the camera. "Thank you, guys and girls. Thank you," he said solemnly.

When he was pulled into the helicopter, Paul Barney also waved into the camera and said, "So I guess I'm lucky now, right?" The film would be carried on British television that night and make him a hero in Great Britain.

24 · A PLACE
LIKE PARADISE

That morning when their helicopter settled in a cloud of dust at the landing area of the hospital at Mariehamn, Finland, each of the six from the raft of Kent Harstedt and Paul Barney felt a great rush of elation. Of the approximately twenty people who had made it onto the raft in those nightmare hours, these six had endured. They had been snatched from the yawning jaws of the dark abyss. They had emerged from hell, victorious.

Even after the rotors stopped whirling, the wind whipped the clothes of those waiting around the ambulances in the landing area. Amid the whirls of dust, the crowd of doctors, orderlies and nurses hovered around these six and two other survivors the helicopter had picked up on the way. They bundled the new arrivals with blankets, with even their faces covered to protect them from the cold. Then, past the shouting crowd of journalists and photographers that were kept at a distance, the orderlies whisked them on gurneys through the emergency room entrance.

But the flash of the cameras continued until the survivors were out of sight behind the hospital doors. Those on the stretchers had stared in amazement at the pleading newsmen. They had no way of knowing that the whole world's attention had turned to the dramatic events on the Baltic Sea.

For six hours the chief physician of the hospital, Anders Fagerlund, had been preparing his crews for the arrival of survivors. Many times he had attended seminars and training courses about the needs of those who had emerged from disasters. After being awakened with news of the tragedy, he had spent most of the night mentally reviewing what he and his staff would have to do to give the most help possible to those who made it off the *Estonia* and through the long night.

Outside on the tiny airstrip at Mariehamn a steady stream of chartered planes had been arriving from Europe and other more distant places, bringing newsmen and others to cover the disaster. Most had gone on to the Finnish island of Abo, where the majority of the survivors were taken. At the request of Dr. Fagerlund, the large group of the newsmen who had come from the world press services gathered in the parking lot. With cameras rolling and a barrage of microphones thrust toward him, he told them that because of the terrible ordeal these survivors had experienced, there would be no interviews granted for twenty-four hours. In the survivors' acute shock, he told the reporters, unless they were allowed to unwind from the experience slowly, whatever they might tell the press immediately following their experience could cause a relapse into their trauma as they watched television replays later.

"These patients have experienced horror beyond anything you could describe," he scolded the press. "They have fought for their lives through rain, darkness, and cold. They have seen their fellow passengers die. They have seen people be washed away. They must be left alone for at least twenty-four hours, and then they are going home as soon as possible to get crisis support."

All international studies imply that early interviews of disaster victims with the mass media only make the shock of injuries worse for them, Dr. Fagerlund said. Previous experience with ship sinkings in Europe had shown this. Each of these survivors at this hospital, he explained, was being assigned a psychologist right then to be with them for twenty-four hours to talk of their experiences and allow the emotions begin to subside.

In that hospital at Mariehamn, these survivors found enthusiastic support from the medical staff, a warm refuge, and what they later described as "paradise." The first thing they wanted was to call their families. When Morten called Fredericke in Copenhagen, she was just waking up and had no idea what he was talking about when he said he had survived. Paul Barney reached his mother in London, and she also had not heard of the accident. "I'm tired, Mom, but turn on your radio," he told her. "Now you know I'm alive."

Paul Andersson and Elmar Siegel tried all morning without success to get through to their families in Estonia. Finally they reached them by going through the Finnish Embassy in Tallinn. When Kent Harstedt reached his mother in southern Sweden, she too knew nothing of the accident. She panicked as he told her what had happened, and told her to turn on television. He could tell that she was in shock. In the ensuing hours his name was not listed among the survivors, and she began to wonder if she had imagined that her son had called to tell her he was alive.

In their exhausted and near-frozen state, the six survivors were given all the medical attention they needed to warm their bodies. But as their bodies thawed, the swelling, pains and aches began. All had some cuts, bruises and abrasions where they had bounced down the side of the ship or from being tossed around in the raft. Paul Barney was in a room alone because his body had so used up his energy reserves that protein was beginning to enter his blood. After the time in the helicopter, his body temperature had risen only to

30 degrees Celsius instead of the normal 37 degrees—which is 86 degrees Fahrenheit—about 12 degrees below normal.

None of the six were allowed to sleep until they had discussed the tragedy with their own private psychologist, who remained at their bedsides for twenty-four hours. In order to minimize the trauma, all the fears and the horror of the night had to come out. Otherwise sleep seems to freeze the events and the emotions in the person's psyche, doctors explained, sometimes for years. But then as they warmed and the tension melted away, they each sank into a cozy euphoria, with all their needs taken care of. The strain had taken a toll that showed up during those early hours. Kent could not remember the month, or whether it was summer or winter and did not ask. Sara at first was unable to remember her pact-partner's name, and asked if perhaps it was Bob. Because Kent kept asking about Sara, she was put in the same room with him and Morten.

By afternoon the press corps had swelled at the hospital as news leaked that among the last survivors were these that had been taken to Mariehamn in Aland. The restrained and polite Swedish press probably lost its innocence that day. The international press had no qualms about being intrusive, even obnoxious, in an effort to get details of a story that the whole world was watching. The phones rang interminably at the hospital, seeking interviews and news. Some thirty journalists stood begging at the doors. Some threw notes toward the survivors' rooms until a pile of them accumulated. In pathetic gestures, some of the reporters sent chocolates or flowers with notes begging for interviews and promising money. A few even dressed like orderlies and tried to bluff their way to the bedsides.

Not until the following day were the six brought together in the same room. During his time with his psychologist, Paul Barney had lamented that the beautiful girl he had seen in the cafeteria before the accident was probably lost. Now as they came into the room he shouted with excitement to recognize Sara as a fellow refugee from the raft. He laughed with her as he explained that through the night he had remembered her face sleeping on the bench before the ship lurched. Because the group spoke three languages, they soon fell to using English. Despite the lack of communication on the raft, soon a real camaraderie began to develop. Only Elmar Siegel was silent. With a start Morten recognized this was the hooded figure on the raft who stared so sullenly when he tried to talk to him. But the young Dane bore no resentment. It was all right if the Estonian at the time preferred to withdraw.

Following that, Paul Barney and Kent Harstedt met separately with the press and told their stories. Kent was in a wheelchair because of a deep cut on his leg and bruises to his back.

From reporters who had come from around the world, the accounts went out, with an emphasis on Kent and Sara's meeting on the side of the ship, their pact to help each other and the promised dinner date, and the ordeal of huddling together during their longest night until rescue came. Inevitably, the press played it as the decade's most dramatic romance. It caught the world's attention, and their faces were on the front pages of newspapers and magazines in far corners of the globe. In reality, Sara already had a boyfriend, and Kent regarded her as a little sister. But never mind, their story, and those of the other survivors, was heartwarming and inspiring to a world that found too much to despair about in the news. When the session ended, one of the television reporters off-handedly mentioned to Kent that the coverage would change their lives. It was to be so.

On the next day the six went their separate ways. Each of their lives had been inevitably altered. But they felt bound together. They had shared a corner of hell, and they had prevailed. It united them in a way that would endure through their lives. For each of them, only five other persons on earth really understood what they had conquered.

Morten was flown to Copenhagen, Paul Andersson and Elmar Siegel to Estonia, Paul Barney to England, and Kent Harstedt and Sara Hedrenius were taken by helicopter to Huddinge Hospital south of Stockholm. On the evening news in Stockholm it was announced that Kent and Sara, as they came to be known with affection, were arriving at the international airport in Stockholm from the hospital in Finland. Because the story of the promised dinner date made on the sinking hull of the ship had caught the world's fancy, the two became the instant heroes of the tragedy.

In an effort to protect them from the horde of journalists that waited, officials essentially smuggled them into Sweden at night. When they reached Stocholm, the helicopter taxied into a hangar, where an ambulance whisked them to the Huddinge hospital. There along with other survivors they received the same encompassing care they had received in Finland.

At the Huddinge hospital, as they mingled with the other survivors, Kent received a shock. In a group suddenly he recognized the young woman whose red skirt he had stepped on and torn as they escaped the *Estonia*. At the time, she had insisted on going back down the stairwell to retrieve her lost shoe, against his shouted advice. He had been sure she had perished with that decision. Now here she was, one of the few who had not only got out onto the deck, but had made it into the water and through the long night till rescue. As they talked about the incident, it gave a sense of relief to a scene that was etched deeply into his mind.

When they both requested it, Kent and Sara were again put in the same room. "I would never have been able to do this alone," Sara explained. They found it helpful to recount details of the experience, prodding each other's memories as new bits and pieces of the ordeal surfaced in their recollections. The media trumpeted their shared room as further evidence of a fated love that had emerged from one of the tragic events of the century. In fact, the bond they shared was not a romantic one, but as brother and sister. Sara's boyfriend frequently visited. Doctors agreed it was good for them to talk about the tragedy. Time after time they relived the experience of when the *Estonia* went down, trying to work through the emotions of the tragedy. They were the best therapy possible for each other.

The media circus that had followed them in Finland continued at the hospital in Sweden. Hundreds of phone calls and telegrams arrived each day, many of them offering thousands of dollars for interviews. "That's disgusting," said Sara, who was unemployed at the time. Some of the other survivors did accept money for their interviews, and no one blamed them.

But the supposed love story of Kent and Sara was the main focus of the media. The press from all the major nations of the world seemed camped on their doorstep, desperately trying to get inside. The hospital had never seen anything like this, and they kept the survivors sealed off on one floor. So many flowers came to Kent's and Sara's room that they could barely breathe, and the flowers were moved to an empty room next door.

After a few days there was a memorial service at the largest church in Stockholm for those who had perished on the *Estonia*. It was filled with the mourning friends and families of the victims. Swedish officials had made arrangements for the survivors who were able to attend to come from the local hospitals. Kent, on crutches because of the wound in his leg, went with Sara and several others. The Swedish prime minister spoke, along with other dignitaries. It felt terrible,

Kent was to write later, to stand at the end of the services as the announcement was made that the survivors should go out first, with thousands of eyes on them as they slowly made their way outside.

Sara's parents picked her up at the hospital a few days later, with the promise from Kent that they would have their long-awaited dinner in a week or so. Kent found his newly won celebrity status unsettling as he left the hospital and went to his parents' home in southern Sweden. Soon they quit answering the phone and would not respond to a knock on their door unless they could peek and see it was someone they knew. When he moved to his old apartment in Lund, Kent still found himself uneasy as everywhere he went heads turned and stared. He began to feel haunted. Finally he went to Stockholm and registered at a hotel under the name of Henrik Wahlstedt, where with the collaboration of hotel clerks he managed to find some peace.

Three weeks after the *Estonia* catastrophe, on a Friday afternoon Kent and Sara met at the Grand Hotel across the bay from the royal palace in downtown Stockholm for their famous dinner. In deference to the interest of the Swedish people they invited the newspaper *Aftenbladet* and the television news show *Aktuel* to take part for ten minutes of the reunion in suite 419 overlooking the harbor, then ushered them away. They kept the location of the dinner a secret until an hour prior to their meeting to avoid hordes of other media. Then, alone, by candlelight, along with champagne they dined on the Swedish delicacy of tongue-fish, a kind of flounder, with raspberry sorbet as dessert.

Afterwards, they sneaked to an outlying pub, The Tall Man's Hat, where they had invited friends. To their surprise, fifteen of the people from Huddinge hospital who had waited on them hand and foot also showed up. The experience at the pub felt "fantastic," Kent said. For them, it brought a kind of closure to the whole experience.

Of the fifty-four Swedes who survived, twenty-eight lived in and near Stockholm. After a month they arranged to meet regularly and share their experiences. In their first meeting, Kent and Sara invited a woman to sit with them. She was recovering from a broken leg. As she recounted her experience of getting on deck, she told of crying out for a life jacket, and being given one. It was then that Kent and Sara both recognized her as the woman with the broken leg whom they had helped. She remembered Kent telling her, "You're not going to die!" With pangs of guilt Kent recalled that after he had put the life jacket on her, they had left her seated next to the door still crying out for more help. Following that, she had fallen into the sea wearing the life jacket, then had grabbed hold of a trailing rope from a raft and held on until she was pulled into the raft. She was among the last to be rescued. Learning that she had survived added one more piece to the healing process that had begun for Kent and Sara.

25 · WAITING LATE

As the day wore on at the ship terminals in Stockholm and Tallinn, the grim crowd of families and friends waiting for word began to dwindle as hope faded for names to be added to the list of survivors. For Estonians, whose small country is situated in a Baltic crossroads and has thus suffered periodic invasions and conquests throughout history, catastrophe was nothing new. For many older Estonians, indeed, the trauma of the *Estonia* tragedy was reminiscent of another Baltic tragedy in 1944 when thousands of Estonians drowned trying to flee the occupying Soviet army by taking to the sea.

At 1:30 p.m. the list was revised downward again. Fifty-four survivors had been identified in Finland. Seven of these were brought to Sweden for hospitalization, but one died en route. In a weird scenario, that afternoon a young Lithuanian couple arrived at the dock in Stockholm, suitcases in hand, ready to take the evening voyage on the *Estonia* to Tallinn. They had not heard of the catastrophe.

By late night it was announced that one hundred one of those on the ship had been saved. But the identities were not yet known. As the torturous waiting wore on, hope faded little by little. Relatives of those not accounted for broke into sobs or hysterics when it became apparent that their wait was futile. In Stockholm, social workers said that one pregnant woman went into premature labor when she learned that her fiancé was not among the survivors.

Early on that morning, friends called from Denmark and asked the wife of Alexander Voronin whether Vassili, Alexander and Vasya had boarded the ship the previous night. Alexander's wife, Larissa, asked at once whether anything had happened. "No, nothing special," was the answer. But when Larissa turned on the radio, the awful shock came blaring from every station that the *Estonia* had sunk, with few survivors. Instantly she swooned to the floor, stunned almost into paralysis. She could not even speak. When she recovered slightly, she sat for hours by the phone, dreading the news that would arrive. She did not even tell her children, Misha, eleven, or Valentin, five. She sat like a zombie, her world in a shambles. Her husband, her son, her father, all so strong and so loved. It was not possible they had all perished.

Larissa hurried to their Greek Orthodox church, carrying thirty-three candles that had been brought from Jerusalem. She knew that in her faith one was supposed to burn the candles when anything very bad or very good had happened, and that they were to be used sparingly — just a bit at a time, and save the remainder for the future. That day she burned all her candles. After she returned home late in the afternoon , the joyful news arrived that her husband, her son, and her father were all safe, each on a different raft and rescued separately.

By late afternoon, when it became obvious that all who would be rescued had already been saved and there were no more survivors, the revision of the list slowly stopped. Yet, perhaps as frustrating as anything else was the confusion regarding who had survived. For the families waiting to hear on the morning of the sinking, it was maddening to learn that some who had been identified as survivors had actually perished, while others who were listed as dead then phoned from Finland.

A case in point was Avo Pitt, the off-duty captain. *The New York Times* for September 30, two days after the disaster, carried this item: "Officials said one of the vessel's two captains, Avo Piht, an Estonian, was among the 140 confirmed survivors of the sinking. They said that Mr. Piht was believed to be in a hospital in Helsinki, but that he had not yet been interviewed." The most credible account came from a crew member who said she saw him on deck handing out life preservers as the ship went down. Some survivors reported having seen Captain Piht in one of the life rafts, and rumors circulated for days that Piht had intentionally disappeared to avoid prosecution in the tragedy. He never reappeared. The evidence strongly suggests that Piht perished on board the sinking ship.

For some, the wait was rewarding. In midmorning, Elmar Oun emerged smiling from the Estline shipping office. His son, Mikael, the relief truck driver who had taken the photograph from the hull of the sinking ship, had called from Finland to say he had been rescued. "It's like winning the lottery," he shouted to the others. At the home of Mikael Oun's mother, she had been anxiously watching the television screen all day that listed the survivors. Her son's name was not among those who had escaped. At the Rescue Center at Abo in Finland, Mikael was coming from thawing out in a sauna at the hospital when he stopped to watch a television report of the accident. He noticed that his name was not shown among the living, so he quickly borrowed a cellular phone and called home. His mother answered, but she gasped in disbelief when he identified himself.

"Mikael, is that you?"

"Yes, Mom, it's me."

She did not dare believe it was really true, afraid a trick was being played on her. Even when he gave her his personal number, the Swedish equivalent of an American social security number, she would not accept the miracle that he was alive.

"Don't you recognize my voice?" Mikael asked, puzzled. Then he laughed. And it was the laugh that she knew. She was finally convinced.

Among those waiting with dread was Susanna Persson of Hjo, Sweden. For the first 24 hours after the *Estonia* went down, Susanna mourned her husband, thirty-seven-year-old Per-Arne Persson, the father of her three children. After all, not only was he on the official missing list, but Per-Arne had already cheated death once in a ship accident a little more than a year earlier. At that time he had been booked on the Polish passenger ferry *Jan Heweliusz*, which sank in a storm in 1993. Luckily for the truck driver, that time he had engine troubles and had missed the ship sailing.

For six years Per-Arne had been driving trucks through Europe, often traveling by passenger ferry. He had been critical of conditions aboard many of these foreign vessels and had three times filed complaints about the situation on the *Jan Heweliusz*, mainly about drunken crew members. Nothing was done, and that ship sank in a storm shortly afterwards with a loss of fifty-four lives. On that day her husband had sent her a bouquet of roses, and they arrived at the same time she heard on the radio that the ship had gone down. His wife spent tearful hours after the sinking of the Polish ship until she received a phone call from her husband that he had missed the ship and was alive and well. Now he had driven his truck with a load to Estonia and was returning from Tallinn. With three driver friends, he had gone to bed early in his clothes, as was his custom so as to be ready for emergencies.

On this blustery day following the midnight accident, In their home at in Sweden, Susanna woke up shortly after six a.m., turned on her radio and got news of the sinking. Terrified, she kept her children home from school as they waited for more word, floating between hope and despair. All that day they sat bonded to the television set, watching the changing lists of survivors, the recovered dead and those still missing. She kept thinking of the *Jan Heweliusz*, wondering it was possible that Per-Arne could cheat death twice. After sixteen hours her husband's boss phoned to say that he had been rescued. A few hours later Per-Arne himself phoned to say he was safe.

"I had decided to survive," he said from the hospital in Skovde. In his cabin on the fourth deck Per-Arne had been lying on his bunk talking to friends when they heard a crash and the ship tilted. Outside the cabin people were running and crawling up the stairs. He stayed calm and managed to reach the outer deck, which by then was almost lying in the sea. In spite of the people screaming around him, he did not panic. In fact, he decided that to preserve his body heat he would stay on the ship as long as possible.

When the ship began to slip beneath the waves, he spotted a group of life rafts that had automatically inflated, popping to the surface with lights glowing atop their tents. Before he could move, a mountainous wave swept over the hull, lifting him and sending him sprawling to land atop an upside-down life raft and injuring his hip.

Around him the cries for help and roar of the sea were deafening. When he saw a woman's hand reach up over the edge of the raft, he grabbed it to pull her in, but her hand slipped away from him. For four hours Per-Arne lay alone atop the raft, freezing and trying not to get washed away. He began to lose hope, but his thoughts kept turning to Susanna, his nine-year-old daughter and his two thirteen-year-old twin boys. He determined to survive for them. Finally, at a little after six a.m., a Finnish helicopter appeared through the rain, hauled up Per-Arne, and took him to the Coast Guard station at Abo.

Unlike Susanna Persson, most of those waiting for word that day were not so lucky as news arrived of the survivors.

26 · THE CAPTAINS

The competence of *Estonia*'s captain, Arvo Andresson, was of course a major issue in considering the fate of the ship. Captain Andresson enjoyed what might be called a mixed reputation. His men saw him as professional, with tight discipline, and well-liked. At forty years old, he looked like someone Hollywood might cast as a sea captain: tall, handsome, with a dark mustache setting off a chiseled and sun-tanned face — an athlete who exuded leadership and power.

When the Russians withdrew from Estonia a year and a half earlier, the Estonian government entered into a joint ownership of the ship with the Swedish private company, Nordstrom & Thulin. The new company was called Estline, and the ship that was re-christened the *Estonia* began service between the Baltic states and Stockholm, thus breaking Estonia's long isolation. Trade, smuggling and tourism flourished. The shipping line became known as "the lifeline" because it opened the way to the West for the first time in half a century. On even-numbered days the *Estonia* sailed from Stockholm to Tallinn, returning on odd-numbered days. To safeguard their investment, company officers hired two Swedish aides to Andresson to be sure he understood maritime safety.

An experienced Swedish captain named Anders Andersson, whose similar name must have caused some confusion, was delegated to assist the Estonian, Captain Arvo Andresson. For six months they worked together until finally the Swedish captain quit. He claimed later that Arvo Andressen was arrogant and strict on his ship, but overall, not very competent.

Later Swedish investigators, indeed, found much to criticize. Following the accident one Swedish story that may be apocryphal claimed that in his first try at docking in Tallinn as captain of the *Estonia*, Andresson nearly smacked his ship into the dock, then supposedly confessed with embarrassment to his Swedish counterpart, "I sometimes get mixed up about 'starboard' and 'port.'"

After a couple of incidents like the near-disaster at the dock, the Swedish captain Anders Andersson complained to the Swedish owners and asked if they couldn't do something about the Estonian captain. "Yes," replied the owners, "you make damn sure you are on the bridge with him when he docks and leaves!"

However, the tug driver who helped dock the ship in close quarters reported later that after the Estonian captain's first gaffe in docking, he learned quickly and the tugmaster never saw him have problems again. After the tragedy, the Swedish press was quick to blame the Estonian crew, but it must be remembered that the Swedes shared a disdain of Estonians as members of an impoverished nation after such a long period of Russian domination. They saw them as somewhat backward and struggling to catch up with the modern world.

The Estonian Andresson had earlier been captain of the ship *Georg Ots* for nine months, running between Helsinki and Tallinn. This route, however, did not take him out into the more treacherous seas of the open Baltic. He had also commanded ships sailing to Africa and the Mediterranean. With the reputation as the best captain in Estonia, he had been put in charge of modernizing the *Georg Ots* and the *Estonia.*

Arvo Andresson grew up in the harbor town of Parnu on the west coast of Estonia. As a young seaman he moved quickly up the ladder as part of the Soviet trading fleet, serving as an officer on several ships in that fleet. He was then chosen for advanced education in St. Petersburg, where he had graduated with honors. When his country regained its independence with the Soviet breakup, he was regarded as the best seaman in Estonia. Estline officials reported it was natural that he be assigned to command the new company flagship.

According to his wife, Captain Andresson was a perfectionist. For two days before going to sea, he abstained from any alcohol so as to be at his best. As captain, he had visited ports in Europe, Africa, Canada and Cuba. "His only fault was that he was sometimes too tender with us and too strict with his colleagues," his wife, Veronika, who occasionally sailed with him, told an interviewer later. "On board Arvo was a completely different person. Too pedantic, often severe. The life of his sailors was never easy."

On the other hand, the Estonian co-captain, Avo Piht, was reported as thoroughly professional and without Captain Andressen's problems. The Swedish captain helping with the *Estonia* spoke highly of him.

Industrious and ambitious, Piht had become a captain at age 29 after studying both in Estonia and the naval academy in Leningrad. For several years he sailed between Estonia and Africa. He became captain of the *Georg Ots* and then the *St. Patrick*, a ship he loved. In December of 1993 he was moved to the *Estonia*, but without his own crew. He was so saddened by the move, that it made him ill. "Well, life is not meant to be easy," he lamented to his wife.

On the *Estonia* the two officers commanded one trip each. It was the country's flagship, Estonia's largest ship and the pride of the small fleet. Each officer had learned to speak Swedish fluently for the tests in piloting they periodically had to undergo. All communication between the commanders and pilots and traffic control took place in Swedish. Each had a tutor, but Avo Piht had more of a talent for languages.

The critical part of the testing, however, dealt with their knowledge of the route in the Stockholm archipelago. On the fateful trip in September 1994, they were scheduled about daybreak of the following morning to reach the maze of twenty-five thousand Swedish islands through which their route wound. They had to know the names of all the nearby islands, the depths, the lighthouses, the distances between each, where they could anchor, and where the other ships on that route would normally pass them. Given a blank map, they had to be able to place all those in their proper position. At five a.m. that morning, Captain Avo Piht was scheduled for his winter exam. to show that without a pilot he could guide the huge ship almost two football fields long through the reefs and rocks of the archipelago, at times passing only a stone's throw from the cliffs and the picturesque shoreline.

Two men who had qualified as pilots were required to be on the bridge when the ship wound its way through these narrow passageways of the archipelago, so a pilot normally accompanied the captains to help guide them. On this trip, the pilot Juri Aavik had returned after serving aboard another ship for two months. Through the past few months, he and Captain Andresson had become friends, and often spent time together when off duty in Stockholm and Tallinn. There is no sign of Aavik having shown up on the bridge during the critical time, however, and it is likely that he was in his cabin asleep in preparation for his morning duties. He was not among the survivors.

Following the accident, the competence of the Estonian crew was called into question by the Swedish press. The Swedish captain who had helped train Captain Andresson undoubtedly had misgivings about the efficiency of the Estonians. For one thing, he complained, they had been trained under the Soviet system. This meant that if a superior officer was not available, a crewman felt it safer to do nothing about a problem than to do the wrong thing and get in trouble. For instance, on most ships the helmsman slows the speed of the ship according to the conditions of the sea, then informs the captain of what was done. On the *Estonia*, however, he would need permission before lowering the speed.

One fault, according to the Swedish adviser, was that the Estonian crew didn't bother to pack the cars and trucks correctly into the ship's hold. If loaded unevenly, the ship would lean to one side. Of course the *Estonia* carried ballast tanks on each side that could be pumped with water on the high-riding side to add weight to recover the ship's trim. On the fatal night, the unbalanced weight was one of the problems, and may have been a major factor. When the ship left the harbor, it was already leaning slightly to the right in spite of the ballast tanks on the port being filled to correct the trim. That fault was to have dire consequences later.

The Estonian captain earned seven or eight thousand Swedish kronors a month, about thirteen or fourteen hundred American dollars. The crew got about half that. To put that into perspective, however, the average Estonian wage at that time was about two hundred fifty American dollars a month. In that depressed economy, a cabin maid on the *Estonia* earned more than the president of the country.

The ship that went down and riveted the world's attention to television sets on that September night and morning was typical of the dozens of passenger ferries that ply the treacherous northern waters of the Baltic Sea. However, it would be a mistake to consider this ship and others like it as "car ferries" in the American sense of the word. Most Americans think of ferries as the open, flat-bottomed barges that load a couple of dozen cars, such as those that cross between San Francisco and Sausalito in California, a twenty-minute run, or between the Battery in New York and Staten Island.

Instead, around the world more than 4,000 of these ships operate each day, built to carry large numbers of passengers in comfort, often overnight, as well as transporting trucks and cars. In fact, they look like cruise ships and offer many of the same amenities, such as cabins, swimming pools, saunas, several restaurants, gambling casinos, conference rooms and other luxuries.

The *Estonia* was approved to carry 1,400 passengers. Although the bow of the *Estonia* looked like that of any ship, it was in reality a hinged prow raised by hydraulics at the dock. This allowed the watertight ramp to be lowered like a drawbridge so that trucks and cars could roll onto one deck of the ferry. Sometimes these ships are called "ro-ro" ferries — roll on, roll off. The car decks are above the water line because drivers must drive onto the ship from the docks.

What was happening to the front of the ship in those critical minutes during the fatal storm can be conjectured from the evidence later reclaimed from the sunken ship. The previous day Swedish inspectors in Stockholm had examined the door seals and found a few minor cracks, but had declared them to pose no danger. The sounds that were heard by passengers and crew alike that night were apparently the locking devices being torn loose by the force of the waves on a ship that had not slowed appropriately. There is speculation also that the locks may have been weakened over the years by inferior repairs and holes being drilled near the hinges. The major cause of the failure, however, as found by the international investigators, was that the original shipbuilder, the Joseph L. Meyer Company of Germany, had miscalculated the strength needed for the bow-locking device to hold up under the battering of powerful waves. Thus the builder used plates that were too thin to last, and locks that were too weak, they suggested.

When the fifty-four-ton bow visor was torn loose and lost from the ship, it exposed the ramp to the full force of the sea. The ramp itself had watertight seals, but with further pounding of the giant waves it worked loose at the top about three feet, allowing water to pour over it and into the car deck. Those crashing, grinding noises reported by the crew were the sound of the bow visor tearing away. The metal-on-metal clamor as the heavy bow visor crashed against the ramp or side of the ship was undoubtedly what alarmed some of the crew. Only the fury of the storm and the pounding, crashing noises of the waves against the ship masked the deadly impact of these failures. After much searching, the bow visor was found a mile west of the wreck six weeks after the accident.

Aboard on that night, in addition to the 186 crewmen, were at least 803 passengers. However, it was a custom for the staff on board to bring friends along without a ticket. Their names were never written down, nor were small children usually listed as passengers. A short time earlier, for instance, one of the employees brought 20 friends along for a birthday party. Thus, it will never be known how many passengers were aboard. The Estonian government put the number of all those on the ship at 1,049, while most official estimates say 989 sailed that windy evening from Tallinn.

27 · THE ANALYSES

Shortly after the disaster on the *Estonia,* numerous theories emerged as to what caused the deaths of at least 852 human beings that tragic stormy night on the Baltic Sea. Almost one thousand people went aboard the ship that stormy evening, and fewer than one hundred fifty returned to land. Those on the ship were aware of the storm, of course, as it pushed through those mountainous waves. But storms are common in those northern regions in late fall, and such ships are built to withstand them.

Speculation on the streets and in the press ran rampant in the days following the sinking. Headlines in the Swedish and Estonian papers asked if the ship could have hit a World War II mine, or had a collision, or had perhaps been the victim of a bomb plot. Other speculation centered on the Russian Mafia and a drug run gone bad, with the Swedish police waiting to intercept a massive shipment of cocaine in the trucks. The British and Swedish press proposed that the accident was caused by poorly trained Estonian seamen. On the other hand, the Estonian seamen were convinced that the Swedish and Finnish shipping companies would stop at nothing to eliminate competitors on the route between Tallinn and Stockholm.

Another version in Estonia was that the Russians, bitter about Estonia's gaining its independence from the Soviet Bloc, had sunk the ship in order to undermine the international reputation of the new country. One rumor that seemed popular for a time had the *Estonia* hitting a Russian or Swedish submarine or other vessel. In order to keep the secret, the rumors say, those countries would go to any lengths to cover up what really happened.

There were also stories about a small smugglers' boat that the crew had abandoned in the storm and that the huge ship had collided with it. One of the wildest accounts, which was published in the respectable Russian newspaper *Segodnja* on May 24, 1995, claimed that a Mafia group had been attempting to smuggle a truck with forty tons of cobalt in it for making nuclear weapons. The newspaper described a complex plot involving members of the Estonian Parliament and an Estonian who had been a lieutenant colonel in the U.S. Army. According to the account, the smugglers had panicked because the Swedish police learned of the shipment and were waiting to intercept it. They supposedly gave orders for the truck with the smuggled cobalt to be pushed overboard, which would require opening the bow doors and lowering the ramp, which for a ship underway would be not only foolish but suicidal. The Moscow newspaper refused to substantiate any of the claims in the article or to give the true name of the author. Swedish and American officials denied having any knowledge of any such shipment.

Such rumors do not die easily. The *Moscow News* of April 25, 1996 carried a similar report that when the *Estonia* left its home port headed for Stockholm it carried about 240 pounds of heroin and forty tons of cobalt for producing nuclear weapons. But when it appeared Swedish authorities knew of the smuggling, a Russian general in charge of the operation ordered the captain to dump the cargo. In order to save his life, so the story goes, Captain Andresson ordered the ship's bow to be opened. An investigator of the tragedy contends that a telephone call between the Russian general and the ship ordered the dumping. On the face of it, the charge seems foolish, and there is no direct evidence that anything like that occurred.

When the lost bow visor was located and brought to shore a few weeks later, examination showed that there had been no bomb or mine or collision. However, because human nature loves a conspiracy theory, there were considerable numbers of Europeans who believed, and even today believe, that the International Investigation Commission was simply involved in some kind of massive cover-up.

By September 1995, such rumors were mostly put to rest by the findings of the International Investigation Commission after extensive research involving models and computerized simulations in a pool in Goteborg in southern Sweden. Their research showed that the weak construction of the visor locks, combined with inordinately heavy seas, was the major cause of the tragedy. Some later findings, however, may have cast doubt on their findings — as will be noted.

For the first day or two following the accident, some newspaper reports suggested that survivors might still be alive in air pockets within the ship. Doctors involved in the rescue effort first made the air pocket suggestion. The rumor then grew. Russia's TASS news agency followed up the idea by quoting the noted Russian submarine designer Anatoly Kuteinikov in St. Petersburg as saying, "Hundreds of people remaining inside the sunken ferry can be saved and should be saved." Kuteinikov claimed that an air cushion always accompanies any shipwreck and might allow survivors inside the *Estonia* to stay alive for at least a week. The emotional debate in the media caused by this report was short-lived, but fervent.

Other experts quickly contradicted the Russian submarine expert. They pointed out that the high pressures at the 240-foot depth of the sunken ship would crush the steel panels, and that a combination of such high pressures and the frigid temperatures of 4 or 5 degrees centigrade at that depth would mean death in only a few minutes. Even if a person did survive at first in such a trapped air chamber, most authorities estimated the person could survive no more than thirty minutes. The mental pictures such reports engendered must have been heart-rending for families and friends of those lost and unaccounted for, with long-lasting results in some loved ones.

After a week, the International Investigation Commission sent underwater robots down to the sea bottom where the *Estonia* lay on its side in the sea bed about 270 feet deep. The resulting sixteen hours of video showed the bow visor missing, the ramp pushed part way in, with the locking devices that held the bow visor shut ripped out of the metal that held them. These catches, called Atlantic locks, appeared to be the root cause of the trouble because they were all torn loose. This discovery answered the question of whether the locks had been fastened or not. They were wrenched from their metal moorings, leaving the ramp at the mercy of the heavy seas.

Then, after two years of study, the International Investigation Commission ruled that the original construction of the ship had been faulty, with the metal too weak to hold the Atlantic visor locks under the stress of a large storm. "The locking device was not designed as strongly as it should have been, according to calculations," the Stockholm newspaper *Dagens Nyheter* quoted the international commission's findings.

Thus the ship's critical bow visor, the huge, top-hinged door at the front of the ship that swung up to allow vehicles to be driven into and out of the ship's car deck, was torn away by the force of the extremely heavy seas that pounded the *Estonia* that night. The commission found that the shipbuilder, the Joseph Meyer shipyard in Papenberg, Germany, did not have proper blueprints for the lock when building the ferry in 1980. This resulted in the company's underestimating how strong the locks should be built and anchored. The report said the lock was built to withstand only half the pressures that it endured that night when the waves pounded so heavily against the bow. That, said the report, combined with excessive speed in the face of the storm, cost at least 852 lives.

Nevertheless, the sealed ramp should have held the water out. The pictures showed a yard-wide gap at the top of the boarding ramp where the waves had pounded the ramp loose without the protection of the bow visor. With the engines going at full force, this scooped up water into the car deck, much as a whale would do swimming with its mouth wide open. With water pouring into the car deck, the ship could not stay stable long. Swedish naval experts cited the "free surface effect" in which a rapidly moving mass of liquid is able to upset the stability of a container. Water sloshing in the car deck would be the equivalent of someone trying to carry water on a cookie sheet, with any motion pushing the liquid to one side and increasing the tilt of the ship until it could not right itself.

Some specialists blame such accidents on the construction of these passenger ferries, which unlike ocean liners, do not have interior bulkheads to contain leaks. Once water gets into a passenger ferry, there is nothing to stop it from sloshing back and forth and destabilizing the ship.

Ninety-four bodies were recovered. With the 137 survivors, that meant that at least 758 of the bodies were still missing, most of them probably still within the confines of the ship.

Almost immediately a furor arose about what should be done with the ship and its victims. Originally the Swedish government hinted that the ship would be raised and the victims then be buried on land. Most of the families of the victims campaigned for this measure, but it soon became apparent that the cost for salvaging the ship would be more than one hundred million dollars. In addition, to try to bring out the trapped bodies was ruled unfeasible. There would be great danger, the Swedish government claimed, and considerable psychological trauma for those divers who would be involved in the locating the bodies in the cabins.

In 1996 the three-country commission from Sweden, Estonia and Finland in charge of the *Estonia* investigation decided to make a tomb of the sunken ship at the bottom of the Baltic Sea. The plans were to seal the ship with concrete in order to preserve the sanctity of the tomb to keep out scavenging divers and curiosity seekers. The wreck would be covered with concrete where it lay to make of it a giant mausoleum. It would be, a spokesman said, like a giant blanket covering a coffin. But the survivors and families of the victims objected vehemently, noting that the investigation was not yet completed and to cover the ship would be to hide needed evidence.

Complicating the whole matter was a massive lawsuit in the international courts, brought by the victims' families against the shipbuilders and Estline, the company that owned the ferry. It was one of the largest lawsuits in European history, and years later was still working its way through the courts. Because of the pending lawsuit, the plan to cover the wreck with concete was put on hold for several years.

In the meantime, other questions arose for shocked observers and the investigation commission. Why were only 26 of the 137 survivors from the *Estonia* women? According to those who lived through the experience, the old adage of "Women and children first" seemed no longer to apply. Sixty percent of those who went aboard the *Estonia* were women, while they made up only 22 percent of those rescued. There are reasons, of course. Men in the Nordic countries serve a mandatory term in the military services and are taught to climb vertical walls such as those offered by the ship that quickly turned on its side. Also, the sinking of the *Estonia* occurred in minutes, and those who made the wrong split-second decision paid with their lives. Most of those who survived were young and strong enough to be able to pull themselves up vertical stairways. Most women did not have the arm strength necessary to get up the barriers to the outer deck.

Yet, in spite of their Victorian reputation as "the weaker sex," nature has generally provided women with the ability to survive better than men, especially in situations of long-term duress. Nature has prepared women biologically to better withstand cold and famine. In the hectic events of the *Estonia* disaster, it appears that strength, agility and determination were the ultimate factors — especially the determined optimism, as exemplified by Kent Harstedt and Sara Hedrenius. Of course, a major factor was the good fortune of being located near an exit to the seventh deck.

An unknown number of children were aboard the *Estonia* with their mothers. Because children under the age of six were not recorded on boarding, we will never know how many there were. Imagine what mothers with children faced as they tried to climb up a nearly impossible escape way, tugging a child or two. Instinct and compassion obviously made that choice for most of them, to stay together and hope for the best.

"There is no law that says women and children first," Roger Koken of the International Maritime Organization told *The Times* of London following the *Estonia* tragedy. "It was an idea that had come from the age of chivalry and conjured up images of the *Titanic*, with fathers passing babies to their wives and then going down with the ship. The *Titanic* took several hours to sink. They had time to be gentlemanly." But he also noted that, lest one romanticize that tragedy, the greatest percentage of survivors on the *Titanic* were from the first-class passengers.

Aboard the *Titanic*, 97 percent of the women in first class survived, along with 87 percent of the ones in second class and 50 percent in third class. It may be argued that it was the end of an age, the twilight of Victorian class structure and sensibilities. On the *Estonia*, of course, there was no class structure. Yet there were luxury cabins on the sixth deck, and the cheapest cabins were below the car deck at the very bottom of the ship.

Of the 137 people who survived the sinking, there were 111 men and twenty-six women. Of those who were found dead, fifty-three were men and forty-one were women. For those missing and presumed drowned, there were 343 men and 422 women. Thus there were forty-nine percent men and fifty-one percent women on board, but of the survivors, only nineteen percent were women. This disparity, of course, was caused by the swift sinking of the ship, the strength needed to get up the stairways, and the panic of the hurried circumstances that resulted at times in the survival of the strongest. Of the 137 survivors, forty-three belonged to the crew. This means that twenty-three percent of the crew and thirteen percent of the passengers survived. Obviously the crew had a better chance to escape because of their emergency drills, their cabin locations near the seventh deck exits, and their youth and physical fitness.

Another major question dealt with the rafts. "How is it possible that so many people died after reaching the presumed safety of the rafts?" was a question that plagued all those concerned about maritime safety. Theoretically, those who reached a raft that was designed to protect them from the weather should have been able to make it through the night. The equipment was fourteen years old, the same age as the ship. Yet the rafts met the requirements for maritime safety, according to the International Maritime Organization.

Just getting the life rafts out of their containers was a difficult task. On the slanting deck of the sinking ship groups of people gathered around the steel life raft containers, tearing with their bare hands at the canvas straps that held them shut. In the dim light the instructions were unreadable. In some spots, no one knew how to get the rafts out of their containers. Crew members had been trained to unloose the bands and free the rafts, but not all the containers had a crewman present.

Atti Hakanpaa, forty-three, found that he was in darkness in the place on deck where he emerged, but he found his way to the life raft barrels.

"There were probably forty people up there," he recalled later. "No one had a clue how to open them. But luckily one of them had a knife, so we could cut off the lines and get out one of the rafts."

Later, as the ship sank, the other rafts automatically popped to the surface. The heavy wind blew some rafts away empty.

"There were only three of us in the raft when the ship went down," Atti said, "and we were only five or ten yards from there. I was very worried that we could be pulled down in the whirlpool, but nothing happened. Instead, we heard a bunch of screaming people. Several of them swam toward our raft. We managed to pull six of them aboard."

There were other problems in how the rafts functioned after they were in the water. A large percentage flipped over in the rough seas, forcing survivors to perch precariously while waves washed over them. According to the international seafaring conventions, the rafts should have each carried one100-foot rope with a life buoy ring, a knife, a device for bailing water out, an anchor, a first-aid kit, a whistle, two light rockets with parachutes, three red torches, a smoke buoy, an electric lamp for signaling, a signal mirror, a table of rescue signals, 1.5 liters of water for each person, and an instruction booklet on dealing with hypothermia. Much of this equipment was apparently missing from the rafts carried by the *Estonia*.

While many of the survivors mention lighting red flares or sky-rockets found in their rafts, little of the other recommended equipment was available. The rope with attached life ring would have been particularly valuable in pulling in those survivors struggling in the water. Those rafts lucky enough to have a crew member aboard were more likely to find the emergency equipment, for they had been drilled in its location and use. Afterwards, one survivor testified that they searched the raft for food or a device to pump air into the raft, but all they could find was plastic bags. There were some instructions on the bottom of the raft, but these were under knee-deep water, and they were only in Swedish.

When the *Estonia* went down, the encased rafts automatically popped to the surface and inflated. Most accounts say the rafts were plentiful, although getting over the high sides was a problem for most people already exhausted from struggling in the water.

"Climbing into the raft was even more difficult than I had imagined," one survivor recalls. "The waves kept sweeping me off all the time. The only person in the raft who could help me was a member of the crew. I begged him to help me get up into the raft but he couldn't. The rope ladder had somehow got stuck inside the raft and we simply had to climb over the side of the raft, which was about two feet above the water. I tried to get into the raft in every possible way. At last I succeeded in getting my feet into the raft. I can't imagine how I did it. Without the help of another person it is impossible to survive in such a storm. Only a healthy, athletic person can do it."

According to international rules, all ships built after 1986 must be equipped with life rafts that have ladders to make entrance easier. In Sweden the rule has been honored since it was passed, but the *Estonia* was built in 1980. Many of the survivors say that the ladders were missing from their rafts, or that those inside didn't know about them in the darkness, or were unable to get them loose.

In addition to the rafts, the *Estonia* carried 10 sturdy lifeboats hanging in davits from deck eight. Because of the severe slant of the decks as the ship turned on its side, the crew was unable to get any of these launched. However, as the ship went down at least two of the rigid lifeboats must have popped loose, for film of the rescues show at least two wooden life boats upside down or filled with water. Some survivors hung onto the keel of an overturned boat and were rescued. Tom Johnsson, the police official from Stockholm who survived, told of floating in his life vest and seeing a lifeboat, but explained that it was "broken." Then a rubber life raft appeared and he was pulled into it.

What were the lessons learned from the *Estonia* to make sea travel safer in the future? One major flaw was the design of the rafts, which tipped over in the turbulent seas before the survivors could even get aboard them. There are now rafts that turn themselves upright automatically, and which have pumps to remove the water. But critics say that unless government regulations mandate such equipment, the companies choose not to spend the extra thirty to forty percent that these rafts cost.

In meetings following the shipwreck, the Nordic countries also agreed that future rafts should bear the names of their ships and a number, visible from the air, to keep track of rafts in a disaster that have already been checked. Much time was lost when helicopter frogmen descended to check rafts that had already been found empty by other searchers. Other steps were also taken to ensure greater familiarity and cooperation between nations in sea emergencies.

As might be expected, several lawsuits against the builders of the *Estonia* and the shipping line made their way through the courts in Europe, some still pending as of this writing. The compensation offered to victims from the insurance companies early on was $24,000 to each survivor. Relatives of those who died were to receive between $6,000 and $169,000 each. In 1996, the insurance company paid the crew members about $18,000 each, while the 400 dependents of crew members who perished shared about $11 million.

The *Estonia* was insured by the Skuld Company of Norway. In fact, the chairman of the international support group for the *Estonia* victims, Gunnar Bendreus of Stockholm, claimed that the Estline company made money from the accident. It was insured, he charged, for $27 million more than it was worth. "It is disgusting that money is being made off the grief of others," he said.

Advocates of the *Estonia* victims' families and the survivors demanded that the millions of dollars in profits paid in insurance to the owners be divided among the survivors and victims' families, rather than to stockholders as the company planned. Little attention was paid to those demands, however, by the company. Other pending lawsuits were expected to drag through the international courts for years.

The band that was playing in the ship's lounge that night was Henryk Goj's Orchestra. Of the five musicians, three died in the accident. Originally from Poland, Goj and his wife had lived outside of Stockholm for many years. Ten years earlier Goj had started his orchestra, playing at bars and hotels across Sweden. But during bad times he worked the boats to Estonia and Finland. His wife and the families of the other musicians had a major problem because of the way Estline, the owners of the *Estonia*, paid their wages. Because it was under Estonian registry, they were paid out of an account in Estonia, which meant they avoided Swedish income taxes. It also meant they were being paid illegally and were thus uninsured, unlike the crew members. Normally a work-related death in Sweden paid relatives about $36,000.

The headquarters of the Estline company were in Stockholm, probably because most passengers were Swedish. The ship was registered both in Estonia and Cypress, apparently at the request of the bank lending the money for its purchase as a protection against creditors.

After being built in Germany in 1980, for its first eight years the *Estonia* was owned by the Viking lines of Finland and sailed under the name *Viking Sally*. Then in 1988 it was bought by Silja Lines and used the name *Silja Star* and two years later became the *Wasa King* before it was sold to Nordstrom & Thulin and the Estonian government and was renamed the *Estonia* in 1992 for the Tallinn-Stockholm route. Business for the company was good and growing. In 1994 passenger travel on the *Estonia* was up thirty-one percent from the previous year.

But some concerns had already been raised about the safety of such vessels. In 1987, a similar ship, the *Herald of Free Enterprise*, had sunk in a storm in the English Channel off Zeebrugge, Belgium, with the loss of 193 lives. The all-important bow door had inadvertently been left partly open. The disaster had erupted a swirl of controversy about the safety of such ships. One of the results was new international regulations that required proper alarms and television for monitoring the bow doors from the bridge. A Safety of Life at

Sea conference in 1990 had drawn up a code whose provisions would guarantee that a ship could remain upright for forty-five minutes after a collision. Although the *Estonia* carried television monitors, most of the regulations had not been carried out. On ships around the world such regulations were — and still are — widely ignored because of the costs involved to comply. The *Estonia* disaster, with the ship going down so quickly, gave dramatic evidence of the need for greater compliance to the regulations.

Overall, apart from the tragic loss of life and human suffering involved, the accident to a modern ship that most people believed couldn't sink brought a shattering of confidence in modern advances. At a time when men had traveled to the moon, the assumption had grown that if we had conquered space surely we were now in charge of the earth and the seas. Just as when the *Titanic* went down, people's faith in technology and progress was called into question. If the *Estonia* was the lifeline for those who lived in Estonia, opening doors to a vision of a better life, that doorway and all the other modern promises suddenly looked not so worthy of trust.

28 · SCANDINAVIAN TRIANGLE

Two and a half weeks after the sinking of the *Estonia*, the Finnish search ship *Tursas* showed a giant metal object on its sonar monitors that looked like the visor of a ship. For seventeen days, the *Tursas* had been prowling the area in search of the missing part of the ship that held the clue to the mystery of the sinking. Repeatedly the sonar had sent pinging pictures of metal objects that turned out to be pieces of other ships gone to the bottom in other times.

On the afternoon of October 18, however, a robot video camera proved that this was indeed the missing bow visor from the wreck of the *Estonia*. The missing part of the bow, which swung upward on hinges to let automobiles and trucks enter and leave by a ramp, lay in the sea mud in 240-feet-deep water a mile west of the sunken giant. This was the fatal failure, the crucial part of the ship that was ripped away by the potent force of huge, storm-driven waves. With that visor gone, the watertight ramp was then wrenched by the force of the waves so that a gap of about three feet opened at the top, enough to let the sea water flow in to the car deck like water over a dam.

Plunging ahead into the waves at high speed with that gap in the ramp, with the sea pouring in, it was inevitable that the car deck was quickly awash in hip-deep water that destabilized the ship. As the water sloshed to the starboard side, it finally sent the ship lurching into an angle from which it could not return. It happened in a region that for at least a century had been known as "the ships' graveyard." Scandinavian seamen in the nineteenth century knew that the area near the island of Uto where the *Estonia* sank was dangerous and mysterious. In 1816 the sailing ships *Bellona* and *Furst Blucher* sank there, followed by *Leonora* in 1824, *Frieja* in 1846, *Wilhelm* in 1849, *Hanna* in 1862, *Hoppet* in 1869, *Fortuna* in 1874, *Frida* in 1880, *Eclipse* in 1881, and *Ilma* in 1890.

The twentieth century shows no better record. In the 1920s, nine sailing or motor vessels went down in the area. During world War II the Finnish warship *Ilmaren* sank in 1941 for unknown reasons southeast of Uto with 247 lives lost. In 1944, the Allied forces sank a German submarine in the Uto archipelago. In 1947, the *Park Victory* en route from Rotterdam to Turku, Finland, sank near Uto with fifty hands missing. By that time seaman were beginning to call the area "the Bermuda Triangle of the Baltic." In fact, in 1946 the motor vessel *Salla* sank there, followed by the *Sparta* in 1947, the *Rhein* in 1958, the *Tercia* in 1962, the *Torsholma* in 1967, the *Ostersjon* in 1968, the *Johan Kolb* in 1974, and the *Simson* in 1978.

It is small wonder that the Finnish ship searching for the missing bow visor of the *Estonia* kept finding so many sunken relics. And only four days following the *Estonia* tragedy, a Finnish cargo ship, the *Gehrwinder II*, hit rocks and went down in that area, but with all hands saved.

The site of the wreck of the *Estonia* has been of continuing interest in the Baltic. Not only do memorial groups plan annual pilgrimages to remember those who died, but constant rumors of mysterious divers planning to scavenge the site cropped up on a fairly regular basis. In 1995, a former diving instructor in the Soviet army stood at the railing of the *Estonia*'s sister ship, the *Mare Balticum*, which now plies the same route between Tallinn and Stockholm. With diving friends, he was planning to dive to retrieve cash, jewels and alcohol in the gift shops. When he leaked his plans to a journalist of the Latvian newspaper *Segodnja*, that newspaper published them and the plan was aborted. A Finnish magazine *Nykyposti* reported_in June 1995 that several groups of people from Estonia and Latvia were planning to send divers to bring up goods that could still be used. Yet after a year the Finnish radar and the Swedish ship guarding the site had registered no attempts to violate the sanctity of the sunken ship.

The wreck is in international waters, but by 1997 formal legal protection to the site had been enacted to make it illegal to disturb the wreck.

The establishment of the place into a peaceful maritime sepulcher has not been without controversy. Gunnar Bendreus, chairman of the International Support Group of the Survivors of the *Estonia,* decried the efforts of some of the media to exploit the interest in the wreck. For instance, in April of 1995 a Swedish television station showed video material that had been taken inside the wreck when divers went down to investigate the possibilities of bringing out the dead.

Some eighty hours of video was shot of the venture, but only short segments were broadcast, and no bodies were shown. The video pictured divers going in through a window, moving through the restaurant, and looking into several cabins.

Bendreus and others protested that families of the victims were repulsed by these intrusions into what should have been sacred territory. Their pleas for protection of the site bore fruit.

So the wreck of the *Estonia* lies at the bottom of the frigid Baltic Sea, encased now with a covering of concrete as a barrier from intrusion, a silent and eerie tomb. As such, it has joined the *Titanic* and the other ships large and small that through the centuries have lost their battles with an unforgiving sea.

29 · WE HAVE TO MAKE PEACE WITH THE SEA

Most of the victims of the *Estonia* tragedy were from Sweden or Estonia, two small and close-knit societies. When word of the catastrophe flashed across the Baltic, it became a collective national trauma that few living citizens had ever known. In the capital cities particularly, there was hardly a person who did not know someone lost on the ship. More than half the passengers came from Sweden, sending the nation of eight million into mourning.

"It is a human tragedy beyond belief," said Swedish Prime Minister Carl Bildt in Turku, Finland, where he was visiting survivors. "We haven't been at war in a very long time … there is no comparison I can think of."

Indeed, eighty-year-old Swedish resident Sonja Herkfelt put the tragedy in perspective. "We haven't lost so many people since Charles XII returned from fighting in Norway," she said, and added after a pause, "I think that was in 1780."

The Finnish press noted that there was a difference between Sweden and Estonia in how the two nations reacted to the tragedy that affected them both so deeply. Two weeks after the accident Estonian society seemed to remain paralyzed with mourning. All else going on in the world was of no consequence, only what happened on board the ship. The symbols of death, the rituals that commemorated it, the nearness of its presence — all these permeated Estonia as the people openly mourned and wept. In Sweden, life went on. A trifle more sadly, but much as before, even in the small communities that were so decimated by the losses in the tragedy.

For the Estonians, the depth of their grief was reflected in the rumors that swept through the country day after day following the sinking. There were stories of Estonians receiving phone calls from the bowels of the ship, supposedly from relatives who had survived in air pockets in the ship and calling on their cellular phones. These ghostly callers pleaded to be rescued by submarine.

For the Estonians, a people who had survived invasion and occupation time after time, this sea disaster was viewed as a natural part of life, something that could be neither predicted nor avoided. It was to be mourned, but accepted as part of the natural order of things. On the other hand, the Swedes began to search for someone to blame. Whatever had happened, the Swedes asked what could be done to remedy it, in order to avoid such problems in the future.

For those who had been fortunate enough to have the will, the stamina, and the luck to survive Europe's greatest peacetime sea disaster of the century, their lives were forever changed. Aulis Lee, who with his wife made up the only married couple to survive the accident, went back to sea one month after the accident. This was on the *Mare Balticum*, which replaced the *Estonia* on the Tallinn-Stockholm run. After a short time, however, Aulis Lee opted to change to another ship, the *Tallink*.

As for changes in his life, the thirty-year-old Lee says, "We do not make huge plans. We are satisfied with what we have. I have had so much luck in my life … the moment I met Aina, or simply each new day I can see. … I have no reason to be afraid of the sea. In case of a plane crash, you don't have a chance, but you can always do something at sea." Aulis is not without evidence that he is lucky: he has been in three shipwrecks on three different ships and survived them all.

His wife, Aina, traveled with him to Sweden two months after the *Estonia* catastrophe. "I was obstinate enough!" she says. "Both on the way there and back I did not sleep a wink. Even now I don't feel safe on a ship." The couple has two children, Kris, who was one year old at the time of the accident and Elise, who was five.

Two years after the accident of the *Estonia*, the insurance company paid Aina Lee as a passenger aboard the ship the 250,000 Estonian crowns for her sufferings, about 20,000 American dollars. Along with her husband's insurance money as a crew member, they were able to build a home.

For Wanda and Holger Wachmeister, the Swedish brother and sister who both survived, the disaster has not made them afraid of the sea. "On the contrary," Wanda said afterwards. "It let me live. Today, I feel like I am here for a purpose, something I'm needed for, but I don't know yet what it is. And I am one who realizes how fragile our existence is." Her brother, Holger, remained determined to return to Estonia and start up his business. When he went, he traveled by ship. His bond with the Estonians, rather than be weakened by the *Estonia* disaster, has been strengthened. "It feels like I have become part of their history," he said.

In that country, among the most mourned was the Estonian singing star, Urmas Alender. In honor of him, Virve Asila, the poet with whom he was collaborating on an album, published the volume *The Bird of the Soul*. It is dedicated to the memory of Alender. In it these lines appear:

> ... *half of my heart died on that day*
> *when the icy whirlpool took you with it* ...

will you truly never come home from there?
  I will throw the ashes that once have been poetry,
into the sea ...
It will reach You — and maybe then I will hear Your
    voice sing my songs.

Alender's father believes his son's fate was destined. "I think you can never escape your fate. It is all written down in the Great Book. In my dreams I have seen Urmas alive and well."

On a green hill in Tallinn, Estonia, overlooking the sea there is a White Cross, dedicated to those who went down with the *Estonia*. On a summer day in 1996 Estonian documentary movie producer Valeria Kaspar approached an old woman in black who had bowed her head at the memorial. "My son's music teacher, Urmas Alender was on that ship," the woman explained. "He taught singing to my son. You know, he seemed so close, like my own son. He could sing of things I thought about and felt. And he always sang in the Estonian language." She was a cleaning woman who, at age sixty-nine, could barely get by with her pension money and her job.

"I come here often," she said, "and I always feel tears come to my eyes."

Hele Mottus, the salesgirl from the ship, survived the sinking but for months suffered from injuries received as she left the ship. During her stay at the hospital she had surgery on her foot and was unable to walk on her own for several months. Her husband, Rene, received money for a plane ticket to fly to Sweden to be with his wife in the hospital. During all the ordeal of the sinking and the terrible night in the raft, she knew she was carrying the couple's first child. The boy, Robin, was born seven months after the accident. Some in the press dubbed the child "The Miracle Baby" because of the circumstances of his mother's survival.

"He helps me to overcome all the horrible things that have taken place," Hele says now.

Her co-worker on the ship, Timmo Vosa, was on crutches for two months as his legs healed. But there were other and deeper wounds that were not healed. When he was able, he went back to work on the *Mare Balticum*, the sister ship to the *Estonia*. After one week, however, following a rough passage, he went to the shipping office and told them he could no longer sail. The haunting memories and the pounding fears were too much. By the following year he was working as a driver for the Japanese Embassy in Tallinn. The wages were considerably less than on his job at sea, but he felt it was a necessary change.

After the accident, thirty-year-old Margus Treu, the engineer who escaped up the ship's funnel, found some changes in his life. "I have started to cherish the things that I have and the people who love me and care about me," he said a year later. "I am happy to have my family, friends, and acquaintances. You never know when the last time is that you see another person."

He is back on the sea again, as fourth mechanic on the *Mare Balticum*, plying the same route between Tallinn and Stockholm. "It was a great feeling to be in familiar surroundings again. Staying at home was driving me crazy," he says. "I don't sleep as peacefully as I used to, yet I have refused the help of psychologists. But I am an optimist and am able to overcome sorrow quite quickly."

The three-generation Russian family that lived through the *Estonia* tragedy faced a jubilant reunion when they returned home intact. The grandfather. Vassili, during a celebration dinner was told by the grandmother, "Well, let's have a wedding now!" The priest had asked her if she had been married in church and advised her to do so.

Vassili did not yield on that issue, but did say, "We are going to celebrate our birthdays twice a year now, one on the day of our birth, the other on the 28th of September."

In the days following the ship disaster, a solemn Estonian Prime Minister Mart Laar asked his people to forgive the sea. "The sea has treated us severely," he said. "But we are a maritime people, and we have no life without the sea. We have to make our peace with the sea."

For Risto Ajassaar, the dancer with the troupe of nine just beginning a three-month engagement on the *Estonia* that night, there was no forgiving. As one who formerly loved watching the waves, he now avoids the sea. He will never take another ship, he says. The last time he saw his manager, the woman who led him to safety up the back stairs to the outer deck and saved his life, was at her funeral. She never made it into a life raft. Instead of sailing again, he took work as a used-car salesman in Tallinn. Nor will Ajassaar dance again. Physically he is able, but dancing brings a flood of recollections he cannot bear to relive; it evokes too-painful memories of his friends he lost in the dark waves.

Some were touched in different ways. Einar Kukk, the only surviving officer from the bridge that fatal night, denied interviews to the press following the accident. At his home in Tallinn, he still suffers aches when he rises in the morning, but he has maintained his cheerful demeanor. He still complains that the Estonian government did not treat the survivors fairly. When he was flown from Finland, he says, he arrived at 11 p.m. without even money for a phone call and had to beg use of a phone to call his wife to come pick him up. He received compensation, but he believes the Estonians were given less than other citizens. "Why?" he asks with a raised eyebrow. "Are we Estonians cheaper, second-rate people?" Following the sinking, he went back to sea, working for Estline again. But he was insulted that he had to compete for his position, and when the opportunity arose he took a job as a marine manager on shore for a different company.

As for his experiences the night the *Estonia* went down, he strangely recollects them with some relish. He never turned to God, he says with pride. Being brought up in the Soviet times, he had not learned to pray. But he never lost hope, and he concentrated all his thoughts on simply surviving. It was Kukk who communicated with the Swede Anders Ericson, who was trapped beneath their raft, filling him in on any possible rescue efforts that appeared on the horizon.

From it all, Kukk emerged with some shocking views. "I would never have believed that such a ferry could sink," he says. "Still, I liked the *Estonia* catastrophe! I liked it a lot! I like extremities, I really do! I like to let the adrenaline flow into my blood. Just a few days ago I went out to sea by a motor boat. There were fourteen-foot waves and the boat was close to turning over. It was horrifying, but at the same time I was proud I came out of the situation."

Now he proudly keeps as mementoes the boots, the trousers and coat that helped save his life. Kukk is one of those men who courts danger for the rush of finally conquering, of surviving.

For others, the recollections are more bitter. What happened in the Baltic Sea that night left an inconsolable void in the life of Kerstin Henriksson. As she sits in her home in the small community of Vasteras, Sweden, she thinks of what might have been. Her husband, Henry, and her thirty-seven-year-old son Per-Olav, hesitated to take the trip on the *Estonia* without a Swedish crew. She was to have accompanied her husband on the trip but decided against it because the weather was bad. So her son went in her place. "He did not want to go," she complains now, "but the travel agents convinced him it was safe." On the day after the tragedy, a letter arrived addressed to her husband from the travel agency. It read: "Welcome home! We hope the trip was pleasant. Hope you will travel with us again." Kersten Henriksson now suffers feelings of guilt that her son, their only child, got her ticket and the fate that went with it.

In a different way another traveler who stayed home remembers the journey he almost made. Swedish legal juries are made up of professionals who exercise judgment and negotiation skills to earn a living. It is a profession. Erik Rosenqvist, sixty-seven, was a member of one such association of jurors from the city of Uppsala. His jurors' association was invited by a similar Estonian group to come visit. Rosenqvist and his wife, Kersten, had planned to go, but they were informed that the Estonian association could host only twenty-six members. Because the Swedish group was double that, not everyone could go. One man prayed that he might be allowed to be included, so Rosenqvist and his wife relinquished their place and remained at home, even though he was one of the leaders and usually went on such excursions.

"Sometimes I think of a person I met in August before the sinking," he remembers. "I told her, 'When you retire, I think you should take your husband and get out on the sea.'"

"'Yes, we are going to Estonia soon to celebrate our fifty-year anniversary,' she said, 'and I am really scared. I don't know how to swim.'"

"'Have you ever heard of any big boat which has sunk? You will eat and drink well.' I said. Later I heard that in the catastrophe she went up on deck and did not jump. Afterwards I regretted those words."

Rosenqvist took up sailing in 1967. He still spends most of his free time at sea in his own boat.

Leeni Lett, age fifty-five, a cleaning woman in Tallinn, lost her daughter, Kaja, in the tragedy, along with Kaja's husband, Aiva, and their two children — including her favorite granddaughter, two-year-old Krete.

Later she wrote to a man she believes is a reincarnated saint of the Buddhist religion, Sai Baba. In her letter she explains that Krete had phoned her a month after the sinking, on October 26, 1994, at 4:32 p.m. Then her letter asked the one she regards as a saint to perform a miracle: "I am not asking any material benefits, only for Krete to come back to me and fill all of our lives with love. It would be God's miracle that would make the whole country of Estonia think and turn towards spirituality."

Lett is sure that Krete phoned her and repeated her pet name for her grandmother. "I was given to understand that she is alive. that is, her soul is alive and with God. You can't imagine the influence on me!"

Kaja worked reclaiming, repairing, and selling second-hand clothes, earning less than a hundred dollars a month. But she and her husband had a dream of opening a store selling fishing equipment. Now every day Leeni Lett burns candles in their home in memory of her daughter's family. At Lett's next birthday celebration, she fixed traditional Estonian dishes: sauerkraut with sausages, meat jelly with potatoes, and of course potato salad. In Estonia, a party hardly ever takes place without these dishes. Then the whole family went to the cemetery where they had erected a white stone in memory of their lost ones. Partly through her efforts there is now a memorial there to all the *Estonia* victims.

In the Swedish city of Norrkoping, where fifty-six retirees took their last excursion aboard the Estonia, on the following Sunday 900 candles were lighted in the packed Hedvig church to honor each of those who perished. It was, as one witness described it, "overwhelmingly beautiful — and terrible."

The lives lost in the sinking were but a small fraction of the others forever affected by the tragedy. Seven-year-old Heidi Kukk — no relation to the only surviving officer, Einar Kukk — went to live with her grandfather and grandmother in the Estonian town of Hiiu outside of the capital of Tallinn. Both her mother and father went down with the *Estonia*.

"I think my mom and dad are down in the ocean somewhere, drinking coffee," she said shortly after the accident. "But I know they will not come home any more. My grandma and grandpa told me everything that happened with *Estonia*. I have started school. It is a special class for children who like dancing and singing.

"Sometimes I cry during the nights, but not too often. I am going to live with grandma and grandpa now. And I have all my things and all my teddy bears in my new bed there. And yesterday morning when grandpa combed my hair, he did it exactly like my mom used to do it. It felt the same way. When I told my grandpa, he became a little bit weird."

Tom Johnsson was one of only three of the sixty-eight police officials aboard the *Estonia* to survive. On the following Sabbath, outside a red wooden church dating back to the 1700s in Skansen, a part of Stockholm, a parade of police cars drove up and dropped off mourners. The police chief read with a steady voice the Old Testament account of the Lord sending his angel to rescue Daniel from the den of lions. He kept his emotions intact until the mourners rose to slowly file from the church. Then Police Chief Sven Smedjegarden buried his head in the police priest's shoulder and sobbed uncontrollably.

In the tiny Swedish town of Lindesberg, perched on the edge

of the hills, thirty-three women went aboard the *Estonia* and did not return. Twenty-two children of the community were left without mothers. Immediately following the sinking, priests, counselors and psychologists descended on the community to provide counseling and support for the families whose lives had changed so drastically. On the Sunday following the tragedy the townspeople came together in their grief in the white frame church. "For us, it is not about mourning for hundreds of people," the Rev. Orvar Homann told them. "It is about our family, those we worked with, our friends."

"We are no heroes, no supermen," Homann said. "But we must find a way to go on, and we must find it together. We must believe there is a tomorrow."

The town itself is an idyllic setting, with the church spire, the beautiful Tinghouse, and the old city hall showing bright through a line of trees. All the women in this club who had traveled together to Estonia worked in local kitchens, schools, or rest homes. All had husbands, children or friends in the town. Every person in Lindesberg knew at least one of the women. The pastor had come from the west coast of Sweden, and he assured the townsfolk that the sea can function as a grave. But to the people of Lindesberg, this made little sense. They were country people, living far from the sea. In Lindesberg one buries one's people in the earth.

Now there are empty tombs in Lindesberg, even though technically the law of the town does not allow this. And in the southern cemetery is a new tombstone shaped like a heart. It bears the name "Maana" and the single word "Why?" There are flowers there, but no coffin or urn or tomb. For this loved one, the East Sea, as the Swedes call the Baltic, has become a communal tomb with the thirty-two other sisters from Lindesberg, and the other nearly thousand citizens of the world who lie there.

Nearby, after a year Lennart Johansson still mourned for his wife, Mona. Big, strong, with wavy hair and a mustache, Lennart still breaks into tears at any mention of his wife's name. For the first year almost every evening his neighbors invited him for dinner so that he would not have to cook. He erected a small wooden cross, near which he put flowers next to the forest. It served until the tombstone he had ordered arrived. He is bitter at the Swedish politicians who at first promised to do everything to recover the bodies, and then decided to cover the wreckage with concrete to make of it a sea tomb that would keep out scavenging divers.

At night Lennart sometimes thinks that perhaps Mona is not dead. As long as no body has come home, as long as there is no proof, he feels there is hope. Perhaps she made it out of the ship, maybe hit her head on something and was knocked unconscious before she was rescued by a passing fishing boat. It could be that Mona Johansson is alive somewhere, he tells himself, and does not remember who she is.

30 · THOSE WHO WERE LEFT

One of the lingering mysteries of the *Estonia* sinking lies with the fate of Avo Piht, the Estonian off-duty captain who apparently went down with his ship that tragic night. At 6 a.m. on the morning of the sinking, Piht's wife, Sirje, called the wife of Captain Andresson and informed her that the ship had sunk. They both watched Finnish TV news for further word. Uncomprehending, they saw the helicopters search the empty sea. There was no ship, only the stormy sea littered with tragic bits of what had once been a proud ship.

They listened to lists of survivors read over the air, but the names had little meaning. On the survivors list from the Baltic News Service it was announced that Captain Avo Piht was alive, but had not yet been taken to any of the hospitals. "At the moment we lack information as to his whereabouts," it said. "Interpol and the security institutions of different countries are all looking for Piht." In those early hours there was some thought that the captains and crew might be held accountable for the disaster.

That afternoon Sirje Piht, a slender, charming, and youthful woman, received a phone call from Rostock, Germany, from a group of Estonian seamen who said they recognized Piht among the survivors from a clip shown on German television. She was at her home in Merivalja, a suburb of Tallinn. The Estonians were in Rostock to take over the new ship that was being groomed to operate out of Tallinn, the *Mare Balticum*. Two days after the accident a Finnish newspaper wrote, "The general director of Nordstrom & Thulin ... has stated to Reuters that Avo Piht is alive and is at a hospital in Finland." Baltic News Service also reported on the same day that "The technical director of Nordstrom & Thulin ... claims that the Investigation Commission is trying to hide the off-duty captain Avo Piht who survived the accident. According to Forsbeg, the members of the Commission fear Piht's testimony."

On that same Friday afternoon Reuters announced that "Bengt-Eric Stenmark, the Chief of Security of the National Maritime Board of Sweden, claims that the International Commission of Investigation has finally succeeded in talking to the captain of the *Estonia*, Avo Piht. His location is still unknown two days after his survival."

When questioned, however, all these sources denied they knew anything about Piht's survival or his whereabouts.

In all the turmoil of three nations looking for somebody to blame in the tragedy, and with the inevitable conspiracy theories in full blossom, rumors were soon flying rampant regarding Captain Piht. Two of the Estonian seaman who saw the German TV clip over and over remained adamant that they saw a Mercedes-type ambulance stop at the hospital entrance. The door was opened and out stepped people wrapped in blankets. The fourth was Avo Piht, his hair wet and a blanket on his shoulders. He was the last man who was shown getting out of the ambulance. "It is out of the question that I would not recognize Piht," said Enn Laane. "After a very serious talk with him on board the *Estonia* I will remember him for the rest of my life."

Similarly, the purser aboard the ship, Tonu Poolakas, was equally steadfast, "I am certain that it was Avo Piht." That morning they watched the TV clip several times, but by the evening news, the clip ended just as Avo Piht stepped out of the ambulance. "Somebody had given an order that Piht should be cut out," the two later agreed in unison.

"I believe the words of these Estonian seamen," Mrs. Piht said a few weeks later. "These men do not lie." Unlike many of her acquaintances, Mrs. Piht did not consult a fortune teller or seer to learn the fate of her husband. She forbade journalists to use the past tense when talking of her husband. Nevertheless, a fortune teller wrote to her to tell her that her husband had been kidnapped, that he was alive and well and would return home.

Through it all she remained upbeat, but resigned. "I would not be surprised if my husband came home in a year's time," Sirje Piht said. "At the same time I am convinced it is not going to happen in ten years." Her son, Egon, who was seventeen at the time of the accident, wanted to go to sea. Instead, Arvo Piht wanted his son to go to the university to study law or economics. "But I want him to follow in his father's footsteps," Mrs. Piht said with a sad smile.

On her table, just as on the table of the wife of Captain Arvo Andresson, a large pile of telegrams and letters expressing condolences accumulated in those early days following the disaster. It was amazing, remarked Mrs. Piht, how many widows of captains live on the coasts of the Baltic Sea. They who know what it is to have a husband taken by the sea can best empathize in a forlorn and lonely sorority.

One remarkable incident shows the depth of mourning of one who was left behind, and his dedication to the memory of his wife. Peeter Barasinki, age thirty-nine, is originally from Poland. Now living in Stockholm, he met his wife Carita when both worked on the Viking line *Athena*. She was a maid, he was a waiter and bartender. They enjoyed their work because they worked two weeks and got two weeks off, during which they were able to vacation together to twenty-one different countries. They often talked about the safety of the passenger ferries, but the possibility of any real problem seemed remote. When she got a job on the *Estonia*, he reminded her, "If anything will ever happen, be careful and make sure you put on enough clothes."

On the night the *Estonia* went down, two friends later told Peeter that Carita came out of her crew cabin on the eighth deck as the ferry tilted. Another girl came out and asked what was happening. "It cannot be anything dangerous," Carita replied. "The alarm has not yet gone off."

Along with Carita, two other young women and one man then tried to get out of the hallway as the ship lurched to the side. The hallway became almost like an elevator shaft, and one of the young women slipped downward. Carita stopped to try to save her. It was a magnanimous but fatal gesture. The other two struggled toward the exit and the deck, and eventually survived. Those in the bottom of the corridor had no chance of getting back up.

After hearing of the accident, Peeter was down at the dock at six that morning, waiting. At 11 a.m. he received a fax that said Carita had been rescued. The fax was mistaken, but he did not learn until eight hours later that she had not survived. Peeter's grief in the following weeks and months focused on why Carita and the others at the bottom of the sea could not have a real funeral. Technically, it was possible to get the bodies up, but the government commissions set up to study the problem abandoned that idea as impractical and unwise.

Beset with grief, Peeter amazingly hired a German camera-equipped diving robot to explore the ship for two days. When it filmed inside the ferry, it showed some fire hoses in the room by the exit. Someone, he surmised, probably tried to throw them to those trapped below as a rope to climb up to the exit. "It felt very good to be there at the place of the tragedy and to be close to her," he said. The venture with the diving apparatus cost him 300,000 Swedish kroner, about 50,000 American dollars.

"I know exactly in the ship where she is, and I have still not given up," he told the Swedish newspaper *Expressen* one year after the accident. "I am thinking of other possible solutions to be able to give my wife a funeral."

As might be expected, some people call Peeter possessed or crazy. For them, he has an answer. He points to one of the main attractions in Stockholm, a museum built around the near-perfectly preserved warship called the *Wasa* that sank almost 400 years ago. At that time ambitious Swedish King Gustavas Adolphus was expanding his empire over the Baltic, and he ordered built the largest and most beautiful warship in the world. It featured two gun decks with sixty-four large cannons and sported more than a hundred carved wooden figures adorning its gun ports and other features. It was, however, built top-heavy in spite of tons of rock stored as ballast in the hold.

Amid pomp and ceremony, the *Wasa* was launched on August 10, 1628, near the royal castle, sailed 500 yards and promptly tipped and sank in the harbor. Contemporary accounts say between thirty and fifty officers, seamen and celebrators drowned. For a couple of decades efforts were made to raise the ship, but they were futile and it eventually sank into the mud and was forgotten. Three hundred years later, in 1956, archaeologists exploring a mound of mud in the bay drilled down and discovered the *Wasa*. The Baltic Sea is only slightly salty, and so the salt worms that eat at wood in most ocean water do not live there. After burrowing six tunnels beneath the hull, Swedish engineers slowly brought the *Wasa* to the surface in near-original state and a gorgeous museum was built around it. A sea chest covered with tar found in one of the cabins, for instance, was opened after 300 years under water, and the wide-brimmed felt hat of some dandy owner waited in stale air inside as if ready to be plopped on at a cocky angle to go out on the town.

The bones of twenty-five of those aboard the *Wasa* who perished so long ago were recovered, studied, then laid in the earth with honors by the Swedish government. Now Peeter Barasinki reminds his critics, "Have you seen what the tomb of those in the *Wasa* says: 'Early passed away, late put to rest in the blessed earth.' It took those victims 333 years to get on shore," he chides. "You know, it is never too late."

Three years following the *Estonia* tragedy, a large monument was dedicated near the *Wasa* Museum to honor the names of those who died in this greatest sea disaster of the century for the area. Smaller acts of memoriam were carried out on a regular basis by those who were left behind. One year after the accident, retired Swedish sailor Thure Palmgren carried a wreath on his own boat toward the spot where the *Estonia* sank. It was there that he and his wife of forty years, Clary, were awakened in their cabin on that fatal night by the sounds of metal on metal. As a seaman, Thure knew it was not a normal result of a ship fighting a storm.

Thure hadn't really wanted to go to Tallinn on that trip. He knew what the Baltic Sea could be like in September. But Clary insisted, saying if he didn't go she would take her mother with her. But on the return trip toward Stockholm when the storm began, they were unable to sleep because of all the vibrations and untypical clanging. When he realized that the metallic crashes he was hearing were not from the sea, he urged his wife to leave and they ran toward the stairs wearing only their underwear. On the deck, in the panic and confusion, they became separated in spite of Thure's frantic efforts. When he last saw her, she was holding on to the railing of the ship. He called for her to jump, but he does not know to this day if she heard him amid all the turmoil.

Before he jumped, he had snapped an extra life vest to his own for his wife when he found her. In the water he desperately shouted her name over and over. Finally, he was pulled onto an overturned life raft, where all night he endured the torture of the bitter wind and the mountainous waves that covered the raft. The next morning he was hauled aboard the *Mariella*.

On a sunny morning one year later, the grieving Thure Palmgren set out in his little boat, carrying flowers toward the spot of the disaster near the Finnish island of Uto. Ironically, once more the sea gods of September sent heavy seas and strong winds. It was dangerous to go out on deck of the small boat. Thus he had to settle for a spot several miles from the actual site of the sinking to drop the beautiful floral wreath.

"It doesn't matter," he said on that memorable morning. "The sea is one and the same. Everywhere."

It is to be expected that he cannot forget. Every day he sees his wife of forty years standing holding onto the railing in the storm. "It is natural for me that Clary should rest in the ocean. To me the sea is as sacred as any cemetery." There is no bitterness toward the sea. His only bitterness is for human error. "With better seamanship, Clary would still be alive and the *Estonia* would still be sailing," he said. "The sea demands respect."

31 · THE SEA FEEDS US AND BURIES US

For three days Elmar Siegel and Paul Andersson rested in the hospital in Mariehamn. There they relived the long night of tragedy with other survivors and with counselors to expose those raw memories so that the experience would not lie festering and haunt their dreams. When they were flown back to their homes in Estonia, they found a nation deep in mourning. Flags flew at half-staff, and every home seemed to have a window draped in black. Everyone, it appeared, had been touched by the tragedy.

In a small apartment in the town of Laivere ten miles south of Tallinn, Paul Andersson's wife, Ingrid, was waiting joyously for him along with his eleven-year-old daughter, Janet, and his nine-year-old son, Heini. Elmar Siegel's wife, Sirje, was also waiting at their apartment with his two daughters.

Three days after they returned to their homes in Tallinn, the two seamen were called to the company offices there, along with all the other surviving members of the crew who were able to attend.

There the Estline directors explained that the sister ship of the *Estonia*, the *Mare Balticum*, would be resuming the run to Stockholm. After expressing his condolences for the loss of their shipmates, the director asked how many of the remaining *Estonia* crew wanted to return to sea on the new ship. After a moment of hesitation, slowly, one by one, the hands of almost all the thirty-six crew member survivors who were present went up.

Like most of the other crew members, Paul Andersson and Elmar Siegel had found a wondrous new life in working on the *Estonia*. After five decades of Russian oppression and resulting poverty, their country was then like a butterfly just emerging from the economic and social cocoon of occupation of the Soviet Union. For Andersson and Siegel, working on the *Estonia* had been their passageway to a decent existence for the first time in their lives. The jobs on the ship provided double and sometimes triple wages as the same work performed on shore in Estonia. The work at sea offered not only an income, but a future for their families. When faced with a choice by the company after the accident, it was either return to the sea on the *Mare Balticum* or go back to land and unemployment. At that time the economy in the capital city was stagnant, just beginning to stir as new-found capitalism began to make inroads into the old system.

Within a month after his ordeal Paul Andersson was back at work as head bartender on the *Mare Balticum*. "I am not afraid to go to sea again," he said. "None of us knows our last hour." After sailing for a short time there, he switched to a ship sailing between Estonia and Finland, but he found himself unsettled and went back to land as a bartender at the fancy Olympian Hotel in Tallinn. While there he suddenly found that he had had enough of serving other people, of the noise, the drinking, and fighting. After staying home for a time he took a job with the Customs Board of the country, earning a much smaller salary than he had on the *Estonia*.

"But I don't hate the sea," he says. "I love the sea." And he gained from the experience in the sea that night. "I am thankful that all that happened to me," he says. "Life has got a completely new meaning for me."

As for his shipmate, Elmar Siegel, when his new ship sailed in November, he was back at his old job as machinist in the engine room. He has no trouble sleeping, as some *Estonia* survivors did. Sometimes he ponders what it was that helped him survive when so many others perished. "I did not lose hope for a moment. I had warm clothes and was convinced the whole time that I would survive," he explains. "That people died around me did not alter my decision to take it easy and wait for dawn. I knew the helicopters would come then."

By 1997, Siegel had changed to working on the ship *Melodia* between Tallinn and Helsinki, Finland. After twenty-right years, the sea is in him and he cannot leave it. "I have lived by the sea since I was a child and have become a part of it," he said. "The sea feeds us and buries us."

"Life goes on," he says philosophically. "The sea is sometimes rough, but it is impossible to work as a seaman on the solid ground. We have to keep the ship going that takes us forward in life."

After Paul Barney left the hospital at Mariehamn, he stopped over in Stockholm for one day on his way to London. In the Swedish capital he wanted to go to a church and show his respect for the youths from the Bible college in Jonkoping. Only an hour before the tragedy, he had visited with two from that group, Mikael and Maria, in the Admiral Pub where they had assured him that giving oneself to Jesus would solve all problems. It was a meeting he was to think of often. There in Stockholm he went to the ancient Klara church, where he lit a candle and sat alone for a long while in deep silence.

When he arrived at Heathrow airport, Paul Barney was astonished to see hundreds of clamoring reporters shouting questions at him. A police escort took him through the lines of newsmen and well-wishers to the VIP lounge, where his mother and sister waited.

As the only surviving Briton, he had become a national hero, with accounts of the sinking and his post-rescue interview dominating television news for several days. The other Englishman aboard, John Manning, sixty-three, also from Berkshire, went down with the *Estonia*.

When he met the press, he answered their questions, then ended with a question of his own. "On board the *Titanic*, they had four hours to get off the sinking ship. That was 1912. More than eighty years later, we had barely thirty minutes. Why has no one reflected over the extremely lousy security on these ferries before this? Why the hell did the Mayday take so long? I heard no alarm whatsoever."

In a twist of fate, on the day that Paul Barney returned to London, a large exhibition dealing with artifacts brought up from the *Titanic* opened there. The next day Paul's face was on the front page of every London newspaper. For two weeks, he endured a whirlwind of television and radio interviews with such notables as David Frost. Finally, after a particularly harrowing reliving of the experience shared via BBC World News Service in a London studio, he shut himself off from the attention. That afternoon he went to a London church to mourn the Estonian girl who had died in the raft just out of his reach. His helplessness, and the sight of her black hair floating in the water, haunted him.

Paul returned to his family's beautiful home among the green hills of Pangbourne, but he has not forgotten. Not long after returning, he played a record he had bought in Sweden that reminded him of the Estonian girl. One of the songs was "In Your Eyes," and it finally brought all the emotions to the surface. He broke down in sobs and let himself weep. He forced himself to listen to the recording over and over to give the feelings free rein so that he would be able to deal with them later.

"Sara and Kent had formed an emotional tie with each other before everything on the raft was chaotic," Paul explains. "It saved them. When I met the Estonian girl on the raft, it was too late. There was no room for human contact then. I have had feelings of guilt over the fact that I was unable to save her life. I have gotten over that now, but the thought hasn't left me."

After several months Paul Barney finally was able to identify the Estonian girl. She was twenty-thrtee-year-old Liia Haaberman, who was separated from her husband in Tallinn. She had no children. Her friends say she was an outgoing person who loved dancing, music, and traveling. She was drawn not only to the high wages on the ship, but to the excitement of the social life on board and mingling with people of different nationalities. Yet she did not trust the *Estonia*, and she had hoped to find comparable work ashore.

On his return to England, Paul shrugged off the label "hero" that the tabloids attached to him. Instead, he told the press, for the entire duration of that longest night on the raft, his first and most powerful instinct was to survive and to get back safely to land.

Following the *Estonia* tragedy, Sweden and Estonia went through periods of national mourning. Paul missed out on that catharsis, and instead threw himself into the making of a television documentary about the sinking. As much as anything else, it was for him a healing time, a coming to grips with the incident and learning to live with it. Slowly he also returned to his work as a landscape architect. He has also become heavily involved with raising funds for aid to the Estonian people.

"I'm beginning to feel more like the person I was," he said three months later. "I am more moody. I definitely get more depressed. I'm not so capable of being on my own as I was. But what happened put a lot of things in perspective," he mused later. "I'm asking myself the basic questions again: Where are we going? What does it all mean? You've got to get something out of the experience, otherwise it would drag you down."

Morten Boje, when he returned to Denmark, faced his own demons about his survival. As the only surviving Dane, he was the center of attention of his own country's media in the same way that Paul Barney was in England. On the raft he had dreamed of his girlfriend, Frederikke, and he found her waiting for him in Copenhagen. To meet the clamor of the media, he called a press conference. In explaining his survival, he was amazingly frank: "I was very selfish," he announced. "That is why I survived, because I was thinking only of myself."

Bombarded with attention from friends and well-wishers, he and Frederikke escaped to Paris for two weeks. But, like Paul Barney, he felt a strong sense of alienation, of loneliness. And over it all, as a burdening sense of guilt hung over him far greater than that experienced by the others. One vivid memory still plagues him: the many hands reaching up for help as he was pulling up people through the near-vertical stairway while searching for his friend, Knud.

"I have realized now that I probably would have died if I had stayed any longer at the door," he philosophized after a year. "But why does one pull up five and not six? What made me decide that now I can't pull up any more people?"

Even more haunting for Morten Boje is the recollection of the fast-drifting raft with a man lying near-naked on it that he and Paul Andersson caught briefly before the wind tore it from their grasp. They had hoped to get the man onto their raft, turn it over, and then transfer to the new raft with the tent raised above them for protection from the wind and the waves.

"When that raft came, I was prepared to kill the man who was lying there on the bottom," Morten Boje told a sympathetic Danish television audience that included nearly everyone in the country. "I was ready to kill to save myself. I know that others experienced it differently, but that is how it was for me and I must accept it. I was driven that far."

His audience, however, did not blame him for such feelings. And Morten, with the help of twice-monthly visits to a psychiatrist, finally put most of the guilt behind him. "I have finally accepted that this is the way I am," he said months later, "and it's okay. I don't feel bad about it any more."

Like the others on that raft, Morten came away from that life-shattering night on the Baltic Sea with one overriding impression: "There is a very big difference in me," he says now. "I am no longer frightened of death. I don't think death is terrible or even uncomfortable. I think death is ... soft."

Following the accident, Morten Boje married Frederikke and went to work as a public relations officer at the co-op company he was representing at the on-board conference. At times, he says, an overwhelming longing fills him. "I long for those two days at the hospital in Mariehamn. It was like paradise, that feeling." In the same way, he feels inseparably connected to the other five survivors on the raft with him. "There are only five other people on this earth who can understand me completely, who can understand what I have gone through."

For Sara Hedrenius, her experiences on the ship and in the sea that night also had a lasting impact. A few days after leaving the hospital, she went to Africa with her father, where he was carrying out a work project. A person who doesn't like the limelight, she found that the peace there away from the media helped restore her spirits. Later she went to Spain to continue her university studies. In retrospect, on thinking back about the offers of money to grant interviews, both she and Kent wondered why they had not done so in order to donate the money to charity. After about a year they did make an appearance on the American television show *Discovery*, with the money going to plant trees in Kenya.

At this writing in 2010, Sara Hedrenius Andreasson serves as a Red Cross Trauma Counselor — helping in such places as Indonesia following the Tsunami there.

For Kent, the *Estonia* tragedy put a focus on his life that had not been there before. "I'm still running fast," he explained a year after the accident, "but I'm thinking more of how I'm running now."

For one thing, the accident left him with a sense of the goodness of life. Because of the circumstances of meeting Sara Hedrenius and the date made there on the side of the sinking ship, the couple caught the world's attention. Their faith in each other during the long night, their cheerfulness, their promised dinner brought the spotlight upon them. Yet he made no pretense of being a spokesman for all the survivors.

"The friendship between the six of us that survived on the raft will always be there, especially the one between Sara, Morten and I," Kent said. "Morten called me yesterday. He is married to the girl he kept thinking of on the raft."

Because of the publicity, Kent and some of the others got letters from all over the world, thanking them for being an example of courage. "Sara and I got to be in some way symbols for the good in society," he says now. "That role feels like a responsibility, and has in a way changed me. I'm trying to live up to the expectations, and I'm thinking more of what I'm doing."

Nevertheless, now Kent doesn't like high bridges, and when he goes to Estonia, he flies rather than taking the ships that runs there.

He feels that he is living on bonus time, and he wants to do something with the extra life he has been granted. After the shipwreck, he became the political adviser for the deputy foreign minister of the Swedish government. After a year he resigned to pursue a career in writing. His own book of his experience in the disaster was published in numerous languages. He writes a column for his hometown newspaper as well as for a Stockholm paper, and has now published a second book about people he has known. By 2010 he had a family and is a respected member of the Swedish Parliament — with a promising future in Swedish politics.

For years he kept on his desk at home in Stockholm the plastic key to his cabin on the *Estonia,* number #4316. As for the lucky coin he purchased that afternoon before boarding the ship, it was lost in his escape. Or maybe, he now says with a smile, he simply used up all its good luck.

Like the other five survivors aboard that overturned life raft, Kent Harstedt is no longer afraid of death. He has seen it close up, and it didn't seem terrible. Indeed, those on his raft had been to the edge of the Great Abyss, and had teetered on the brink. In the end, they had survived, they had been for endless hours cheek-to-jowl companions with a hovering, beckoning death. And they had come away alive. Afterwards most of them had emerged forever fearless of that journey to darkness and light that waits for all.

EPILOGUE

The mystery has deepened. In the years since the tragic loss of the *Estonia*, a growing body of evidence has emerged that casts doubt upon the official version of the sinking. After a decade of testimony, suspicions and investigations, a growing international scandal was still brewing in the face of evidence that the Swedish government was covering up the facts in the tragedy. Several independent researchers concluded that the accident couldn't have happened as explained by the official body.

Immediately following the tragedy, the prime ministers of Estonia, Sweden and Finland set up a Joint Accident Investigation Commission (JAIC), comprised of three members from each country. After two years of testimonies, meetings and investigation, the commission issued its report in 1997. The findings held that the vessel was seaworthy and properly loaded. The problem, said the commission, was that the builders of the ship — Meyer Werft shipyard in Papenburg, Germany — had not provided bow visor locks strong enough to withstand the force of extreme seas that occurred on the night of the sinking. This weakness caused the bow visor to be wrenched off, pulling open the ramp that normally lowered in port to allow cars and trucks to roll onto the ship. Combined with the high seas, the rush of water into the lower decks caused a severe list to starboard and sent the ship down quickly stern first.

In the face of numerous lawsuits against the ship-building company, the report also stated that at the time of the *Estonia*'s construction, no regulations were in place regarding bow visor strength. This presumably absolved the ship-building company of responsibility in the accident. The report also placed no blame on the captain or crew of the *Estonia*.

One of the oddities of the commission's report was that, although it depended heavily on testimony of survivors — whose identities were not revealed — for its findings, the report omits testimonies from some witnesses because they are contradictory and "confusing." The report states: "Some details deviate from what the witnesses actually stated. ... The Commission has edited some detailed statements in order not to confuse the reader in cases where witnesses have made obvious mistakes."

What happened with the committee itself raises some interesting questions. There were bitter disputes among the committee's members during the investigation, and its conclusions have been widely disputed since. For instance, Andi Meister, the Estonian transport minister, resigned in protest. Uno Laur, the Estonian president's personally appointed representative, resigned silently. Priit Mannik, head of Estonian Security Police, resigned silently. Olof Forssberg, head of the Swedish Board of Accident investigation and law expert, was removed. Bengt Schager, psychologist, resigned in protest of the findings. Christer Lindvall, of the Swedish Ship Officers Association, resigned in protest against the commission's conclusions. The JAIC's version of events caused a storm of controversy, not only from the victims' families but from the shipbuilder, Meyer Werft of Germany. Both groups asked for further investigation to reveal what they suspected were other forces at work in the tragedy. In the maritime industry, also, concerned observers contested the official version.

For example, two months after the official version of the tragedy was published in 1997, naval architect Anders Bjorkman challenged the official version by publishing his book, *Lies and Truths About the Estonia Accident* His book concludes that although the *Estonia* could have had 2,000 cubic meters of water on its car deck when it sank, this could not have been the cause of its sinking. "There would have been 18,000 cubic meters of air trapped below the car deck! According to the JAIC all the watertight doors below the car deck were closed!" he wrote.

To further complicate matters, the shipbuilding yard that was blamed in the JAIC report for faulty construction of the *Estonia*, Meyer Werft, faced with an onslaught of huge lawsuits by families of the victims of the sinking, initiated another report from a group called "The German Group of Experts." The findings of this investigating body were very different from the official version, calling its findings "misleading." The conclusions of the German Group of Experts in 1999 were that the *Estonia* was not seaworthy at the time of sailing due to inadequate maintenance and lack of repairs.

This group even took its findings to the Swedish people, with two exhibitions of evidence in Stockholm. In those meetings, one of the commission members reported, "Many of the relatives and survivors pleaded for us to assist them in finding the truth."

When the official report was released in December of 1997, a storm of controversy erupted. Jutta Rabe, an investigative journalist for the prominent German news magazine *Der Spiegel*, met with Henna Witte in Stockholm to compare notes. Witte was the lawyer for the approximately one thousand relatives and survivors of the *Estonia* catastrophe. Both had investigated alternative causes of the sinking. They agreed their investigations did not correspond in any way with the official findings being proposed by the JAIC. Witte and Rabe had both found numerous leads that pointed to an outside attack. They decided to work together, but found numerous obstacles placed in their path by state authorities. They agreed that in three years of investigation, more energy had been expended by official groups in concealing and hushing up rather than trying to bring the truth of the catastrophe into the open.

In May 2000, a conference organized by survivors and relatives of victims dismissed the official report. After the conference, American entrepreneur and diving expert F. Gregg Bemis Jr. of Santa Fe, New Mexico and Jutta Rabe offered to organize a $200,000 dive of the *Estonia* to search out new evidence that would explain what really happened that tragic night in September 1994 in the Baltic Sea. Bemis owned the largest school for commercial divers in the world. In several decades of diving he had explored such wrecks as the British ocean liner, the RMS *Lusitania* sunk by a German U-boat in World War I off the coast of Ireland.

In August of 2000, this dive team of Bemis and Rabe set out to explore the wreck site of the *Estonia,* being careful to remain in international waters. This was because the governments of Sweden, Estonia, Finland, Latvia, Denmark, Russia, and Britain had declared the wreck site as a "Final Resting Place" and off-limits to divers. So with helicopters swooping above them, the Bemis/Rabe research ship was stopped by a flotilla of Swedish military ships. The trip leaders were warned by stern Swedish officers that they were violating Swedish law and might be facing arrest. Because they were in international waters, however, Bemis informed the naval officers that he was willing to take that risk and ordered their divers to proceed. Following the dives, Swedish officials issued arrest warrants for Bemis and Rabe.

In several days of exploring the wreck, the divers brought up clear video and incontrovertible evidence of an explosion on the starboard side of the *Estonia*. The divers brought up two steel sections cut from the bow, each about two feet square that showed signs of a detonation. This contradicted all the official investigations. In addition, their video plainly showed bodies scattered on the sea floor around the ship. The earlier Swedish reports said no bodies were to be seen, and that no bodies would be brought up for burial — bringing howls of outrage from grieving relatives.

The steel pieces from the *Estonia* were sent to three laboratories for testing: the Southwest Research Institute in San Antonio, Texas, the Material Testing Laboratory of the State of Brandenburg, Germany; and the DN Institute for Materials Testing and Material Engineering in Clausthal-Zellerfeld, Germany. "I am convinced the sinking of the *Estonia* was not an accident," Bemis told the press. "I think the strength of the bow visor had nothing to do with it."

The results of these dives became the most serious blow to the official version of the *Estonia* catastrophe. Bemis and Rabe disclosed that all three independent laboratories determined that the fragments brought up from the vessel showed unmistakable evidence of bomb damage. Former Royal Navy officer, diver and explosives expert Brian Braidwood said the laboratory results provide "indisputable truth that the samples were exposed to the effects of an explosion." It should be noted that Braidwood worked for the shipping and insurance industry and was retained by Meyer Werft, the shipbuilder, but was highly respected in maritime circles.

The results of the Bemis-Rabe dive raised further skepticism of the official report. The chairman of the Finnish section of the Joint Accident Investigation Committee, Kari Lethola, raised an interesting point. "If it is proven that there was a bomb, then that would be a good case to reopen the investigation. But then it would be better if it was carried out by the police because it will be an investigation of 852 murders."

When the results of the technical analysis became public, Lennart Berglund, chairman of the Foundation of Estonia Victims and Relatives, called for the investigation to be reopened. "To us, it's now clear without a doubt that this hole has been caused by a detonation," he said at a news conference. "There is no other possibility. There is still a lot of evidence down there. Their [the Swedish authorities'] major argument was that there was nothing new — now there is something new." The reluctance of the Swedish government to reopen the investigation remains puzzling. Sixty-one members of the Swedish Parliament have asked that the investigation into the wreck site be reopened, only to be voted down each time the issue came up. In 2001 Bemis appealed to the Admiralty of the World Court to look into the validity of the *Estonia* agreement that banned research on the site. After studying the case, Bemis reported, "They found it very interesting, and said it certainly deserved further investigation. But ultimately they said their body was allowed only to bring cases brought by states, and that I don't qualify as a state."

In order to bring attention to the situation, the reporter Jutta Rabe became involved in the production of a $6 million theatrical film called *Baltic Storm*, dealing with the tragedy. It featured American star Donald Sutherland, playing an investigative reporter based on Rabe. However, a review of the movie by Gunnar Rehlin in the American show-biz magazine *Variety* was lukewarm: He wrote, "'Baltic Storm': The real-life 1994 sinking of the ferry *M/S Estonia* in the Baltic Sea, which claimed 852 lives, has been turned into a standard conspiracy thriller. English-lingo German pic finally opened in a couple of Swedish cinemas in February, to negative reviews and lackluster B.O. [box office]. For Anglo markets, the only hook is name presence, with TV its likeliest avenue. ..."

In spite of that failure to raise awareness of what happened with the ill-fated ship, the international furor has not died down. Of course by 2004 a major question remained: if there was a bomb that sent the *Estonia* to the bottom during a storm, who did it? And why?

Immediately following the sinking, rumors ran rampant throughout the Baltic. One prevalent theory was that the Russian Mafia involved in drug trafficking had sent a large load of contraband aboard the *Estonia*. Somehow these drug lords got wind that the Swedish police were ready to swoop down upon the illicit cargo and make major arrests with this evidence. To avoid this, a bomb was secreted aboard with a timing device that was activated when police plans became known. Proponents of this theory cite the fact that fifty Swedish police were aboard after attending a conference in Estonia. Were they aboard to make major arrests? Only one of those police officers survived.

If this theory is correct, why is the Swedish government so intent on stifling any further investigation? Yet, some observers see a strange Russian influence in all of the decisions that were made regarding the investigations.

An even more intriguing theory is that the Russian Mafia was smuggling nuclear fission materials out of their country for sale to third world terrorists or rogue governments. If this was so, the Baltic governments might not want it known that their sea traffic was a major player in such world-threatening tactics. This might account for their reluctance in exploring the causes of the *Estonia* sinking.

Another rumor current at the time said that during the nighttime storm the *Estonia* probably rammed a Russian or American submarine that didn't belong in the area. An international incident would have resulted, something Sweden and Estonia would not have wanted. However, the results of the Bemis/Rabe investigations probably eliminated the possibility of such an accident.

One other possibility that gained some currency in the months after the catastrophe was that the ferry had hit a mine that was still adrift, left over from World War II. It is true that some of these explosive devices still exist, on land and sea. But if this were the cause of the sinking, all of the governments in the investigation would have embraced such a finding, because it would have exonerated them, the shipbuilders, the Mafia and anyone else remotely connected to the event. Such has not been the case, with the governments involved apparently not really eager to know what actually happened on that tragic Baltic night.

Probably the most far-fetched theory proposed that the burgeoning economy in Estonia and the growth of shipping there posed a threat to competing companies of Estline, the joint-owned Estonian/Swedish company that owned the ferry. The Swedish, Finnish and Russian private shipping interests might have viewed the resurgence of the Estline Company as a rival that would take away business. In light of the enormity of such a criminal undertaking, however, most observers agree that such a conspiracy would involve so many people as to make secrecy impossible.

And therein lies the weak link in most of these conspiracy theories. It seems a part of human nature to search for conspiracies in events that impact major populations, ranging from presidential assassinations to flying saucer cover-ups. Part of the attraction of such speculation is undoubtedly the titillation factor, that all of us love to speculate amid the belief that things are not always what they seem.

Fueling these emotions these days is the constant headlines dealing with what mindless terrorism has done to people's lives around the globe in recent years. Following the unthinkable terrorist strike on New York City in September 2001 that took nearly 3,000 lives, a bomb aboard the *Estonia* did not seem so improbable.

Yet there is an axiom that if more than three people are involved in a secret conspiracy, the secret will not long endure. Again, human nature comes into play. People brag, they get drunk, they confide to others, and eventually the truth emerges.

So which of the above theories reveals the actual cause of a huge ship that went down in a storm, taking 852 souls to a dark and watery grave? Perhaps there was another as-yet unnamed conspiracy at play? Or was the JAIC commission correct, that faulty structure of a critical part of the ship was to blame, along with faulty maintenance? The fact remains that either an accident claimed the *Estonia* with most of its passengers, or that somebody or some group with no limits to what they would do to achieve their aims were ruthless murderers that night.

Thus fifteen years after the *Estonia* disaster, huge questions remained nagging at the international community. For instance, how did the official investigation fail to detect the bomb damage? The detractors of the commission's finding maintain that its members were covering up a sinister underworld crime, with some governments bringing pressure to make sure that the real facts never come to light due to political consequences.

Yet, in spite of international outcry, after all this time the Swedish government was still refusing to reopen the investigation. Even in the face of heavy criticism, that government wants the tragedy to just go away forever, but the *Estonia* mystery and the controversy refuse to die.

ABOUT THE AUTHOR

The son of a Norwegian immigrant, Jack A. Nelson grew up in Bellflower, California. However, during college he became a heartfelt Utah resident after discovering the wild places of that lonely land. As a youth, he danced the Squaw Dance with Navajos on the reservation at the prodding of his cousins who ran the Dennehotso Trading Post. A former reporter, Nelson taught journalism at California State/Humbold, the University of Utah, and then settled in to teach writing for twenty-five years at Brigham Young University. With a master's degree in creative writing from the University of Utah, he has published four other novels with New York publishers. As an outdoor writer, Nelson served for thirteen years as Utah editor of *Western Outdoors Magazine* while teaching, along with writing an outdoor column for a local newspaper. He lives with his wife, Patrice, in Provo, Utah.

For research on the *Estonia* tragedy, he and his wife spent a month in Sweden and Estonia interviewing survivors and exploring details of the disaster. He also worked with Valeria Kaspar, a documentary film maker in Tallinn, Estonia, who provided invaluable help in seeking out and interviewing those who were affected by the losses that devastated two nations.

The future of publishing...today!

Apprentice House is the country's only campus-based, student-staffed book publishing company. Directed by professors and industry professionals, it is a nonprofit activity of the Communication Department at Loyola University Maryland.

Using state-of-the-art technology and an experiential learning model of education, Apprentice House publishes books in untraditional ways. This dual responsibility as publishers and educators creates an unprecedented collaborative environment among faculty and students, while teaching tomorrow's editors, designers, and marketers.

Outside of class, progress on book projects is carried forth by the AH Book Publishing Club, a co-curricular campus organization supported by Loyola University's Office of Student Activities.

Student Project Team for *Flashes in the Night*:

    Michael Bullwinkle, '08

    Salvatore Mastrocola, '09

    Amy Choi, '10

    Dan McDevitt, '10

Eclectic and provocative, Apprentice House titles intend to entertain as well as spark dialogue on a variety of topics.

Financial contributions to sustain the press's work are welcomed. Contributions are tax deductible to the fullest extent allowed by the IRS. To learn more about Apprentice House books or to obtain submission guidelines, please visit www.ApprenticeHouse.com.

CPSIA information can be obtained at www.ICGtesting.com
Printed in the USA
LVOW121623030212

266967LV00002B/18/P

9 781934 074213